SHANE SHEBA AND SKY

PAUL VINER

Printed in the United Kingdom

Cover design and layout by www.spiffingcovers.com

This book is dedicated to all of the poor innocent, abandoned, injured, disabled and abused dogs struggling to merely survive on our planet.

And to the caring individuals who work tirelessly and selflessly to rescue, home, heal and care for them.

I know that not everyone is in a position to help dogs.

But I also know that everyone is in a position not to harm them.

PROLOGUE

Please Allow Me to Introduce Myself

My half-century, the big fifty, is rapidly approaching. So far so good. I'm about to officially become a quinquagenarian, and luckily there are no apparent outward signs of a mid-life crisis to those around me. Although I must admit that I utterly adore the Triumph Speed Triple RS, I have no intentions of donning a full set of black leathers and roaring off into the sunset on one of the 1050cc beasts. Well I'd like to, but two reasons prevent me. One, I can't afford the £13,500 price tag; and two, I've never taken the time to learn to ride a motorbike.

But the 'crisis' was there, lurking menacingly deep within my troubled mind.

For men of a certain age, the 'crisis' can manifest itself in many guises, not always blatantly obvious to those around them. Some men may confuse the 'crisis' with mental health issues, a taboo subject that most would find far too embarrassing to talk about, suffering alone in silence as anxiety, sadness and feelings of loneliness start to creep into their everyday lives, the lives that they may feel have now turned mundane. Men do try to fight back, often to the amusement – and sometimes the entertainment – of those around them.

When, and if the 'crisis' does hit it doesn't always have to take the form of a much-maligned expensive two-seater open-top sports car, accessorised with driving gloves, and Matt Monros 'On Days Like These' blaring out from the speakers.

To the sufferer, the car symbolises success and youth, as apparently these are the two essential needs of a man (and generally it is men) experiencing the onslaught of this unexplainable mental anguish.

Psychologists have also identified another significant symptom of the 'crisis' – sufferers may demonstrate an increasingly random and erratic decision-making process, which may explain the purchase of expensive and unnecessary items.

Apparently, so I had been told, the 'crisis' strikes when you are at your lowest ebb. To maximise its desired effect, it inevitably kicks you straight in the teeth when you're down, it envelops you in a lonely darkness that there seems to be no escape from.

I had suffered from, and to this day still do, the sleep disorder insomnia. My condition was now being aggravated by the addition of even more sleep deprivation, if that was at all possible. My mind was continually working overtime to try and make sense of, and to come to terms with, the strange changes happening to me – my grossly exaggerated feelings of general hopelessness and being 'stuck in a rut'.

I also started to think in depth about my own mortality. At times I honestly believe that I even welcomed it, in fact, I'd go as far as to say that I looked forward to my own demise.

Scarily these thoughts led to a dangerous obsession with death, and, in the end, the morbid thoughts that I was having inevitably culminated in a bout of depression.

It soon became easy to comprehend as to why 84 men a week committed suicide, many of them too afraid to speak up about their mental health. Probably they knew that they'd have been told to 'man up'.

I have to admit that maybe – no definitely – it was these feelings that I was now personally experiencing that forced me into having to take drastic action; I had to refocus my seemingly humdrum life. I was already feeling despondent, and suffering unexplainable feelings of guilt, helplessness and worthlessness. These unwelcome emotions were the scary invisible enemy that were making me feel even more confused about my mental state. But more to the point, sadly I was embarrassed and found it impossible to talk openly about the dark demons lurking within. However, there were other peculiar thoughts – strangely I suddenly needed to feel needed, I felt entirely worthless to those around me; in the blink of an eye my expiry date had expired.

CHAPTER ONE

How do you feel about getting a dog?

Before humans die, they write their last will and testament

I had met Toni, my wife-to-be, on Good Friday, 9th April 1982, at the tender age of 17, at a somewhat disreputable local discotheque. I believe the younger generation now call them nightclubs. We got engaged eight months later and married at St Mary's church, Great Parndon, Harlow on 9th June 1984, at the ripe old age of 19. We decided in 1985, when we were 21, to start a family of our own. We had indeed had a bit of a whirlwind three years.

From the moment of the birth of our first daughter, Kealy, in August 1986, our lives rapidly had to become – and rightly so – dedicated entirely to the needs of our children. We were eventually blessed with two more daughters, Gemma, born in June 1988, and Leah, April 1991.

Throughout our daughters' childhoods, we strived, in fact, more often than not we struggled to provide for them the best that we could. Somehow, and goodness only knows how, we managed, sacrifices needed to be, and usually were made, but I'd like to think that we gave our daughters the best start in life that we possibly could.

In 2012 we had been living in our family home on a large estate in Old Harlow, Essex, for 24 years. Toni and I had recently spent our entire life savings – in fact, a small fortune – in renovating it to just how we wanted it, with a high-spec, sleek contemporary design.

But it wasn't about the house or the decor. Our endeavours had foolishly been based solely upon trying to please the other one, when the reality was that separately we had both grown to despise the estate that our home was situated on. The trouble was, as we were later to find out, we didn't want to hurt each other's feelings, so each of us remained silent.

We were sitting having a meal to celebrate Toni's birthday, accompanied by several bottles of wine, in our favourite local restaurant, The Hand and Crown, a 16th-century inn, in High Wych, Sawbridgeworth. The copious quantity of alcohol consumed must have given us the necessary, long overdue kick up the arse we needed to engage in a much-needed, meaningful heart-to-heart conversation. We opened up to each other about exactly how we felt, and thank goodness we did. Without haste we put our home on the market. It sold for the full £225,000 asking price almost immediately. We received the offer on Saturday 27th October. That glorious day was now going to be a double celebration, it was also my parents', Janet and Roy's, golden wedding anniversary. To mark their landmark 50 glorious years of marriage we had a surprise party lined up for them at my father's favourite pub, The Bull in Sawbridgeworth, Hertfordshire. Family and friends had been sworn to secrecy and invited to join us at 7 pm for a fun evening.

2012 had been a year full of love, happiness and celebration. My eldest daughter Kealy had granted me the most precious honour that a daughter could bestow on her father – the privilege of walking her down the aisle of St Mary Magdalene Church, Harlow, on her beautiful wedding day on the 26th May.

We eventually found the house of our dreams and moved into it on 3rd April 2013. For the first time in 27 years, Toni and I now found ourselves almost living alone, but most importantly for us, at long last we were both unconditionally contented with the place that we now called home.

In late August, after a short break, I resumed my beloved career as a street trading enforcement officer in East London. Life for us was as good as it could be.

Our three daughters had all grown up into beautiful and caring young ladies. For us, we now felt that our roles as parents had diminished, as the girls had all forged successful, fulfilling lives and careers for themselves, far away from the parental nest.

Now at the age of 49, we knew that our maternal and paternal desires had not deserted us, but until the time that our lives would eventually be graced with grandchildren, there was nothing that we could do about it… or so we thought.

Christmas Eve 2013. Toni and I were excitedly looking forward to our family joining us en masse over the next few days to celebrate the season's festivities. My brother Gary had driven down from his houseboat, Moondance, which he had moored on the River Great Ouse in Ely to drop off his Christmas gifts for the family. The three of us were sitting next to our Christmas tree; the main lights in our lounge were switched off, allowing the three hundred or so small LED lights to illuminate the room, randomly flickering on Toni's favourite fairy tale setting. I had knocked up a saucepan of mulled cider, to my own secret recipe, which was soon consumed by the three of us while we reminisced about the very hectic year that had gone before us.

Toni got up and went to pour the three of us each a sherry, a drink we traditionally only tolerate at Christmas. When she sat back down she broached a subject that weirdly I had been contemplating over the previous few weeks, but had not mentioned to her. Here we go again, my lack of communication problem.

"I've been thinking."

Toni opened her sentence almost with an air of caution.

"How would you feel about us getting a dog?"

Her sudden question hit me like a bolt out of the blue. Gary stifled a laugh and looked straight at me.

"Honestly? That's strange because I've been thinking along the exact same lines for some time now as well. What breed of dog do you like?"

Gary was now looking on completely bemused at the discussion unfolding right in front of him.

My imagination was instantly going into overdrive – the loyal, loving companionship of man's best friend, beautiful countryside walks, exciting new adventures and hopefully meeting a whole new circle of like-minded friends.

But more importantly for me in my current mental state of mind, it would be the re-establishment of someone needing me; almost the role of becoming a parent to a toddler reinstating itself, albeit this time to a four-legged whippersnapper.

"I've always loved Scottish Terriers, so my choice would be a little black Scottie dog, a boy; I already have a name for him, Winston. Let's get Christmas out of the way then maybe we can look into it. One thing's for sure; he'll give us both a new purpose in life."

Toni had obviously already put a great deal of thought into it.

Our quest would mean us entering into completely uncharted territory, and we were more than aware that this was going to be a daunting and unknown adventure for us. For me, this could prove to be just what the doctor ordered. Who could ever have thought that my mental issues might hopefully be cured by a dog?

We have never had the pleasure of a dog being part of our immediate family unit. The thought of taking on the role of dog parent filled me with both excitement and trepidation. The prospect also made me feel very nervous; it was going to be a huge responsibility. Strangely it brought memories flooding back to me of how I felt on the day back in 1985 when Toni and I had first spoken about the prospect of us having children and starting a family of our own.

One thing was for sure, our lives were going to change beyond all recognition, the well-being and welfare of our new family member were going to be paramount and have to take priority. No more sporadic, spur of the moment weekends away; we certainly couldn't just spring on our family that we needed a babysitter for Winston the Scottie for the weekend. Also, there was going to be an added financial commitment. Money was tight for us as it was, and serious funds were going to have to be found and allocated. As of that moment, I didn't have the foggiest clue what this figure would be. Any interests that we had would also have to take a back seat. For me personally, seeing my heroes the Sex Pistols or the Anti-Nowhere League – punk bands that I had followed faithfully since I was a teenager – live in concert would only happen if there were any spare pennies available in the kitty. Oh, and then there was my wardrobe. I would need to acquire a whole new collection of all-weather dog-walking attire, wind and waterproof over trousers, a waxed jacket, Wellington boots and maybe even a hat. I was either going to look like a proper country gent or a complete and utter prat. Sod it, maybe the 'crisis' had hit me, although I would not be strutting around town in a vest top and skull bandana.

Many of our family and friends have dogs or have had dogs, and both of us get immense satisfaction and pleasure from spending time interacting with them. A beautiful little mongrel, or to give them their new politically correct title, mixed-breed, had graced my parents' lives for 13 years. They named her Tess, and from memory she had cost them £5 from a local breeder in 1983. Tess had the kindest of hearts and was the gentlest little soul, and she had led a very fulfilling and relaxed life with them until she very sadly crossed the Rainbow Bridge in August 1996. Her ashes are now lovingly kept under an antique urn in their garden. My brother Gary and his partner's lives are continually blessed with dogs; their usual breed of choice up until now has always been Labradors.

With Christmas over, we held our annual New Year's Eve party. Far too much alcohol was quaffed throughout the course of the evening. We listened intently to our guests as they each drunkenly – and loudly – spoke of their aspirations for the coming year. For us, there was the anticipated excitement of Winston.

We had a lot of partying and merrymaking to look forward to in 2014. June 9th was our 30th wedding anniversary and a garden party for about 120 guests to be hosted in our home was already planned. Our celebratory summer holiday had also already been booked – in August we were to fly off to the small Greek island of Skiathos for two weeks. Then in October it finally happened. We were both going to reach the dreaded grand old age of 50. Now to put the icing firmly on the cake, we were at some point during the year hopefully going to become the proud guardians to a four-legged house guest.

CHAPTER TWO

Our Search for Winston

They leave their homes and all they have to those they have left behind...

As the new year began, we started researching in earnest the obligations and requirements that we were going to have to fulfil and undertake to give a home to a puppy. Daily we trawled the internet with an intense fire lit within us, continually searching for reputable breeders of Scottish Terriers. I was spending as much of my spare time as I possibly could to seek the elusive Winston. But my endeavours were to no avail.

The weeks were rapidly passing, and before we knew it, they had morphed into months; the cold winter was a distant memory and long behind us, and the beautiful spring months had blossomed into life.

During one of my regular, methodical online search sessions trying to find Toni's dream Scottie, I accidentally stumbled across a website for the rehoming of abandoned dogs. Something about the site sparked my curiosity. Luckily I took the time to start glancing through the images and reading the heart-wrenching backstories of the dogs, whose scared faces almost seemed to be pleading to me from my computer screen. They all appeared to have one thing in common – their eyes, their sad dark soulless eyes full of despair, fear and sorrow.

I typed 'rescue dog' into the search engine, and was horrified at the results that rapidly loaded onto the computer screen. I clicked onto various countrywide dog rescue websites, and it very soon became blatantly obvious to me that there was an abundance of beautiful dogs – of all breeds and varying ages – that had been sadly forsaken through no fault of their own. These poor little souls had all been let down by us, humans. I began to research in greater depth, and my findings left me reeling in shock. Those poor dogs whose profiles I had looked at were some of the fortunate ones; they had at least been given the chance of life by being rescued by a dog rescue sanctuary. I just couldn't comprehend what I was reading. In the previous year, over 110,000 dogs had been picked up by local authorities in the UK; shockingly, and very sadly, over 7,000 innocent abandoned dogs had ended up euthanised when the standard seven-day deadline imposed by local authority dog wardens for their owners to come forward to reclaim them had expired. Just seven paltry days to live, and who cared?

Those 7,000 poor beautiful little souls had been given no chance. Twenty dogs a day, nearly one an hour.

The next statistic horrified and saddened me even more. Worldwide during the same period over 2.7 million dogs and cats were killed because rescue shelters were too full; there were just not enough adoptive families available to give them all homes.

7,397 a day, 308 an hour, five every minute…

In fact, in the time that it has taken you to read this one short sentence, another two innocent souls have been sent, through no fault of their own, across the Rainbow Bridge…

What I had just read stirred emotions of both sadness and anger within me. Did we really need to buy a pup from a breeder when there were so many poor abandoned dogs that simply need a loving home and family, but most importantly a chance of life?

Stuff it; there was absolutely no way that I was giving my money to a breeder. Looking at the horrendous plights of the stray dogs, one thing soon became blatantly obvious to me – you can't buy love, but you can rescue it.

We drastically needed to rethink about the dog that we wanted to share our home with. I picked up my laptop and headed downstairs. Toni was quietly sitting engrossed in reading her latest East London gangster crime thriller novel.

"Can I have a word?"

Toni looked up, took off her glasses and lay down her book.

"Is everything all right? You look upset, what has happened?"

I sat down next to her and lifted the top cover of the laptop; the browser instantly went straight to the rescue site that I had been previously looking at. I passed my computer to Toni and she started looking at the pitiful, moving images of the dogs in front of her and read their heart-wrenching stories. We have been together since we were teenagers, and can almost hold a conversation without speaking words; her eyes were full of tears when she looked back at me. She nodded her head.

We now had a new quest, to find and give a home to a poor, abandoned stray dog.

I set to work immediately trying to find out the names of all of the dog rescues and animal rescue sanctuaries within a 20-mile radius of our home. It was now a case of us not just feeling sorry for the dogs; we were actually going to do something positive to help.

I emailed each of them to express our interest in rehoming one of the stray dogs in their care. I asked each sanctuary the same set of questions, relating to any specific personal criteria or details about our home that they required with regards to their adoption processes. Eventually, we signed up to five rescues and filled in their relevant online adoption forms, stating our experience – or as it was in our case, total lack of experience – and any preferences or specific dog requirements such as sex, breed or age. For us now it was going to be a case of waiting for the right abandoned dog to arrive at the rescue.

We were fully aware that inevitably our future family member was going to be a dog that had been badly let down by its so-called ex 'loving family', dumped through no fault of its own, simply discarded like an unwanted by-product of our modern throwaway society. Was it simply because it was no longer loved? Or had it grown too old? Well, that's easy, chuck it out and get a nice new cute puppy. Maybe it had become ill, or had it shown its teeth in self-defence when receiving a cowardly, heartless unprovoked beating? Maybe it howled and cried when it was chained up in the garden for 24 hours a day, locked out in all weathers. Or could it be that it didn't get on with the new partner who hates dogs? Perhaps it didn't match the new wallpaper or even the designer handbag, blah blah blah. There's just no bloody justified or valid excuse to abandon a family member. Taking on a 'rescue dog' doesn't mean that it is damaged, it means that it has been badly let down by us humans.

Now, my every spare waking minute was spent in pursuit of our dog; even while on duty at work I was continually using the various online search engine apps on my mobile phone to find our dog. The illegal street vendors in East London must have had a field day, with my attention focused elsewhere I was not hunting them down; in fact, I was missing (or ignoring) the illegal, secretive deals that they were often conducting right in front of me, as I gazed intently at the small screen on my mobile.

Every day I would spend my one-hour lunch break hiding out in my favourite pie and mash shop on Hoxton Street. Pie, mash and lashings of liquor, or bowls of jellied eels, covered in black pepper and chilli vinegar were my comfort foods – sitting there for 60 minutes in solitude, trying to make sense of, and comprehend the horror stories that I read on how the 'featured' dogs had found themselves, through no fault of their own, in such wretched and sorrowful states, and now in the care and safety of the rescue sanctuaries. Every day, anger consumed my mind. Do some sick, vile, inhumane individuals honestly believe they have the God-given right to inflict pain and suffering on a dog, just because it is there? Every day after my lunch I popped into the pub opposite the pie shop, for a pint and whisky chaser, to help numb my sadness and anger.

***

Spring soon turned into summer; it was now June. So far, despite our best efforts, we had had no luck in our quest in finding a dog locally. So on a sunny Sunday we made a visit to the world-famous Battersea Dogs Home in south-west London. We were keen to see first-hand how the whole rescue process worked; also it would give us the chance to meet any dogs that they may have available that would be suitable for us. Before we could express an interest in any of their dogs, we would need to be formally interviewed. Luckily, they had a cancellation. We were ushered into a side room and joined by one of the rescue's dedicated rehoming team. The interview took about 30 minutes, during which time the required interest-of-adoption forms were filled in. An online search was carried out on our property, and from what she could see the lady ascertained that our home was more than suitable, but she did point out that our house may require a more in-depth check by a local agent at a later date. For the time being, we were issued with our unique membership number and told that we were now free to go and select a dog.

We headed off to view all of the available dogs. Gemma was drawn to a kennel housing two beagles. They both became animated, letting out their baying howls as we read their notes attached to the door on their kennel. On hearing the commotion one of the kennel assistants came over to us.

"Gorgeous aren't they?" she said

"They're beautiful," replied Gemma.

"If you should be interested we would prefer that they are rehomed together. They are brother and sister, and due to their sad past they have come to rely upon each other."

We were novices, and at that moment in time taking on one dog was going to be unchartered territory for us. Two dogs? That would have been plain silly, and irresponsible.

A few kennels along I spied a beautiful Shar-Pei. The notes on her door said that she was not ready for rehoming at that moment due to her ongoing surgery. She'd had one facelift, and was due to undergo her final corrective operation the following week. She'd hopefully be available for adoption early to mid-July.

Knowing that we were flying off to Greece in the middle of July meant realistically that we had reached the break-off point in our dog rescue quest. It would have been unfair to rehome an abandoned dog, and then send it to boarding kennels just four weeks later. It would have been far too confusing and distressing for the poor dog.

We were going to have to scale back our search for the foreseeable future.

Sadly, for us – but positive for the world of abandoned dogs – Battersea did not have many other available dogs in on that particular Sunday. Before we left, we were told that the 'dogs available' page on their website changed daily, so we would need to check frequently for new arrivals and their availability for adoption.

I honestly believe that everything in life happens for a reason. Unbeknown to us, just seven weeks later our dreams would all come true.

CHAPTER THREE

Shane

If with my paws I could do the same, this is what I would ask...

Sunday 10th August 2014 had begun like every other lazy Sunday does for us, with a pot of freshly brewed coffee and a full English breakfast.

We had only arrived home the previous evening from our two-week holiday on the beautiful Greek island of Skiathos. The 14 glorious days of our lazy holiday had been spent swimming in the warm Aegean Sea, or nonchalantly sunbathing and lounging about on the sun-kissed beach. Lunchtimes consisted of us enjoying the local cuisine, always washed down with a bottle or two of locally produced wine. Over our favourite mezes, our topic of conversation was invariably the excited anticipation of us one day – hopefully very soon – finding a suitable rescue dog to share our lives with us.

One day we did venture off-piste, we hopped on a small boat so that we could visit the small island of Skopelos. Toni wanted to see the filming locations of the 2008 film Mamma Mia. During the crossing, the owner and self-proclaimed captain of the boat took great pride in showing us a well-thumbed, slightly blurry photograph showing what he claimed was him, way in the background of one of the opening shots of the film. He had some crudely printed copies that he kindly offered to autograph for his adoring fans. He was selling these for five euros; if you wanted a photograph with him, that was for the knock-down bargain price of two euros.

Never in my wildest nightmares would I ever have imagined us, in the blistering midday sun, climbing the 198 steps carved into the rock of a sheer cliff face, trying to avoid snakes all the way up, just to see where the wedding procession had been filmed at the stunningly located Agios Ioannis Chapel.

Once Toni had rung the bell outside the chapel and seen all that she wanted to, we plucked up the courage to start on the treacherous 100-metre descent.

Relieved that we had made it unscathed, we headed straight back to the safety of the boat. Several welcome glasses of ouzo were quaffed as soon as we boarded, before setting sail to head to our next port of call, the harbour in Skopelos town. The Ouzo was purely medicinal of course, to counteract the shock of our terrifying mountaineering experience.

Anyway, back to Sunday, I fired up my laptop. I had already decided that today I was going to kick off my search by logging into the Mutts in Distress webpage. I had already taken the time to fill in their online application form several weeks earlier, just in case a suitable dog for us was brought into them for adoption while we were away.

The series of events that were to follow would change our lives beyond all recognition.

Suddenly, there staring back at me from their current 'dogs for rehoming' page was a photo of the most handsome-looking dog I had ever seen – Shane. I hadn't seen this stunning looking boy before. Full of anxious excitement I read his profile:

Shane is a Belgian Shepherd Dog (Malinois type). Shane is about two years old and will need a home where he can 'do something'. He is a working breed and has a working brain. Shane would not make a fireside pet and needs to go to training, perhaps do agility and be a companion to a real 'doggy' person. During his time with us, he has proven to be very affectionate towards people. Shane loves to be made a fuss of. He walks beautifully on his lead and is at his happiest when he is chewing at his 'Kong'. That's his favourite toy, and doesn't like to be away from it for too long! He does not like to be shut in or shut out for too long. He wants to be with someone who will make him their hobby, their companion and share their life with him. He has ignored other dogs as they come in and out of the kennels. Not yet tested with cats. We will update that as we find out. Nice dog for a real 'dog person', who can give this youngster time, training and work of some kind, maybe do a few fun dog shows with him? Shane is not suitable as a guard/security dog. Shane is a pet who will do well in obedience.

Shane's profile sounded perfect. For me, this really was love at first sight. I enlarged his image on my computer to full screen and called Toni over to view his profile photo.

"Toni, you've got to come and take a look at Shane."

My voice was full of excitement; I had everything crossed and was hoping and praying that Toni's initial thoughts about this beautifully stunning dog would be the same as mine.

"He's beautiful, what breed is he?"

"He's a Malinois, a Belgian Shepherd."

Toni shrunk the photo and carefully perused through Shane's profile; luckily she also liked the words that she read.

"Well, he certainly isn't a Scottie. Do you think, honestly, that a couple of novices like us could take on a Malinois? It sounds like he is going to need an experienced handler, we haven't a clue. However, nevertheless, he sounds absolutely perfect. Let's give Mutts a call to see if he is still available, and if they would at least consider letting us adopt him."

Toni was obviously as excited about meeting Shane as I was. Unable to contain her excitement, she immediately picked up the phone and rang Mutts. She mentioned that we were interested in popping over to see Shane; no, in fact, we couldn't wait to meet him. The initial response was not quite what she was expecting.

"Shane? You're interested in offering our Shane a home? Really? Listen I have to tell you that Shane does have some issues, but if you are genuinely interested we will sit down and talk about him when you come over. Would you like to make arrangements to pop over and meet him at some point next week?"

The lady seemed to be entirely taken aback by Toni's enthusiasm and response.

"We'll be over in 15 minutes."

Hurriedly we got ready, jumped into our car and headed to the rescue sanctuary. It was a dismal day, the heavens had opened, and driving was treacherous due to the flooded roads. The wiper blades were just about managing to clear the windscreen as we meandered along the potholed, winding country lanes to the dog rescue. On any other day I would have turned back, but not that day – we were on a mission, potentially our first, and as time would prove, not our last, dog rescue mission.

For reasons unknown, we both felt extremely anxious as we slowly pulled up in front of the reception area of Mutts. I parked our car next to a kennel block. It was still pouring with rain, with faint rumbles of thunder far in the distance. We got out and put up our umbrellas, in a half-hearted attempt to offer a bit of protection, then turned onto the sodden paddock and walked past a row of six kennel units, each of them individually housing a dog.

We both carefully scrutinised the inhabitants, hoping to catch our first glimpse of Shane. The dogs became animated with excitement as we passed them, jumping up and barking greetings at us, the two strangers in front of them. It was almost as if each of them were begging us in anticipation to give them a home, their sad little faces imploring us, 'Please pick me, please choose me, please take me home with you.'

It was both distressing and sad looking into their kennels, but for those poor doggies, it must have been much harder spending their life looking out.

Unfortunately, we couldn't see Shane amongst them, so we headed back towards the reception area. We closed our umbrellas and shook ourselves down before entering, wiping our feet on the muddy hessian mat before introducing ourselves to the lady behind the counter, which was adorned by one of the sanctuary's resident cats. We explained the reason for our visit. High-pitched squawks, screeches and greetings of "Hello!" were being hurled at us from a macaw, perched on a branch in the large aviary behind us.

The lady who Toni had initially spoken to on the phone was summoned to come and talk to us. After introducing herself, she began to tell us more about Shane.

"Right, no messing, I'm going to cut to the chase. Shane is really not a 'people' dog; in fact, he can be very dismissive of potential families who take an interest in him. Often he will grunt and turn his back on them. We do not force the issue as we don't want to upset or aggravate him."

She paused. We could see that telling his story, maybe for the umpteenth time, was upsetting her.

"He has had a dreadful start to his young life. Shane had initially been found abandoned by the local dog warden. He had been dumped in a ditch of slurry; it took us days to clean the grime and muck off him. From the condition that he was in when he first arrived here, we could tell that he had been very badly treated. We have tried to offer him as a service dog, but sadly it proved to be unsuccessful, his temperament just wasn't suitable. Guard dog training also failed due to his aggression."

Yet again she had to compose herself.

"Shane was rehomed once, but sadly the owner gave him a violent beating one evening, so he was immediately removed from their 'care' and came back here to us. Oh, and another thing I am going to need to forewarn you about is his teeth, or more to the point, his lack of teeth. All he has left are ground-down stumps, which means that his food needs to be moistened. On the subject of food, he wolfs it down; he finishes his bowl in seconds. I am going to be perfectly frank with you, we'd love Shane to find a home, but because of how he is we have almost resigned ourselves to the fact that he will never leave here."

Our heads were spinning; the lady had been brutally frank and honest in her introduction of Shane. Maybe she was preparing us for the worse, trying to protect us. It was clear that so many times in the past he had rejected people, or hadn't shown any interest. She could see that we were excited, and was obviously worried that true to form, he might stubbornly not want to interact with us.

"He also has an obsession with his rubber 'Kong' toy; it's his comfort blanket, it seems to give him a sense of security. The only time he puts it down is to eat or drink, so please, at no point try and take it from him. Right then, if you are sure you want to meet him, and are ready I'll grab a lead and go and get him, at least then we can see if he takes to you, and if by a miracle he does, how you all get along with each other."

With nervous anticipation, we stood waiting in the foyer, hoping against all the odds that he wouldn't reject us. Then at the end of the small corridor, he appeared – we had our first glimpse of Shane. He sat obediently on the other side of the little safety gate while the lady from the rescue made some adjustments to his collar and lead. When he was ready, she opened the gate. Shane looked towards us, tilted his head to one side, and then literally dragged the poor lady down the corridor, his paws slipping, unable to get a proper grip on the shiny surface of the tiled floor. We could clearly see his beloved rubber toy gripped firmly in his jaws. Not wanting to invade his space or scare him I stepped back. I then extended my arm and slowly offered my hand to him. He gently started sniffing me, then, although I knew that I shouldn't have, and for reasons I can't explain, I knelt down in front of him, the so-called anti-social Malinois. Like a complete and utter fool, and to make matters potentially even worse, I gently put my arms around his neck and embraced him. Shane's face was now right up against mine. I could smell the distinct odour of his rubber 'security blanket', his jaws gnawing ferociously at it, a strange slippery, squelchy, squeaky sound emitting from his mouth as his stumpy teeth chewed intently.

Still kneeling, I leant back and cupped his face in my hands, caressing and gently stroking his powerful jaw with each of my thumbs. Now I found myself staring straight at him, his face no more than a foot from mine. He had now stopped chewing on his Kong, but it remained in his mouth.

My eyes, the windows to my soul, couldn't hide the instant adoration and infatuation that I felt for the stunning dog that I was embracing.

It turns out that dogs are experts at reading body language; they instinctively stare into our eyes, read our posture, they even read our movements. Intuitively they understand so much about us without our even knowing. They mysteriously seem to know exactly what we're feeling; I'd go as far as to say they can read our thoughts.

"Hello, gorgeous boy."

The words came spontaneously to me; there was nothing else I could think of saying to him. Shane by this time had now sat down of his own accord and didn't seem at all uneasy at the affection that I, a total stranger, was showering upon him. Toni moved in and joined in stroking, and offering her own words of comfort and encouragement to the handsome dog sitting in front of us. Suddenly, Shane dropped the beloved toy that he had held firmly in his mouth. It bounced on the floor, he looked down at it, then back at us.

The lady from the rescue looked shocked, in fact, confused that he had voluntarily discarded his Kong. While he was distracted interacting and playing with us, she reached down, picked up his beloved toy, and hid it in her pocket.

"Well that's very strange, not like him at all."

A knowing look engulfed her face; she smiled and gently shook her head. She had worked with rescue dogs for many years and had probably seen it all. Just maybe, with her vast experience, she instinctively knew that Shane had finally chosen his own family.

"Would you like to take him for a short walk? If you head out of the main gates, you could take him along the lane. It will give you some quality time alone to all get acquainted with one another a bit better."

What a silly question, and one that we certainly wouldn't need asking twice. What a privilege, the chance to take Shane out alone, just the three of us. The lady gave us stringent instructions on how to walk and handle him correctly, fitted a second lead to his collar, and issued us with an essential piece of kit – several scented poo bags, just in case.

Luckily, during the time that we had been talking the rain had stopped falling; a clean, fresh earthy fragrance filled the countryside air as the three of us headed off together. Shane had done this walk many times with the kennel maids and volunteers who lovingly took care of him at Mutts; in fact, he took charge as he led us out of the large wooden main gates of the dog rescue.

Shane was even more stunning in real life than he was in his profile pictures, if that was possible. Such a distinguished, proud-looking boy. He almost strutted with an arrogant swagger as the three of us headed along the quiet country lane.

Toni asked if she could take a turn in walking him. Damn it, I was in my element. Reluctantly I passed her his lead to enable her to take full control of him. Toni was a natural in the way that she handled him.

Shane was an absolute gentleman; he walked perfectly, no tugging or pulling. I felt so honoured to be in the company of such a handsome dog. In my mind, I knew that Shane was already our dog. We headed further up the quiet lane. Shane, still leading the way, had now positioned himself between us, and as we strolled along, his head continually turned back to look at us. Maybe it was just a small reassuring glance as if to say, 'Don't worry you're safe with me.'

Had we passed his audition? Had he now definitely made his mind up that we were going to be his chosen family? I would like to think that we passed with flying colours.

"Well, what do you think of him?"

Toni, still holding his lead, looked down at Shane, then at me.

"What can I say? He's gorgeous. I think Shane will be perfect for us, and us for him."

We had walked a fair way along New Barn Lane, and again, just as when we were in the foyer a few minutes earlier, I knelt in front of Shane, who had sat upon a command from Toni. Yet again I put my arms around his neck and hugged him. I had inadvertently managed to kneel straight in a puddle; the dampness seeping through my jeans brought me back to my senses. I looked deep into the loving eyes of the noble dog in front of me.

"You've got a home son. Welcome to the family, mate."

To this day, I swear that he understood the words that I had said to him, for he responded by giving me one almighty lick, straight on my lips. So much for him being anti-social and dismissive, he just seemed to crave the love and attention that we were showering upon him.

Proudly, yet reluctantly, with our new family member, we turned around and started to head back to Mutts in Distress. We knew there were a few more formalities that needed to be finalised as part of the adoption process.

As the three of us walked across the car park, the lady who had been assisting us came out of the reception area to see how our interaction with Shane had gone. She didn't need to ask the question, what with Shane's tail wagging excitedly and our faces beaming with smiles from ear to ear; she saw exactly what she wanted to see. As we got closer to where she was standing, she retrieved Shane's beloved toy from her pocket, then handed it back to him. He almost snatched it back from her, then turned and looked up at me. For some unknown reason he opened his mouth, his rubber toy dropped to the floor. With a look of sheer panic on his face, he quickly retrieved it; again, the sound of his stumpy teeth chewing on the rubber filled the air. I could see how important that little toy was to him; maybe it had been his only companion that had got him through some of his traumatic, darker days.

"Well, by the look of it that all went perfectly for the three of you. I'll settle Shane back in his kennel, and then we can complete the adoption paperwork. Come on Shane, heel."

The lady gave him the firm command, turned and attempted to lead him back to his kennel. However, Shane had ideas of his own; he seemed reluctant to leave our company and pulled on his lead to try and drag her back towards us. Eventually, after another couple of firmer commands, he begrudgingly followed orders and trudged behind the lady back to his kennel. As he walked away from us, I shouted words of encouragement and comfort to him, he looked back towards us, but his demeanour had changed, his poor little tail was now firmly between his hind legs.

Once he had been settled back in his kennel, the lady returned to complete the final pieces of paperwork with us, and to sort out the adoption fee.

"I can't see any notes on the system, but I'm assuming that you have you had your home check done?"

"Sod it."

The 'home check' is an essential part of Mutts in Distress's adoption process. Before being allowed to adopt a dog, a visit to the potential new owners' house is carried out by one of the members of staff or volunteers.

The importance of the check is to ascertain that the dog's potential new home will offer a suitably safe, secure and loving environment. All aspects of the dog's welfare are thoroughly covered in detail during the visit. Things such as where it will sleep, how long it will be left on its own, boarding arrangements when the family go on their holidays, ages of household members and any other pets that they may have. Advice is also given with regards to the importance of obedience or agility classes, exercise, pet insurance and recommended local vets. Security is paramount - during the visit the garden is checked to ensure that there are no potential escape routes and that there is adequately high fencing all around.

"No sorry, we haven't got that far, our application form was approved, but as we hadn't shown any interest up till now in one of your dogs, our house hasn't been checked yet."

Damn, now we were both panicking that we may lose the chance of giving Shane a home. We had fallen head over heels for him, and he seemed to like us, there was no way that we could let him down now.

"Not to worry, do you honestly think your home is suitable? For Shane's sake, I don't want this to fail."

"I don't see any reason why not; we've been checked and passed by five other rescues. Our garden is more than secure, six-foot fences all around and no escape routes."

My answers were honest: yes, we had been home-checked by other rescue sanctuaries that we had signed up with, but understandably, Mutts needed to be 100 per cent sure for themselves about the future welfare of any of the abandoned dogs in their care. We now needed to pass the rescue's own strict and stringent criteria.

"Right, I finish work at three, if it's all right with you, I will stop off on my way home and do the check."

Her very kind offer put us at ease. Shane needed a home, and the staff were going to go above and beyond to try and help make sure that it happened for him.

"If all is okay – and I'm sure that it will be – then tomorrow you can come back and complete the final parts of the application form for the formal adoption of Shane."

***

Our family had all descended on us for a cold buffet and drinks to hear about our holiday on Skiathos, and for us to bore them with our many holiday photos. At just after three the doorbell rang. Standing there, armed with her clipboard containing the home-check forms, was the lady from Mutts. Toni invited her in. Our family, the nosey buggers, were all curious as to who she was.

"Sorry, hope that I am not interrupting a party?"

"No not at all. Anyway, Shane getting a home is far more important."

"Who is Shane?" Kealy asked.

"I'll explain later."

As I showed the lady through to the garden to complete our home check, the girls instantly encircled and start interrogating Toni. She excitedly told them all about the beautiful dog that we had found, and were hoping to adopt.

"Well it's all very secure, even Shane won't be able to escape. There's plenty of room for him to play in, although I doubt very much that he will venture around your garden too much. He has some very odd ways about him, all probably due to his horrible past."

She then took out her mobile. I could see that she was emotionally animated with excitement as she called the founder of the rescue sanctuary.

"All's good; they have passed. It looks like our Shane has found his furever home."

I'm sure that I heard a cheer from the recipient of the call.

We were just about to say our goodbyes and make arrangements to finalise the paperwork and make the necessary plans to bring Shane home the following day, when Gemma raised a concern that she had.

"Don't forget we have a surprise planned for you both for next weekend. Just maybe it would be easier all round if you were to collect Shane Tuesday week?"

Everyone looked at Gemma, then their eyes all became fixed intently upon us, scrutinising our faces in anticipation of our responses.

We could tell that our family had something extraordinary lined up for us, and they had all obviously put a considerable amount of work into whatever the surprise was that they had planned for us. Not wanting to jeopardise their efforts, we reluctantly agreed to wait a week until we collected Shane, but regardless we were still going to go to Mutts first thing in the morning to complete the adoption process. At least it would save us from having to rush out in the morning to buy everything that we would need for him.

"If we can please complete everything and sign him over to you tomorrow, then we will be more than happy to keep him for one last week. At least Shane will no longer be an abandoned rescue dog; he will now be your dog, just staying with us as a holiday boarder. You'll be able to come and visit him every day, and take him out for walks."

Unbeknown to us at this point, that day was going to prove to be a joyous double celebration. Not only was Shane going to join our family, but Kealy had an announcement to make – she was pregnant. I cannot put into words how thrilled I was at the thought that I was going to become a grandfather. Time to crack open the champagne, but only fresh orange juice for Kealy…

***

At last, Monday morning finally arrived. Full of childlike excitement we got ready and hurriedly headed back to Mutts to be there for their opening time of 9 am.

Upon arrival, there were a few other members of staff milling about whom we hadn't met yet. We were introduced to a couple of the senior members of the team by the lady we had spoken to yesterday. Everyone was so genuinely thrilled to learn that their Shane had now finally found a family and home of his own. Bless them, the staff were so dedicated to the forsaken dogs in their care.

We filled in the last of the handover and disclaimer forms, were issued with his microchip details, and paid the relevant adoption fees. We then selected a dog tag, a circular shiny chrome design, which we had engraved with Shane's name, his new home address and three emergency contact phone numbers.

"Would it be possible if we could see him please before we go, and just maybe take him out for a walk?"

"Of course, he's your dog now. Wait a sec, and I'll grab a lead and go and fetch him for you."

Just as with the day before, at the end of the small passageway the handsome, sorry, our handsome Shane appeared. Our newly adopted ex-rescue dog. It was becoming a habit, but yet again I dropped to my knees and called to him.

"Come on Shane, good boy."

In his excitement to get to us, he again dragged the poor lady down the hall. He almost leapt into my waiting open arms, with his cherished Kong in his mouth. As with yesterday, his beloved and revered 'comfort blanket' was soon discarded; in fact it was almost spat out onto the floor.

Behind me, I heard a jangling sound; another one of the staff members was already getting a second lead ready.

Today was going to be different though, for today we would be walking our dog.

Shane proudly stood between us, his new family, and for once he had no rubber toy firmly gripped in his powerful jaws, spoiling his handsome features.

"I give it three months, and he'll no longer need his comfort toy."

My comment almost had an air of arrogance about it.

"No chance," one of the senior members of staff replied.

"That bleeding toy goes everywhere with him; he will never be without it."

The August sun was shining, as yet again the three of us headed off on the same walk along the peaceful country lane that we had done just 24 hours previously.

We stopped and took the time to snap some customary selfie-type photographs. The older generation really should not attempt this manoeuvre – six attempts it took me just to get the three of us in the picture. Anyway, these were going to be plastered all over our social media accounts, for us to proudly show off our new four-legged family member to all our family and friends.

In all, we were out walking for about 30 minutes before we started to head back to Mutts with Shane. We reassured him all the way back that we would visit and walk him every single day.

As we arrived at the reception area Shane's toy was again handed back to him by one of the kennel maids. Then it was the hard bit; we had to say our goodbyes to him. Both of us gave him a huge cuddle and a kiss on his forehead before he was reluctantly led back to his kennel. Only this time it was his holiday boarding kennel.

We were just bidding our farewells to the staff, and thanking them for all that they had done for Shane, when the lady who had taken him back to his kennel came charging back into the reception area. The poor lady was red-faced and looked panic-stricken.

"Shane's gone berserk. He is trashing his kennel and everything in it. He doesn't want to stay, is there any way at all that you can take him home today? I'm terrified he will do himself a severe injury."

Toni looked at me. Gemma's voice and strict instructions were echoing round and round in my mind, my train of thought disturbed by one of the kennel maids.

"If you could please take him today and settle him, at least then he could come back to us just for the weekend."

The staff were all concerned for Shane's well-being; they were more than aware that he could seriously hurt himself given the way that he was behaving in his kennel.

"Shane's welfare comes first. We are not going to leave him, so could you go and get him for us please?"

I had made a decision and would explain all to our family later. But there was another, far more significant problem. Knowing that he wasn't coming home with us that day, well in theory anyway, we hadn't prepared our house for him, and we certainly had not yet purchased all the essential items that we would need for Shane.

As one of the staff members went to get him, another one grabbed a pen and paper and quickly scribbled down a shopping list of everything that we would need:

- Lead
- Collar
- Car seat belt harness
- Dry food (kibble). His favourite brand was listed.
- Wet food, again, the brand that the rescue had found most beneficial to his health was listed.
- Food bowl

- Water bowl
- Hairbrush. Shane loves to sit and have his hair brushed!
- Toys
- Treats
- Poo bags
- Dog insurance

Toni took the list from her.

"Thank you very much. We'll also need to add a bed to the list as well for him."

"I really wouldn't bother. Shane just sleeps on the floor; he always has done."

Then, there he was, the now all too familiar sight of Shane at the end of the passageway. This time he was jumping up at the gate. In fact, I'm surprised that he didn't leap straight over it. The second it was opened for him he excitedly bounded down the hallway towards us; anyone would have thought that we hadn't seen him for days in the way that he lovingly greeted us, running around in circles and leaping up at each of us in turn.

We gathered together all of his paperwork and veterinary records. Shane's newly printed dog tags were temporarily attached to the collar that we were being lent, along with a lead, until we purchased him new ones of his own.

A few final words of advice were given, such as the importance of not walking him for at least an hour either side of him having his breakfast or dinner, and not to bathe him for a few days, to allow him to get his scent around his new home. Reassuringly, we were told that there was always someone there, 24 hours a day, to offer help or advice if ever needed. Finally, the lady told us that it would be in Shane's, and our own, best interests to attend obedience school with him. The class teachers were all Mutts staff members or volunteers, all fully qualified dog trainers.

With our heads spinning from the sudden series of events that had happened over the last few minutes, we proudly led him out. We said our goodbyes to the staff, each of them giving their emotional farewells to Shane.

"Good luck Shane, you really are an exceptional boy."

"We are all going to miss you, Mr Shane."

"Be happy little man."

They also commanded him that he had to come back and visit them occasionally.

I opened the rear car door and without any prompting Shane leapt straight in. He seemed to know exactly where he was going. He was going home, to his new, furever home.

We drove straight to the pet store, and proudly with Shane at our sides we entered totally alien and unknown territory. Up until now we had never had cause to visit such an establishment.

"What a beautiful dog."

That was the welcoming greeting we received from a young female staff member as we walked in. With obvious bewilderment etched on our faces, we started to look at the vast shop, stacked with items that we had never in the past had to concern ourselves with.

"Have you had him long?" she asked.

"About 15 minutes," I replied.

"We're new to all of this. He's our first dog."

She raised her eyebrows and initially laughed, but the dazed, vacant expressions on our faces must have said it all. Her demeanour instantly changed, now she seemed to look at us with both pity and disbelief at our naivety at taking on such a huge commitment as a Malinois; obviously not the ideal breed for a couple of complete novices.

"Would you be able to help us please? We have a list of everything that we need."

I explained to her the story of how we had been caught entirely unawares by Shane, and how he had unexpectedly come to be with us. After listening intently to our tale, the shop assistant took the small piece of paper from us. Slowly she led us around the store, filling a trolley with everything that we were going to need for Shane that had been written on the list.

Throughout the store we both noticed that Shane was continually receiving admiring glances from fellow customers and staff. One thing was blatantly obvious, he was a very noble and proud-looking dog, and the cheeky little sod bloody well knew it.

We took time to select him a suitable collar and matching lead, containing absolutely no leather or studs, just sturdy plain nylon; we also added a half check chain, something that the assistant said we would need as we were contemplating obedience lessons.

As we were meandering around the store, we arrived at an aisle with shelving laden with dog beds. Toni started looking through them; she lay a few that she personally liked on the ground. Shane stood next to her and carefully examined each of them one at a time. He then plonked himself down on what appeared to be his favourite, a soft brown bed with a paw-print design.

"He's picked the one he wants, we will get him a bed; I know that they said he sleeps on the floor, but I want him to be comfortable," said Toni.

After paying for our purchases, and thanking the assistant for all her help, we loaded up our car and headed for home. This was going to be Shane's first experience of his new home; we were both extremely anxious as to how he was going to react.

I needn't have worried; I opened the front door and the three of us walked in, Toni first, then I followed behind Shane. Once the door had been securely closed, and the security chain engaged, I unclipped his lead and let Shane loose.

"This is your home now mate. Go and explore," I said to him.

We both stepped back and watched as he ran excitedly from room to room with his beloved Kong firmly clenched between his stumpy teeth, meticulously sniffing and inspecting every solitary square inch of his new domicile.

When he had covered all of the downstairs rooms, he headed for the back door and stood there poised, staring intently out into the garden, his Kong hanging loosely from one side of his mouth. A damp imprint of his nose had formed where it was being firmly pressed against the glass; the fine, warm water vapour from his mouth was causing a small patch of condensation as he exhaled in excited anticipation of exploring outside.

Toni went over and unlocked the patio door and opened it for him. She stood aside, but deep down was not expecting Shane to venture out too far after what the lady had told us yesterday.

Nope, not Shane. Like a bat out of hell out he charged, full of childlike elation. He bounded frantically up the few stone steps, stopped, looked back to where we were standing then hurtled himself around the lawn at full pelt.

Shane made a few random strategic stops to sniff the grass and shrubs, he cocked his rear right leg as high as he could and scent marked his new domain. This was now his very own garden.

I followed him out, and I have to admit that the scene unfolding right before my very eyes, of an ex-abandoned dog discovering his new home, brought a lump to my throat.

I could see a small distinctive red object lying in the centre of the lawn. Blimey, it was Shane's revered Kong. Had it already been discarded?

Excitedly Shane carried on playing, his tail continually wagging, a wag that went from the very tip of his tail all the way to his head. His body – and I know that this sounds silly – appeared all soft and wiggly. Now and then he would momentarily run frantically around in a circle barking, but in a rather feeble high-pitched bark. He didn't know what to do next, one moment he was bouncing from side to side, then he would drop to the ground and roll onto his back, his head thrashing from side to side and his legs waving aimlessly around in the air. After rolling back onto his belly he would leap up, facing me, his bottom in the air and his chest almost touching the grass, then the whole game would start again.

Not wanting to disturb him, I rolled and lit a cigarette, and sat down in the shade.

Eventually, he stopped and stood still, panting heavily with his tongue hanging out. He looked over towards where I was sitting on a small wall.

Down the steps he bounced, and he walked over to join me. Without me saying a word, Shane sat in front of where I was sitting, staring lovingly up at me. Momentarily I closed my eyes, nodded, then with both hands I slowly reached forward and started to caress his head, before rising to my feet, my eyes remaining fixed on his gaze. Before I knew what had happened he leapt up, placing his paws on my shoulders, I put my arms around him, and yet again he planted one of his now trademark sloppy kisses straight on my face.

Was this Shane's unique way of saying 'Thank you'?

He was still panting from his manic exploration session of the garden, his warm breath covering my face. I removed my hands from his waist and gently grasped both of his front paws in my hands.

"Down Shane, there's a good boy."

Shane sat; I leant forward and reached behind him and turned on the garden tap, the water rushed out and bounced up off the paving slabs, splashing his rear end and tail. He turned, and I cupped my hands under the flowing water. Shane moved forwards and took some much-needed sips from the palms of my hands. Then he began snapping at the cool liquid as it cascaded from the brass tap. When he had quenched his thirst, I turned off the tap. Shane scrutinised the area then plonked himself down on his side, strategically positioning himself in the cooling small puddle that had accumulated.

Toni now took her turn in sitting watching him, as I went and started to unload the car. Our cupboards were soon laden with a whole array of products that they had never seen before.

I found the small bag that contained his new collar; this was the part I that was looking forward to, transferring his name tag, with our address – sorry Shane's address – and contact details onto it. With immense pride, I placed it lovingly around his neck, as if presenting an Olympian with a gold medal. What a handsome boy he looked.

Now was the tricky bit. We had to let our daughters know that we had done the complete opposite to what they had instructed us to do yesterday.

I called Gemma first to let her know our fantastic news. Gemma was the only one of our daughters that still lived at home with us, and she would now be sharing her home with Shane.

"You've done what? I really do have the most disobedient parents on the planet."

Gemma was disgruntled at us for not listening to her simple request, but I knew that deep down secretly she was thrilled that Shane had joined our family.

As I have already mentioned earlier, Gemma, along with Kealy, Leah and my parents Janet and Roy, had arranged a massive surprise for us for the following weekend. Now she was going to have to readjust their meticulously organised plans to incorporate Shane's well-being for a few days.

We spent some time making the obligatory social media announcements – to me it seems that in our modern society every action that you take has to be announced to your awaiting audience. You then wait in anticipation, hoping to receive a multitude of 'likes' and congratulatory messages.

I know this next bit will sound ridiculous, but after spending a fun couple of hours playing with him in the garden, we both had to pluck up the courage to take Shane out for his first proper walk, now that we had formally adopted him. To us, walking him correctly where there are going to be members of the public, and potentially other dogs, was going to be a huge responsibility, and one that we were not going to take lightly.

Tentatively I attached Shane's new lead to his collar. I could feel my OCD kicking in as I checked, then double checked (in fact, from memory, I think that I even triple checked) that I had fastened it correctly. Once I was happy that all was secure, the three of us headed off down the road to the field adjacent to the 12th-century Harlowbury Chapel, with its distinctive brick-buttressed flint walls and Norman arched doors and windows. Together we sauntered around the perimeter of the grassland a couple of times, and on the second lap I lost my virginity with regards to having to pick up poop, noting that we needed to buy much, much bigger poo bags next time.

Of course, we needn't have worried about taking him out; throughout the whole time that we were strolling and playing over the field, Shane behaved graciously and impeccably to all of the two- and four-legged – in fact one even had three legs – walkers that he encountered.

We headed back along Old Road towards home. Once we were back indoors we removed Shane's lead, and headed back out into the garden. As we had been advised earlier, we left it just over an hour before giving Shane his dinner, in his shiny brand new stainless steel bowl.

Blimey, he wolfed it down; in a matter of seconds the whole bowl of meat and kibble was devoured, the bowl licked clean of every last morsel. I immediately set about researching on online dog forums for ways of slowing a dog down when eating. I soon found the answer that I was looking for. First thing in the morning I would go back to the pet shop to purchase Shane a 'slow feeder bowl'.

At about 5 pm Leah came round to be introduced to Shane. She had arrived with a bag chock-full of gifts that she had been out and bought for him.

"Hi Pops! Bloody hell, he's a big boy!" was Leah's cheery, yet somewhat shocked greeting.

Within minutes, Gemma arrived home from work, also laden with presents, followed shortly after by Kealy.

Shane was an absolute gentleman; he greeted each of them with courtesy and eagerly played with the vast array of toys that they had each kindly bought for him.

The girls instantly fell for Shane; I'd challenge anyone to be able to resist his charms. I spent time giving a full and true explanation of what had happened earlier at the rescue sanctuary, so they fully understood and accepted why we had to bring him home earlier than we had promised.

My daughters all listened intently, and appeared saddened when I told them about Shane's 'security blanket', the red rubber toy that was his constant companion, his pacifier.

"I'll know when he is at peace with us, the day when he no longer relies on his Kong. That is the day I'm waiting for, when his home gives him the security that he needs, not a toy from his traumatic past. It will take time, but it will happen."

I don't know why, but in my mind I looked on that toy as a threat, even a challenge. I should just let Shane chew away on it to his heart's content; it was not doing him any harm. However, to me, it was as if it helped him with his demons, the demons that I wanted exorcised from him.

Love and kindness were going to be his cure.

To break the sombre mood that had fallen over us, Gemma was eager to try and walk him; she clicked his lead onto his collar.

"Come on Shane, walkies."

Bless her; we would have to work on the commands that she gives.

We sat and watched as she led him up and down the lawn. Kealy and Leah then each took it in turns to walk him around the garden. The whole time Shane was relishing all of the love and attention being freely bestowed upon him by his new family.

He walked perfectly by each of their sides as they strolled, and occasionally broke into a jog around the lawn. Sporadically he hopped, then he broke into what I can only describe as a dressage horse's gait; his legs appearing to reach the ground one after another, he somehow raised his front legs in perfect synchronisation with his hind, each time he lifted his leg his paws hung limply in front of him.

Remembering the lady saying that he loved his fur to be brushed, I retrieved the brush that we had purchased for him earlier.

I sat down on the grass and called his name. He looked at me, he spied the brush in my hand and bounded over, dropped his Kong and sat bolt upright. I started to groom his soft tan fur, over and over; each time that I tried to stop, he nudged me with his nose. After about 20 minutes, with my wrist aching, Gemma took over; again she was unable to stop as she also received a nudge when she tried to take a break. Leah and Kealy both take a turn. For such a noble, butch-looking dog he was indeed in touch with his feminine side when it came to his grooming sessions.

Darkness slowly engulfed our garden, and our resident bats were putting on their nightly aerial display way above our heads. I looked indoors at our kitchen clock. Blimey, it was 11 pm already. Kealy and Leah said goodnight to Shane, then us, before heading back to their own homes. Gemma climbed the stairs to bed as she had an early start in the morning.

The first day of Shane moving in with us slowly drew to an end, and it was time for us to turn in for the night. We located his bed to a draught-free area of the hallway. Shane had already been out into the garden for a wee. I called him into the hall, and he looked at his bed, then up at me. Again he looked down before plonking himself onto the inviting soft, plump paw-print covering. Shane looked back up at me then rose onto his paws and turned around a couple of times, lay down, got up, turned around, then lay down again. He had now ended up back where he started in the first place; he must have at long last found his most comfortable position.

Shane looked completely contented; he rolled over onto his left-hand side and stretched out his legs. He breathed a heavy sigh and made a gentle, continuous slurping sound with his lips. Bless his heart; my little man appeared to be so untroubled, relishing the soft comfort and sanctuary of his very own bed. He started chewing gently on his beloved toy, only now it seemed reminiscent of when a baby is trying to fall asleep, sucking on its dummy.

I went over and lay down next to him, his body remaining motionless, but his head lifted, his eyes meeting mine, looking adoringly back at him. He rolled over onto his back – not the most glamorous of positions – and for the next five minutes I stroked his belly. Every now and then I must have hit a ticklish spot, because his eyes would roll back, and one of his hind legs would involuntarily kick out like mad.

"This is your furever home mate. Goodnight my precious boy."

Eventually, he rolled back over onto his belly; I leant forward and planted a huge, sloppy kiss on his forehead – something else that I was now going to have to get used to, fur in the mouth.

I headed off upstairs to my bed. Every time I looked back at him, he was lying there looking back at me, his head slightly raised, and his ears pricked up. His eyes glared at me. The last time I glanced at him he yawned, and then laid his head down on his front paws.

To reassure, and enable him to move about the house safely, I left the landing light turned on and our bedroom door open.

Blimey, what an exhilarating, exciting, yet exhausting day. That day Shane had entered our lives in the most profound way, but as time would eventually teach us, that is one of the beautiful things about dogs, they change you, for the better, and you never ever see what is coming.

***

Six o'clock Tuesday morning, I heard a scratching sound from the landing. I jumped up and opened the bedroom door, which must have blown shut during the night, only to be met by Shane. The carpet was all scuffed up where he had been clawing at it; there were also a few claw marks on the paintwork on the bottom of the door.

Cheekily he gazed up at me; before I knew what was happening, he stealthily dodged past me, ran into our bedroom and leapt straight up onto our bed, startling Toni.

I roared with laughter. Shane plonked himself down, his head on my pillow. The cheeky little sod had made himself well and truly at home.

I went over and joined them for an early morning cuddle.

I couldn't help myself. I lay there looking adoringly at him, but there appeared to be something strange. Shane seemed different, he was missing something, but initially I couldn't place my finger on it.

Then it dawned on me; it was his Kong. I went downstairs and there it was, lying discarded next to his bed, his one solitary companion that had given him a sense of security for as long as the Mutts team had known him had been left behind. Had his demons started to depart already? Was his tortured soul beginning to heal after less than a day with us?

***

Straight away we set about developing a structured daily routine for Shane.

Early morning walk, breakfast, playtime, sleep. One hour lunchtime walk, a bit of playtime, sleep. Late afternoon he had his dinner, a two-hour evening walk, and then finally bed.

Shane appeared to be settling in with our family life so well; he had after one short day well and truly planted his paws under the table and made himself right at home.

By day two he was already letting his presence in his home be known, barking when the doorbell rang, or when people walked past his house. It was as if he was protecting and guarding his domain and family. His bed had now been relocated upstairs to the landing; our bedroom door was always left ajar so that he could hear us, and freely pop in and join us whenever he wanted to – which now seemed to be him jumping up on our bed every evening.

I had read about the separation issues that some dogs, especially rescue dogs, could suffer from, and to be honest, was reluctant at leaving Shane alone for any length of time.

The various ways that dogs' issues can manifest themselves include constant barking or howling, defecating or urinating in the home, or they may chew and destroy their owner's artefacts. More often than not, they will display these or other distress behaviours within a very short space of time from being left alone.

In preparation for a worst-case scenario, I had researched several ways of overcoming the separation issues Shane could potentially display.

Of course I needn't have been worried. Shane had no anxiety or separation issues. He knew full well that we were coming home to him. He'd spend his days waiting for us, either lying on ours or Gemma's bed, making himself comfortable, rolling up the continental quilts to make a comfy nest.

***

Friday 15th August soon arrived. Gemma had already secretly made arrangements for a friend of ours to both dog and house-sit. He was an ex-soldier who had spent time during his distinguished military career working with both German and Belgian Shepherd dogs.

His recent spate of visits had all been a ploy – he had made Shane's acquaintance and gained his trust, now he was relishing spending some quality time with him. Upon his advice, Gemma left a couple of t-shirts that I had recently worn on Shane's bed.

7.30 am, and our family arrived en masse. They were armed with chilled bottles of champagne. We still hadn't a clue what the surprise they had in store for us was. Upon strict instructions, we had each packed a case with items of clothing for four days. However, we noticed that very strangely they all had suitcases with them as well.

A minibus arrived at 8 am and we all boarded together, cracked open the champers and headed off to Kings Cross St Pancras.

Our surprise was finally revealed to us as we all boarded the Eurostar. Our amazing family had secretly arranged for all of us to go to Paris for four days – this was going to be the family trip of a lifetime.

Why hadn't I guessed that they were coming with us when Gemma had initially said during our home check about not bringing Shane home on Monday, and leaving it until a week later? Surely if I'd thought about it logically, she would have babysat him for us?

We arrived at the Gare du Nord late afternoon. As we were heading to the ticket hall, I spotted a small squad of about six police nationale officers, standing scrutinising the commuters jostling through the station. By each of their sides was a Malinois, but bloody hell the dogs looked like they were on steroids – they were absolutely massive! Each of the officers had a firearm secured in a holster on their belt. I was later told by one of the officers that they are a standard issue SIG Sauer Pro SP 2022, but to be honest I found the firearms far less intimidating than the dogs. I just had to go over; I felt as if I had joined a secret society, no funny handshakes, all you required was a Belgian Shepherd to be a member. The police were very accommodating and keen to show off their hounds. We spoke for some time, in English, as I can only just about get by speaking French. One of the officers told me the reason they mainly used Malinois in the force was because of their 'keen nose' which can find drugs and bombs when they are specially trained to do so, at the French national centre for police dog training (CNICG), in Gramat, south-west France. To the individual officers, there was a more personal reason why the Malinois was primarily used as a police dog – they have a strong protective instinct.

I felt safe in the knowledge that in addition to the security measures we already had in place in our house, on the rare occasions that Toni was ever going to be home alone, she now had Shane there to protect her.

The squad went on to proudly show me how the quick-release muzzles the dogs wore would drop to the ground within seconds. Blimey, if they set one of these hounds on you it would be goodnight sweetheart in the blink of an eye. One of the handlers allowed me to take hold of the lead. He then walked a few steps forward and called his dog; the power it exerted as it lunged forwards was unbelievable. I could have spent an afternoon talking to the policemen, but we had to head to our accommodation, the First Hotel Tour Eiffel, located on the Boulevard Garibaldi.

For four glorious, sunny days, we were treated to many of the fantastic, historic sites that the City of Love had to offer. A trip up the Eiffel Tower, Notre Dame, the Louvre; I must say that I was somewhat surprised at how small the Mona Lisa was, the Sacré-Cœur, personally my favourite part of the city, and a slightly awkward visit to the Place Pigalle, at the foot of the Montmartre hill, to name just a few. Gemma specifically wanted to visit the Pont de l'Alma road tunnel, the scene of the fatal crash involving Diana, Princess of Wales.

Paris's vast array of restaurants and the cuisine they had on offer was undoubtedly one of the highlights of our trip, from family-run bistros to sitting on the banks of the River Seine, eating croque monsieur, washed down with several glasses of cold bière de Printemps.

One particular meal that I'll never forget, in a traditional Parisian restaurant, where the waiters wear crisp white shirts, black bow ties and white aprons, started with Leah perusing the hors d'oeuvre section of the menu. She proceeded to order two dozen escargot – edible land snails – for us to try. Yup, they really were as awful as they sound.

It was early Monday evening when we arrived home from our fantastic Parisian city break. Toni and I were so anxious to see Shane, hoping that he had behaved himself in our absence. As we walked in he leapt straight on us, tail wagging. He just didn't know which one of us to kiss first.

"You missed us then, mate?"

Silly question really.

"How has he been, any problems?"

"None at all. I've had an absolute blast with him over the last few days; what a stunning boy, a credit to his breed. I even took him for a drive down to my old regiment based in Windsor. I felt so proud to be seen with him. I'm going to get out of your way. Shane, it has been a pleasure, sir."

We said our goodbyes and went back indoors to be with Shane.

CHAPTER FOUR

Shane's Adventures

To a poor and lonely stray, I would leave my happy home...

Just a mere ten short days ago Shane had come to live with us and the transformation in him was astounding, even though we had been away from him for a few days.

Already we could see that his beloved Kong was slowly playing a less significant role in his life now that he had a home, a loving family and stability. Moreover, what about the stories of Shane being dismissive and anti-social? Really? He adored our company and had interacted lovingly with every single guest that had visited our house.

I had spent time researching the more in-depth characteristics of the Malinois breed. While reading through the many posts available on the favoured online search engines, I suddenly came across an article about Shane, written by one of the principal cast members of the popular reality TV show The Only Way Is Essex. Bloody hell, my boy's a celebrity in his own right.

***

Wednesday 20th August, we decided to visit the obedience school that had been recommended to us. We had been told that it is normal practice for new dogs to the class to turn up and sit on the sideline with their handler and observe for the first couple weeks, to see the disciplines taught and how the classes were structured. We arrived early because, to be honest, we weren't entirely sure where the hall was located. As we arrived a lady was unlocking the door, she looked around, greeted us and complimented us on our handsome-looking dog.

"Thank you, yes he is a stunner, isn't he? We were advised to bring him here for obedience lessons by the dog rescue that we adopted him from."

Shane took a strange, animated interest in the lady, his tail wagged excitedly.

"That's fine, were you told about just sitting and watching for the first couple of weeks?"

"They did tell us, yes."

"Look there's nobody else here yet. While we're waiting for the rest of the class to turn up let's do a bit of basic heel work on the field."

I couldn't believe how kind it was of her to put herself out for us.

"Right then, if you are ready, then please sit your dog nice and straight by your left-hand side, say his name, then say the word 'heel' nice and firmly and lead off on your left foot. I want to see what we have to work with. Some of the poor dogs from rescues have had no training, and when they are adolescents, we may have a bit more work to do with them. Do you know if he is social with other dogs?"

I did precisely as I had been instructed, and got Shane to sit nice and close to me, his right shoulder almost touching my left knee.

"We were told that he is great with other dogs, so no problems as far as I'm aware. Shane, heel."

I gave the command firmly and set off, almost military style, left foot first as instructed by the lady. We had only taken a few steps when the lady called to us.

"Sorry did you say, Shane? Not Shane from Mutts, my Mr Shane?"

I halted with Shane and looked around. The lady seemed genuinely surprised.

"Yes, this is Shane, and yes he did come from Mutts. He joined us ten days ago."

"I volunteer at Mutts. I have worked with the lovely Mr Shane for about a year now. I used to take him for walks along the lane. I honestly didn't even recognise him. He has changed, he looks different, his face has changed, and where is his Kong?"

I was baffled; or, bless her, was the poor lady confused? If she had spent as much time interacting with Shane as she claimed, then why hadn't she recognised him straight away? Was she getting him mixed up with another dog with the same name? How could his appearance have changed so much in such a short space of time? Far too many questions were spinning around in my head.

Shane had left his Kong at home; in fact, it was his own decision to never bring it out with us when we went for our walks, almost as if he didn't want anything imposing upon our special alone time together, when we were out strolling through the countryside fields.

For the next 15 minutes, the obedience class dog trainer gave Shane and I an intense one-on-one lesson; she had us formally walking up and down the field, doing close heel work, and getting me to sit Shane smartly by my side upon a firm 'Sit' command.

Slowly the other handlers and their dogs started arriving for the evening's class. We followed them as they headed into the hall. Shane and I took a seat on the sideline to observe how the lesson was structured and to watch some of the disciplines that we would eventually have to learn.

Once everyone had arrived, and paid their week's £4 lesson fee, the trainer got the class underway. Firstly, she got the dogs and their owners to form a circle in the hall; the first discipline was to be the 'weave'.

Before the first dog commenced its initial lap, Shane and I were introduced to the group, and kindly invited to join in as guests.

Shane had the time of his life. He was a young, fit and active dog, but at obedience school he got the vitally important mental stimulation that every working breed dog needs.

School also gave him the chance to meet up with some of his old mates; a few other ex-Mutts dogs attended the same obedience lessons.

The following week we paid Shane's first year's membership fees, and he attended school religiously every Wednesday evening. Shane's progress/record card was soon embellished with a multitude of silver stars as he rapidly progressed and excelled his way through all of the various school disciplines.

***

Shane joining our family had made our mundane lives feel fulfilled and complete; our mere mortal existence had become ignited with a whole new passion and lease of life. Our energies now entirely focused on Shane's welfare and well-being. He was an intelligent, young, fit and powerful dog; he yearned for mental stimulation as well as his physical exercise. Come rain or shine, every evening we would head out on at least a two-hour walk

Valuable time was allocated and spent every day honing his obedience school skills. However, for us, our utmost pleasure was being able to introduce him to a whole new world of adventures that he had never experienced before as a poor abandoned stray.

We knew that he had a multitude of fun times to catch up on, and we were adamant that for Shane, there was never going to be a dull moment.

Welcoming and accepting a dog into our lives was going to be a suck-it-and-see learning curve for us; only so much could be learnt from the multitude of online advice forums and web-based training videos.

One article that did catch my eye was about how the hierarchies in packs of wild animals become established and how they survive in the harsh, volatile wildernesses they make their homes. I decided that I was going to try to take things back to basics, and incorporate some of the ways wild dogs live into Shane's training.

So then, firstly Shane's a dog, his ancestors roamed freely in packs, and they hunted for their daily food requirements. Finally, they are social pack animals who establish hierarchies, with an alpha or dominant male at the top of the pecking order, the rest of the pack are his followers.

The basic principles of being a pack animal actually sounded uncomplicated, in fact, the main aspects of our own little pack are already firmly established.

We provided Shane daily with a nutritionally balanced diet, so in theory, the hunting aspect was already addressed.

Toni and I were the pack leaders, so the alpha male is in place. Who am I kidding? Obviously that role goes to Toni.

However, what about the roaming freely aspect? I pondered long and hard on how I could integrate this into Shane's daily exercise regime. Then it hit me like a bolt out of the blue, how silly of me not to have thought of it earlier. I planned a whole new structure for our evening strolls to incorporate my concept.

The first time I put my plan into action I could see that things needed simplifying, the second was far more successful.

I prepared Shane for his walk and opened the front door. I gave him a firm 'Sit' command; this allowed me to exit our house before him. 'Heel' was the next command given; Shane stepped out of the front door and sat tightly next to my left leg, looking up at me awaiting my next order.

The next words I spoke to him were not given as a command but expressed in a much gentler tone of voice.

"Where are we going to go tonight, mate?"

Damn, far too many words, I needed to come up with a short easy word to use when I wanted Shane to lead me. In the end I decided to use 'Follow'.

At first, Shane looked up at me bemused, but he soon learnt what my new command meant. For the first few days, to make it a bit easier for him, I would take one step back, allowing his lead to hang freely, preventing me from determining our initial direction of travel in any way.

Once he had gained his confidence, Old Harlow became his oyster. Upon hearing his new command, Shane would firstly glance around at me; then he would look to the left, then to the right. When he had eventually made up his mind, he would head off in the direction that he wanted to go, his tail wagging. Throughout, I kept his lead loose, again so as not to influence his choice of route that we were going to take.

For one hour I would duly follow my little man; wherever he wandered, I'd be right there behind him. Shane would take me across fields, through woodlands, up our busy local high street, along the old overgrown towpaths of the River Stort. Occasionally, if the mood took him, he would end up even splashing about in the river. More than once I have to admit that we ended up in places that I had never ventured to before.

After one hour of dictating our route Shane would be called to heel. Obediently he would come and present himself at my left-hand side. Shane knew that he was now on training time. For the next hour, I would dictate the route, our home being the final destination. Shane knew that he now had to walk to my strict commands; he genuinely appeared to take delight in the mental stimulation that he was receiving in the form of my instructions.

Importantly though, he had also had one hour of nomadic freedom, being allowed to revert to his ancestral instincts.

***

Sunday 24th August, the bank holiday weekend, a mere two weeks after Shane had come to live with us. We were taking him to a family fun day, held at the rescue where he had lived most of his life. In amongst the afternoon's festivities, he should also get the opportunity to meet up with a few of his old two- and four-legged friends.

We set up our camping chairs next to the small fenced-off area on the field, and for the first half hour watched the impromptu fun-filled events. Wishing to partake, Toni proudly led Shane into the arena and entered him into the 'Best Mover' class.

Mid-afternoon and the three of us were sitting at the side of the show's ring watching the 'Prettiest Bitch' class. The afternoon's host, Pat, the founder of the sanctuary, had taken a brief break and was on her way to get herself some food from the BBQ. She had spent the afternoon auctioning donated items to raise much-needed funds for the dogs in her care, during the breaks for the judging of the dog show classes.

"What a handsome boy," she commented as she passed us.

"Thanks darling," I responded, thinking that she was paying me a compliment.

"You saucy bloody sod."

She laughed at my cheek and then stopped to talk to us. I introduced her to Shane, and yet again, just as when we had taken him to obedience school for the first time a couple of weeks earlier, he received the same reaction.

"Shane? Our Shane? I didn't even recognise you. Wow, you're looking fantastic boy, well done you; you've obviously landed well and truly on your paws this time."

Pat spent a few minutes interacting with Shane, and questioning us how we were getting on, and more importantly, how he had settled down in his new home. Shane relished the attention he lovingly received from the lady who had saved his life and cared for him for so long.

She headed over to the BBQ and ordered herself and quickly scoffed a burger before she had to return to hosting the day's events.

Before she went back into the ring, Pat turned and walked back over to where we were sitting.

"I'm going to be completely honest with you, for the first few days, we didn't even empty his kennel here. With his track record we were expecting him to be back with us within a day or so. Then I heard through the grapevine that he had been attending school. All I kept hearing was how good he looked, and that he seemed so contented. Now to see him today with my own eyes..."

Her words gently trailed off. Shane had a special place in her heart, she had even named him after one of her family's dogs; apparently he had also been a bit of a rascal.

At long last, she could see that Shane was happy, and deservedly so.

Over the coming months, we became very close to Pat. A friendship that we were later going to come to rely on to help us through the unforeseen, dreadful times that lay ahead.

We entered Shane into a few more of the classes throughout the afternoon; in fact, he received a runners-up rosette in the 'Best Ex Mutts Dog' category.

Shane did get to meet up with some of his old gang. He was thrilled when he saw his special friend, Noel, a Staffy, who had arrived at the rescue a few days after him. Strangely, Noel was also rehomed a day after Shane. Within seven months there was going to be an unfortunate sudden end to their unique, on-going bond.

Sadly, unbeknown to the three of us, this would be the only time that Shane would ever have the pleasure of spending a fun-filled afternoon at the annual Mutts in Distress fun day.

***

A mere four weeks after Shane had joined us I returned home from work early. Shane was asleep on his bed, which during the daytime is positioned at the top of the stairs; evening time it was moved to the foot of our bed.

My key going into the lock had awoken him from his slumber, and as I walked through the front door, he leapt up, shook himself down, and bounded down the stairs making his own unique happy grunting sound. I knelt, threw open my arms and embraced him, the same greeting I had bestowed on him every day since he had come to live with us.

As he had excitedly descended the stairs he knocked his beloved Kong; it bounced all the way down, right alongside him. After we had finished our hellos, I picked it up and offered it to him; he turned his head away from me.

As much as I despise the toy, I know that it is special to him, so I always pick it up and give it to him.

"Here you go, boy."

Again I tried to give it to him. This time he took it, begrudgingly, in his mouth. Immediately he practically spat it out with contempt; it bounced as it hit the wooden flooring in the hallway.

"What's up, mate?"

Confused by what had just happened, I picked up his beloved little red rubber security blanket and took it into the kitchen; Shane followed me, not once taking his eyes off what I was doing.

I opened the door to the cupboard under the sink, where his food and treats were stored, and placed his Kong next to them. Shane knew precisely where his toy was; he would see it whenever the door was opened to enable us to prepare his food, or when we retrieved a treat for him.

He feels safe now; I honestly believe that he knows we will never harm nor abandon him; for the first time in his life he is at peace with the world, his demons have finally left.

Shane never touched his Kong again. To this very day, it remains in the cupboard, next to the doggy treat tin.

***

Monday 22nd September. Shane and I had just gotten home from our early morning walk; while over the fields we had fun playing fetch with one of his favourite balls.

I removed his lead and he went over to his water bowl to quench his thirst. Within less than a minute he began violently vomiting, starting initially with a deep hollow rumbling sound emitting from deep within him. The water that he had just drunk was then forcibly expelled all over the floor.

"Are you all right, mate?"

He looked away, almost as if he was embarrassed at what he had done.

"Don't worry, son."

I reassured him, as I wiped up the mess with a tea towel.

I pondered ringing the vet; I now know that I should have done so straight away, but decided to keep an eye on him.

About 30 minutes later he went for another drink; again it was followed by the same deep retching, then projectile regurgitating. Luckily at this point, he had not yet had his breakfast.

After the second occurrence, I immediately rang his vet. Initially, the advice that they gave me was to starve him for 24 hours, ensuring that he drank plenty of water.

Hadn't they listened to a bloody word that I had said?

They continued with their advice, which was, after 24 hours slowly introduce a bland diet, little and often, of boiled brown rice and chicken to help settle his stomach.

Sod this, is this just standard advice robotically given to anyone?

Don't they take any bloody notice of the individual case's symptoms being described to them?

I was confused. I was well aware of a bland food diet if your dog has an upset tummy, but surely they could hear that this was different. He was bloody vomiting after a small drink of water.

"I'm sorry, but you're really not listening to me. I'm worried, this is happening whenever Shane drinks water. He's violently throwing up; also, I think that he is in pain while he's doing it."

The receptionist pretended to listen; again putting me on hold while she went to speak to a vet. When she resumed our conversation she reiterated the bland diet instructions, and to keep a close eye on him.

I could feel myself getting extremely angry at the way that this situation was beginning to unfold.

"Look, I know you vets are the experts, but I'm worried. Can you please arrange an emergency appointment for him as soon as possible?"

Luckily they had had a couple of cancellations, so I got him ready and drove him straight to the surgery.

Upon our arrival the vet examined him thoroughly. Shane became very agitated when the vet pressed on his abdomen. Nothing unusual, the vet explained, if he had a stomach ache then naturally he would feel a bit tender.

I asked if they could give him some water, they needed to see for themselves that his body was unable to retain even small quantities of fluids.

A bowl of fresh cold water was brought in by the nurse. Tentatively Shane sipped it, and yet again it was violently discharged.

The vet agreed, at long last, that I was right to be concerned. He decided that to be on the safe side he would anaesthetise Shane and X-ray his abdomen.

Surprisingly the X-ray showed nothing untoward. The vet was concerned that Shane was beginning to show the early signs of dehydration, his eyes were now very slightly sunken, and his gums were sticky, due to his inability to take in fluids.

"We will keep him in for 24 hours to monitor him."

He went on to explain that an IV catheter was going to be fitted to administer both a small dose of pain relief and some urgently needed fluids in the form of sodium chloride.

Bloody hell, Shane must be feeling anxious, and now I've got to leave him in the hands of a total stranger. At least when one of my daughters had ever been admitted to a paediatric ward, Toni or I could stay with them. The veterinary practice didn't have such facilities.

I was told to say a brief goodbye and leave without making too much fuss.

At about 5 pm our phone rang. I could see by the caller display that it was the vets. Anxiously I picked up the receiver.

"Mr Viner? Hi, it's the vets. Look I'm going to cut straight to the chase, we're becoming increasingly worried about Shane. For some unknown reason he has started deteriorating rapidly."

How the hell could he be? He was fine first thing this morning playing over the field; now they're telling me that they are worried?

"With your permission, I think we need to operate; we need to ascertain exactly what's going on inside. The only other option would be to transfer Shane to a specialist referral clinic to carry out a full abdominal MRI scan, but in my professional opinion I'm not sure if he will last that long."

My head was spinning. Our dear Shane lying there, his weakened body shutting down. Of course I gave permission, they had to do whatever they could to help him, they just had to save him…

Toni and I got ready and raced straight to the vets; we needed to be near Shane, we were far too worried to remain at home.

As we arrived at the surgery, we were each offered a coffee. I took mine and headed outside for the first of many cigarettes. We both knew that for us it was going to be a very long anxious wait.

After what seemed an eternity the door that led to the operating theatre wing opened. Standing there in his bloodied green surgical scrub top and trousers was Shane's surgeon. He pulled off his brightly coloured scrub cap with cartoon cats emblazoned on it, his procedure mask hanging loosely around his neck. In his hand, he held a small sterile plastic bag.

"Mr and Mrs Viner, please come in."

Nervously we got up and followed the surgeon into the small consultation room adjacent to the operating theatre.

"Well, here's the culprit."

He handed me the small bag. Inside was a little green object, about 50mm in diameter.

"It appears to be the remnants of a section of a tennis ball. As you can see, Shane's bodily acids have started trying to break it down. Looking at it, I'd guess that it has been there for quite some time. It's strange that it didn't show up in the X-ray; anyway, we found it deep in his stomach. I can only ascertain that it somehow became dislodged when you were out on your walk and playing this morning. It obviously went on to cause the blockage that presented itself in the form of the vomiting. We're going to have to keep Shane in for 48 hours to monitor him."

We each breathed a massive sigh of relief. Shane was out of danger.

"Can we please see him?"

"Sorry not tonight, he's just coming round from the anaesthetic, he's groggy and we don't want to over-excite him."

Relieved that all seemed well, we reluctantly left the surgery, entrusting Shane's care and temporary well-being into the medical team's hands.

Our home felt so empty and lonely without Shane. We had fallen head first into the beautiful world of dog companionship; to us, our house without Shane felt like a garden without flowers.

First thing in the morning we received a phone call updating us about Shane:

"He has slept well and is walking unaided. He has been outside and is passing urine and faeces without any trouble. His scar is clean, with no apparent signs of infection. While with us he will be given a diet of veterinary-recommended food. Does he have any food allergies or intolerances that you are aware of? We will keep you updated throughout the day as to his progress, and all being well he should be discharged tomorrow morning."

What a relief! Hopefully, he would be home where he belongs in the morning.

That evening we were permitted to visit Shane. Bless his little heart, he was so thrilled to see us, and he loved the little teddy bear get-well present we had bought for him en route.

With a nurse accompanying us we were allowed to take him outside for a very short walk to enable him to relieve himself.

Just in case he may have needed it, I had taken his 'Kong' with us. I kept it hidden in my jacket pocket, and as he had shown no outward signs of anxiety, I didn't offer it to him.

Saying goodbye to him was so hard. He sat there staring forlornly at me as I hugged him. Shane knew our bedtime ritual, and his being left alone in a veterinary cage played no part in it.

The next day we brought Shane home, wearing his plastic lampshade, sorry Buster Collar. Before leaving the surgery, his nurse issued us with a bag of painkillers, antibiotics and a few tins of the high-protein food that vets give to recuperating dogs. We made an appointment for him to have the stitches removed in seven days. During those seven days we had to try and keep him as calm as possible, and we could only take him for very short walks.

The Buster Collar was to prevent him from licking or chewing at his scar, but bless him how disorientating it must have been for him having to wear it. His peripheral vision was obviously marred, and he was forever walking into doorframes, or our legs, which soon bore the battle-scar bruises of the sharp plastic edge of the collar.

I had kept the Mutts team fully updated with regards to his progress, and upon mentioning the issues with the collar, one of the volunteers very kindly brought him round a 'Comfy Cone Healing Collar' – what an absolute godsend.

Shane soon made a full recovery from the tennis ball episode; the only lasting effect was that he had recurring bouts of colitis. Although upsetting initially for our little man, we soon got the condition under control with a carefully maintained and balanced diet, which included boiled chicken, sweet potatoes, boiled fish, brown rice, blueberries and sardines. Bloody hell, he ate better than I did.

***

It was now mid-October, well the 14th to be exact, Toni's 50th birthday. We were heading to Mersea Island, Essex, to celebrate. I had already reserved a table at her favourite fish restaurant for a fresh seafood lunch.

Shane was now back to full strength, the tennis ball saga a distant memory. A fresh growth of fur covered the scar on his belly from the surgery to retrieve the section of tennis ball.

That day Shane was going to experience his first ever trip to the seaside. He sat in the back of the car for the hour's journey, gazing both excitedly and intently out of his window at the ever-changing Essex countryside views.

As soon as we arrived, we eagerly headed straight to the beach; I don't know who was more excited, Shane or us. It was so beautiful to watch him behaving like an exuberant child, playing with the washed-up driftwood and tossing the dried-out seaweed all around. He would drop down and roll about on the soft, warm sand, his legs akimbo thrashing about like a raving loony, but throughout he always seemed to keep one eye fixed firmly on the imposing vast expanse of water.

After about 30 minutes of frolicking around on the sand, we started to edge our way with him closer to the shoreline. Shane shook himself down, displacing most of the sand that had stuck to his fur, although a small clump remained stuck on the end of his wet nose.

Slowly we moved closer to the giant waves that were breaking and crashing angrily onto the beach, they hissed menacingly as they slowly dissolved into a frothy white foam. As the water ebbed away it created a clattering sound, as thousands of pebbles found themselves suddenly being involuntarily dragged into the murky depths of the North Sea, to be spun and washed back up onto the beach, in a constant never-ending cycle, until they eventually found themselves broken down and turned into golden sand.

Seagulls hovered overhead, their squawks and high notes adding to the percussion of the waves.

At first, Shane just stood and stared in bewilderment at the vista of the never-ending water disappearing far into the horizon in front of him, with his mouth wide open, his tongue licking at the droplets of saltwater spray that continually settled on his lips.

Eventually, he plucked up the courage to slowly move a little closer to the water's edge. I kicked off my canvas slip-on pumps, the sand felt cool and squishy between my toes. Together we were now getting closer to the tideline; the sand had turned into pebbles, Shane was faring much better at walking on them than I was.

"Ouch, ouch, sod it, ouch!"

The words flowed both freely and angrily as I hobbled across the vicious little stones. Although smooth in texture, they embedded themselves deep into my lily-white feet. Luckily no onlookers were watching my pathetic attempt to enter the sea with an air of macho dignity.

The breaking waves were soon lapping at our feet and paws; the cold water felt so invigorating and strangely inviting. I am sure that I must have been a hippy in a previous life, for at this moment in time I was so at one with nature, standing there in the sea, the peace and tranquillity of the moment cleansing my soul. I shook my head to bring myself back to reality and looked down at Shane; I moved my hand down to his collar and unclipped the heavy-duty clasp.

"Off you go son, have fun and go play in the sea."

He didn't need telling twice. Shane started chasing the waves as they broke, leaping excitedly in and out of the surf. I sat down, just out of reach of the breaking waves, and watched him. I hadn't seen him have this much fun in the two months that he had now been living with us. Toni joined me sitting watching Shane; neither of us spoke, we just sat there admiring our handsome boy.

Eventually, he strutted out of the sea, just like a canine version of Ursula Andress from the James Bond film Dr No. He positioned himself directly in front of us, stretched, circled several times to get his aim accurate, then decided it would be fun to shake his body vigorously. We rolled back onto the pebbles, trying as best we could to try and elude the deluge of seawater rapidly approaching us, our attempts to remain dry proved to be of no avail; we just lay there soaked, and both roared with laughter. I swear to this day that the little sod smiled at his handiwork as he plonked himself down and curled up into a soggy wet lump. I clipped his lead back on, and we walked back to where our bag was. I poured him a bowl of fresh water, and Toni got his towel out and rubbed him down. He sat there motionless, nose pointing towards the sky and his beautiful brown eyes closed.

I rolled myself an Old Holborn cigarette and slowly fell back on the sand and took a long hard drag. I closed my eyes; the sun felt so warm and therapeutic. I wiggled my head from side to side; as the back of my skull slowly embedded into the sand, an exaggerated crunching sound echoed in my ears. Soon my newly formed inverted pillow felt so comfortable, I wish that I could stay there forever, without a worry or a care in the world. As I lay there, every now and then the skin on my face was cooled by the foamy sea spray mist that blew in from the rampant North Sea.

When I finally smoked my cigarette as far as I could we packed our bag and slowly started to head back along the beach. It was now time for lunch.

Luckily, it was a beautiful sunny autumnal day, so we sat outside the restaurant on a wooden picnic bench. It felt as if we were on the Essex Riviera, if there were such a place, watching the fishing boats, small yachts and speed boats all bobbing about in unison moored up in the marina, or out on the River Blackwater.

The waitress appeared with our seafood platter lunch. The large oval plate was crammed full of artfully arranged lobster, crab, shell on prawns, peeled prawns, large crevettes, cockles, rollmops, smoked salmon, oysters and mackerel, accompanied by a green side salad and a small freshly baked rustic loaf of bread. We washed our seafood feast down with a chilled, half-decent bottle of Chardonnay. We had brought Shane's lunch with us – to allow him to join in with the seafood theme, we gave him a bowl of sardines topped with a scattering of blueberries. I know that it sounds gross, but he loved it.

Afterwards, the three of us popped along to The Victory for a quick pint before heading home.

The day's excitement had been far too much for him. As soon as he hit the back seat, Shane crashed out; he snored for the entire journey home.

***

Our birthdays are just 11 days apart in October, with Toni being the eldest, as I regularly remind her. We were both reaching our half-centuries and we had decided that the most precious gift that we could give each other was Shane.

Bless his little heart, on each of our special days the poor little man had the indignity bestowed upon him of being adorned with a large, bright yellow ribbon; then he had to sit with us and have a photo taken.

It couldn't have upset him that much, for without any prompting, his birthday gift to each of us, wearing his ribbon, was to lovingly plant one of his big special kisses on our faces.

***

Shane's life with us just kept on throwing new and exciting experiences at him. In early November he joined us on a family weekend break to a large 12-bedroomed Victorian mansion in Burwash, East Sussex. He had tremendous fun charging around and exploring the vast expanse of warren-like rooms within the building, each of them warmed by roaring open log fires.

The enormous, intimidating building sits within the red-bricked confines of its perimeter wall, with its entrance through imposing massive double iron gates, with an adjacent gatekeeper's lodge. The estate also has several outbuildings for staff, and mock-Gothic follies can be stumbled across strewn around the grounds in random locations.

The mansion is situated adjacent to Rudyard Kipling's home, Bateman's, which the National Trust now manages. An ancient boundary hawthorn hedgerow separates the two, acting as a wildlife corridor, linking the two adjoining estates semi-natural habitats and allowing the movement of wildlife throughout the Sussex countryside.

We had full, access-all-areas run of the many acres of perfectly manicured lawns, adorned with their rose beds, the rose bushes all meticulously pruned in readiness for winter. The estate also had its own small woodland; autumn is such a beautiful time of the year to explore forests, with the stunning ever-changing colours of the ordinarily green deciduous trees and shrubs taking on hues of red, yellow, purple, orange, magenta and brown. The air was full of the scent of pine and wildflowers, strangely even the rotting and decaying wood that had been discarded by the trees added a comforting aroma to our saunter through the boscage.

As we rambled on, the only sounds we could hear were the branches blowing in the wind creaking overhead. Our feet shuffling through the fallen leaves would every so often snap a large twig that had dropped from the tree canopy, causing the wildlife to scurry away. There was also an added eerie sound of the wind whistling around the trunks of the trees, causing the discarded detritus to form into small brown clouds that danced within the woodland.

Shane was bemused as he watched the local wildlife preparing to bed down and hibernate for the winter, scurrying all around us and chattering as they leapt from branch to branch way above our heads; grey squirrels anxiously seeking nuts that they could secrete away for the bitterly cold months that lay ahead.

During the day, we took him on long treks across farmland or along narrow country lanes, where we would always stop and enjoy the welcoming hospitality of the local pubs, where the ruddy-faced landlords would pull us a few pints of locally produced ale, and serve us bowls of fresh, piping hot, homemade soup.

The weekends rambling through the forests allowed me to finally put my wet-weather dog-walking attire to the test. Green waxed jacket and fedora hat, Wellington boots and waterproof over-trousers. There is a child hidden within all of us, bursting to get out at every opportunity; come on, who can honestly say that they don't enjoy splashing about in puddles? Well, I'm not ashamed to admit that I do, and Shane did as well, so there we were, in our element, it's only mud, and it'll wash off. I had already put two soft towels over the old cast-iron radiator in the boot room. For Shane, there was a full body rub down for him when we got back to the mansion.

Afterwards, I lit the log fire in the drawing room and we crashed out on the faux fur rug; the stone fireplace had now become our little sun. For an hour or so we lay there watching the flames curl and sway, crackling as they burnt the dry wood. I indulged myself with a decent Cognac, paired with a Cuban cigar – purely medicinal mind you, to ward off the cold.

5th November, Guy Fawkes Night, Shane and I headed out at about 7.30 pm. We walked across the field adjacent to Harlowbury chapel. Fireworks were shooting up and adorning the black night sky like glistening jewels.

Shane sat and looked up as the rockets flew up with a whoosh and exploded high in the starscape. He never flinched or moved, but quietly sat in amazement, watching the noisy, colourful display unfolding in front of his eyes. His head followed the bright white trail of the rockets as they shot into the air, then would tilt to one side as they exploded, condensation vapour billowing from his mouth. It became more exaggerated as the fireworks exploded, the whizzing whistles and deep thuds adding to the visual display. Although it was a bitterly cold evening, we stayed there for nearly an hour watching the exciting aerial spectacle being performed way up above our heads.

I could almost imagine him replicating the sounds of excitement you hear kids make at organised firework displays, the 'oohs' and 'aahs' in time with the cracking explosions. Afterwards, we headed to a local pub. Hot jacket spuds and tomato soup with a side of crusty bread were on offer. I also ordered a double Irish whisky, no ice, to help warm myself up.

Shane was now a regular feature by my side, my shadow. Whenever I ventured out, Shane would loyally be with me, and he was also becoming a bit of a local celebrity in his own right. The doormen at one of the local pubs we often passed on our Friday night stroll would always wait eagerly for his visit. We didn't frequent this particular establishment as it mainly catered for the younger generation, with thumping loud music and continual rounds of 'shots' being downed by the patrons, but the doormen would always have a sausage treat waiting for Shane.

"Here you go, mate," they'd say, two shaven-headed brutes going all coy over my little man Shane. He would duly sit and enjoy their affection and attention, eagerly anticipating the meaty gift they'd always have waiting for him.

Luckily the local pubs in my area are all dog-friendly, and Shane was welcome in all of them, and treats were always freely given to him when he strutted in. In fact, Shane would get his cheese and biscuits, sometimes even a sausage, before I got my pint; it was probably because he was better behaved than I was.

***

There is an old saying that 'time flies when you're having fun'. Well we were having an absolute blast, and the months were passing rapidly. It was now December, and a bitterly cold winter had hit us. Just 12 months earlier the subject of us getting a dog had been raised; now our lives were complete, Shane had made them complete.

One thing was blatantly for sure, Shane was by no means an anti-social dog; he absolutely adored and relished human attention, from small excitable young children through to frail elderly folk, strangers always seemed to be drawn to the handsome hound faithfully with me wherever we went. Thoughts of how my caring, intelligent dog could now use his unique people skills to aid others continually ran through my mind.

In the weeks leading up to Christmas Shane would excitedly charge downstairs every morning, where he could be found patiently sitting, tail wagging and mouth salivating in anticipation of the small edible gift he was about to receive from his doggy chocolate advent calendar. Gemma had bought it for him. She usually would have bought one for Toni and me to share, but not this year, that tradition had been passed onto Shane, and we certainly couldn't begrudge him. Bless his little heart, how he relished chewing on the morsel-sized treat, once we had found the correct window to open that is.

The run-up to Christmas is one of my favourite times of the year; now I had an excuse to walk the streets where I lived every evening admiring the decorations and Christmas trees that adorned the Victorian houses in our neighbourhood. Shane and I would wrap up against the crisp, bitterly cold December evenings and head off together.

One of the things that I looked forward to and relished on our strolls was the comforting aroma that filled the streets of burning wood and coal that emanated from the chimneys of the small terraced cottages; the distinct scent brought fond memories of our weekend away at the Sussex mansion flooding back to me. For me to be able to immerse myself in my memories even deeper, I now needed to head to one of the local inns in Old Harlow for a hot toddy and a warm-up, sitting next to their comforting fire burning in the hearth. To this very day, the distinct redolence of an open fire evokes and brings back thoughts of happy, fun-filled times with Shane.

Christmas Day finally arrived, and Father Christmas had been extremely kind to Shane. He had obviously been a very good boy to have received such a bountiful stocking packed full of goodies.

His body still had the sweet aroma of the cologne finishing spray that had been applied yesterday at his Christmas Eve treat, a pampering session at a local dog groomer. He'd had the full works – hair trim, bath and shampoo, blow dry, claws trimmed and teeth cleaned.

Shane being Shane had made an instant fan club; the two female groomers had fallen head over heels with him.

"What an absolutely gorgeous dog. Throughout his entire pampering session, he just sat motionless, his eyes almost closed, lapping up the attention. I don't think I've ever met such a macho-looking dog who enjoys his fur being brushed as much as Shane."

Those were the words the parlour's proprietor gushed to us when we went to collect him.

Anyway, Christmas Day, our family all arrived in dribs and drabs during the course of the morning. Festive drinks were freely served, mainly snowballs for the ladies, always adorned with glacé cherries, and pints of bitter for the men, as we prepared for the Yuletide celebrations that lay ahead.

Shane had the indignity bestowed upon him by Gemma of having to wear a red bow tie, adorned with large white spots that she had purchased for him from a high-end fashion establishment. Clipped to his collar, he paraded proudly around the lounge, as if he was showing off his gentleman-about-town attire.

We had all splashed out on gifts for Shane, this was his first, and sadly unbeknown to us, it was also to be his last, family Christmas. We all wanted to make this day as special for him as possible. Sturdy cuddly toys and extra-tough rubber toys were the order of the day; although Shane had no teeth, the immense power that he had in his jaws could shred even the most heavy-duty dog toy in a matter of minutes. Soon, in a scene reminiscent of when my daughters were young and still believed in Father Christmas, our wooden floor was completely covered in toys, shiny bows and discarded wrapping paper. Shane loved tearing at the brightly coloured paper that had been used to wrap his vast array of presents, grasping the gift between his front paws and ripping the paper with his stumpy teeth. More often than not, one of us would have to step in to remove a piece of paper from his mouth. Leah reached behind the couch where she had hidden her gift. Shane sat bolt upright as she presented him with her present; he licked her hand, his way of saying 'Thank you' then sat and stared at the glistening paper, emblazoned with Disney characters.

"Go on Shane, open it, it's for you," Leah said.

Well, he certainly didn't need telling twice, he leapt straight on top of the large present and began to rip and tear at the Disney-themed wrapping paper. It didn't take too long before a beautiful new dog bed was unveiled; brown high-raised sides for a sense of security and added warmth, and a full faux sheepskin fur interior covering. Shane hurled himself into his new bed and stretched out. How comfy he looked; he now took up most of the available floor space in the lounge.

Gemma walked over to Shane, lying there like Lord Muck, with her carefully wrapped gift for him.

"Here you go Shane, merry Christmas."

Gemma has professional gift-wrapping skills, and there was no way Shane could open her present on his own, there was probably a whole roll of sticky tape securing the paper together.

Gemma moved to where Shane was sitting and plonked herself down with him; he gazed up at her as she started to help him unwrap the gift she had bought him. A dark olive green box soon emerged from beneath the shiny paper. 'Barbour' was emblazoned in large white letters across the top section. Gemma slid off the lid, removed the white protective tissue paper, and pulled out a green waxed dog coat, complete with a brown corduroy collar, an exact copy of the waterproof jacket that I wear when I walk Shane.

"Now we're twins, son."

I couldn't wait to take him out wearing his new jacket.

One of our gifts to Shane was an extra-tough plush rabbit; he eagerly tore open the wrapping paper that covered it. The rabbit lay there on the floor in front of him; he growled, crouched then attacked it, shaking it vigorously from side to side. Once he was sure that he had disabled the imminent threat posed to his family by the rabbit he left it alone.

For the next three months that little rabbit was to be his constant companion whenever he went to bed, and just maybe, in the harrowing days that he was to endure all too soon, it was to bring happy memories of his first family Christmas flooding back to him.

CHAPTER FIVE

Therapy Dog

My bowl and cosy bed, soft pillow and all my toys…

On a freezing cold Sunday in early January we were out for a walk with Shane, our planned final destination, a few lunchtime pints in the Queens Head, Churchgate Street. As we were strolling through the small park next to St Mary's church, we spotted a young lady with two little boys looking over at us. I could see that the boys were pointing at Shane; the lady was shaking her head while talking to them. Slowly they started to head towards us, when they were a short distance away the lady called over to us.

"I'm really sorry to trouble you both, but would it be possible for my son to stroke your dog please?"

The poor lady almost seemed embarrassed at asking, but for us how lovely that a young lad wanted to meet our hound.

"Of course it would," I shouted back.

We turned and started to walk towards the young family. When we were fairly close to the three of them, I gave Shane a firm a 'Sit and watch me' command.

Obligingly he sat down tightly next to my left side, looking straight up at me.

I could see that the lady felt awkward at disturbing our walk, so I tried to break the ice.

"Hi, I'm Paul, this is my wife Toni, and the handsome dog next to us is Shane."

"It's very kind of you and thank you so very much. My youngest son has autism, and he is absolutely obsessed with anything to do with dogs. Sadly we can't have one, due to our tenancy contract. We've been out for over an hour and walked for a couple of miles in the hope of meeting a dog that he can stroke. I've asked several people if my son could say hello to their dogs, and for a variety of excuses they've all refused."

"Of course he can stroke our dog; in fact, I think that Shane wants to meet your son."

I knelt and put a reassuring arm around Shane, and positioned two of my fingers into his collar to stop him from making any sudden movements towards the young boy who was about to approach him. I knew Shane and was more than confident that he would relish the attention he was about to receive, but I had to take all the necessary, responsible handler precautions.

"Okay mate, come and say hello to Shane."

Excitedly, the young boy – I'd guess that he was about four years of age – bound over. Shane remained motionless, and didn't bat an eyelid.

"Right mate, listen to me and do exactly what I tell you. To start with move your hand slowly towards Shane, and gently stroke and tickle him under his chin."

I can still remember the distinctive woolly rainbow-coloured gloves that the boy wore, and I'll never forget the sheer look of joy on his face as he touched Shane for the first time. His brother, who looked about seven, came over and joined us. Toni and the boys' mother were quietly looking on, not wanting to intrude upon or interrupt the moment of pleasure for the two small lads.

Toni reached into her pocket and took out a few of the small kibble treats we carried when we were out with Shane.

"Do you want to feed him?" she asked.

Full of excitement at the prospect of being allowed to feed Shane, the boys reached out and each of them took some of the small pieces of biscuit from her, Shane's gaze firmly fixed on where his treats now were.

"Right, hold your hand flat, put a couple of pieces in your palm and slowly, one of you at a time, give them to Shane."

The boys listened to my instructions and followed them to the letter.

"Gently Shane," I commanded him.

Although a gannet at breakfast and dinner, Shane knew how to accept and take food when it was given to him by hand, he never lunged or mouthed roughly at the person giving him his favourite titbits.

As he licked the food from the youngest boy's hand, sticky drool covered the multi-coloured glove.

"Wow, look mum! I've got wolf spit on me."

"He'll never let me wash that glove again," laughed their mother.

We spent about 15 minutes talking with them; they thanked us, and the boys bid fond loving farewells to Shane the Wolf.

We walked the short distance through the churchyard to the pub for our well-earned drinks and a chance to warm up.

As we were sitting drinking next to the roaring open log fire in the pub, the answer to the question that I had been pondering in early December suddenly came to me.

"Seeing Shane with that little boy really struck a chord with me. Shane was helping that lad, just as we have helped Shane. Maybe in life's grand scheme of things Shane should give something back to society, let him now help others."

"What have you got in mind?" Toni asked.

"I have been thinking about it for some time now and managed to find an interesting article the other day about a charity called Pets as Therapy. There's been a whole lot of research into the health benefits for the elderly, sick or special needs kids interacting with dogs. The dog with their handler visit people in hospitals, schools and even prisons. I wonder if Shane would be suitable?"

"Well tomorrow's your day off, why not do some research, you've got nothing to lose. Fancy another Guinness?"

We spent a couple of hours drinking in the pub, then the three of us headed off home for our Sunday roast.

Monday morning arrived. Shane and I were back from his regular one-hour early morning walk. He snuggled down on his bed in the lounge close to the radiator, and I sat on the couch opposite him. I was going to drink my strong cup of black coffee, then set about researching the required criteria to apply to Pets as Therapy.

I soon found the website I was looking for, and the initial wording sounded very promising. There didn't seem to be any barriers in place that could prevent Shane from becoming a registered P.A.T dog.

I set about filling in the online application form. The first section involved filling in my details, the second, and the most critical part, was about Shane. There were 18 questions in all; I soon completed the easy part, his personal details, which included particulars such as name, age, breed, sex, and any known medical conditions and when we took ownership.

Now here came the crucial set of questions. These were all based around his temperament.

My dog walks on a loose lead – Yes

Is your dog worried by sudden noises – No

My dog loves being fussed – Definitely yes

My dog is happy to be groomed – Yes, his favourite treat

Always under control when on a lead – YES

My dog takes titbits gently – YES

Does your dog have a good temperament with people and children? – Most definitely, yes

Does your dog have a good, reliable temperament with other dogs? – YES

My answers were honest, and Shane seemed to tick all the right boxes. Blimey, this was a walk in the park, he'd easily get this gig in the bag.

I clicked on the declaration that I agreed to the Registered Volunteer and Pets statement and their T&Cs, then submitted his application form, and awaited the confirmation email outlining the next part of the process. It didn't take long. I responded to the link that was emailed to me, and a standard reply bounced straight back informing me that the local area coordinator for our area of Essex would be in touch in due course. At this point, I had to pay Shane's first year's subscription fee of £19.

A week later, while on duty at work, my mobile rang. I didn't recognise the number.

"Mr Viner?"

"Speaking, I'm warning you this had better not be a bloody PPI sales call."

"No, I'm very sorry to trouble you and hope that I haven't caught you at an awkward moment. I'm your area coordinator for Pets As Therapy, and I am just giving you a quick courtesy call to make arrangements for Shane's assessment."

Sod it, what a great first impression she must have gotten of me. Shane's the perfect gentleman and here I am, his handler and potential visit partner, behaving like a complete and utter prat and having a pop at her.

"Look I really am sorry about that, I'm having a mare of a day at work, and bloody nuisance sales calls have plagued me all day."

"Please don't apologise; I hate them as well, if now is not a convenient time to talk then I could call you back some other day."

Now was more than convenient. I quickly grabbed my Evidence P.N.B to scribble down the details the coordinator gave me.

Arrangements were made for Shane's assessment to take place on Monday 23rd February at 10 am. I was also given the name and address of the lady who would be conducting Shanes P.A.T. appraisal at her home in a small town called Little Burstead in Essex, a few miles off the A127. We had a couple of weeks to fine tune and hone his skills.

***

Sunday 22nd February. Shane and I had been kicked out of our home – well a slight exaggeration there.

Toni, my mum, Gemma and Leah had planned a surprise 'baby shower' for Kealy, and by all accounts, it is a ladies-only affair, so Shane, my father and I were seeking refuge in one of Shane's favourite pubs, The Queens Head, Churchgate Street.

As per usual Shane was attracting a lot of adoring attention from the other patrons in the pub. His afternoon was spent walking around the bar, being stroked by all and sundry and sitting, cutely staring with his puppy dog eyes at anyone with any form of food or bag of savoury snacks. Just watching him I knew that he would pass the following day, Shane had experienced violent physical and emotional pain in his past, but he was a resilient forgiving dog who was so appreciative of his new life. For him, becoming a therapy dog was his calling, it was going to give him the opportunity to help others and open up a whole new world of exciting adventures for him.

At 5 pm we finished the final dregs of our beers and headed for home. The house was still full of Kealy's family and friends, a clutter of cackling and chuckling ladies; like us, a few of them may have consumed too much alcohol. Remnants of party games they had been playing lay strewn on the floor, including a pile of heavily soiled nappies.

"Pick up a nappy, sniff it and try the contents," said Leah, who had definitely had one glass of rosé wine over the top.

"You what?"

"It's a game, Pops; the nappies are all full of brown stuff, you have to guess what it is."

The room erupted into roars of laughter at my apparent disapproval of such a 'game', but I didn't want to come across as a total killjoy, so I humoured them.

"Bloody hell, I think this one really has got shit in it."

I apologised to the ladies for my bad language.

"No, you're wrong dad, that one had chocolate spread," said Gemma.

My dad and I declined the offer to join in with any more of the games and retreated with Shane to the kitchen, where I cracked open a decent bottle of rioja.

***

It was the morning of Shane's assessment. We had arrived at the assessor's home early. Before I knocked on her door, I spent a bit of quality time walking Shane, with him following my strict commands, I was fully in charge. Today was a working day, no playing or fun stuff, and he was going to have to listen carefully to my every word.

The lady peered out of her window, waved and came out to introduce herself to us. I produced the documentation and items that I had been asked to bring, which included my passport, Shane's up-to-date inoculation card, his grooming brush and a bag of his favourite treats.

Little did I know that his assessment had commenced from the very moment that I had shaken hands with and greeted the lady.

"Right dearie, I'm going to briefly go through with you all that Shane is going to have do this morning. There will be several tests, each carried out once and only once, and if he fails any of them, then I'm afraid that I will have to defer him for another reassessment test at a later date."

After a full explanation, she perched herself down on a low wall, she made a few grunting sounds, and I heard her mumble to herself about her 'sodding aching back'.

The assessment disciplines for Shane were: walk on a relaxed lead without excessive pulling and the use of head collars or check chains; accept being stroked and handled and having his paws, tail and ears checked by the assessor; take a food treat gently without snatching from the assessor; respond appropriately to a sudden noise or disturbance in the room/assessment area while being tested.

For Shane and I together the disciplines were: demonstrate control of the dog on the lead while holding a conversation with the assessor; groom the dog's back, chest, stomach and tail; demonstrate that I could restrict/restrain the dog by holding its collar or holding him/her firmly; present the dog in a fit, clean and healthy condition.

On top of the disciplines above, if Shane showed signs of any of the following behaviours – jumping up, pawing, or putting paws up, pulling on the lead, reluctance/backing away when being fussed, vocalisations, such as barking or growling, mouthing, licking or taking food greedily – he would also be deferred to take his retest at a later date after he had received more training.

"Okay dear, just to get him ready I want you to walk him to the first lamp post to my right, turn, get him to sit, call him to heel, then walk past me to the lamp post on my left, turn and get him to sit."

We did exactly as asked, thinking that she was letting us both settle down and relax. Again, I didn't realise that this was part of his assessment, and as far as I could tell Shane was calm and doing everything correctly.

The assessor reached down behind the wall she was sitting on and picked up an old biscuit tin.

"Right mate, it's now up to you son, the test begins."

Shane looked up at me, his face beaming with confidence. I winked at him.

"Righto, now we're going to act out a sudden noise scenario. Inside this tin is a handful of marbles. Believe me, it makes a hell of a noise when I shake it. The idea of this exercise is to replicate a metal tray, or surgical equipment being accidentally dropped onto the ward floor. Shane must not overreact, bark, or show any form of aggression or excessive fear of the sound. If you are ready, then please bring him over and sit him just to my left, but looking away from me. Oh, once he is sitting, I do not want you to give him any more vocal commands or reassurances until after I have shaken the tin."

I positioned Shane precisely as instructed. Bloody hell, under any other circumstance when I know there is the potential for a sudden noise that could shock him I'd be constantly telling him to 'watch me' and offering exaggerated words of comfort to reassure him. Not a chance during this exercise, I would have to leave this one all down to him.

The lady raised the tin and shook it. Shane jumped to his paws and spun round to face the direction of the noise; the lady looked at me as if to prompt me.

"Good boy, sit and watch me."

What a star. Shane sat down, snuggled up close to my left leg, and looked straight up to my face. I gave him a wink, a gentle stroke on his head and a nod. The assessor was scribbling frantically on Shane's assessment form.

"Right, please could you walk Shane to the lamp post to my left, turn and walk straight past me to the lamp post on my right."

Just as we were passing the lady – I must add that at this point Shane was obediently walking to heel on a loose lead – she dropped the tin right behind us, it hit the ground with an almighty crash. What the bloody hell was she playing at?

"Leave it."

Shane had initially been startled. To be honest, so was I, but he listened to my command, we continued to the right-hand lamp post, and turned, with Shane still right up tight to my left leg. Upon my command he sat.

I was getting the serious hump now. If she didn't want Shane to become a therapy dog then just end the bloody assessment.

I was staring straight at her; she reached back down behind the wall, this time she picked up a wooden walking stick.

"Okay, walk Shane past me to the opposite lamp post please."

"Shane, heel and watch me."

I was ready for her, the gloves were off, if she wanted a fight then so be it. She hadn't told me that I couldn't speak to him during this test, and if she was going to try and set him up to fail, then I was going to do everything that I could to help him pass.

"Watch me, good boy."

Over and over I repeated the words, my voice getting louder as we approached the lady. She raised the stick and banged the end on the floor with a heavy thud a couple of times as we passed. Shane was tuned into my words and ignored the sound of wood on concrete. Again she scribbled on his form.

"Sit your dog. Okay, now again walk back past me please."

Now I knew she was playing games. Shane was obviously going to fail, but let's have some fun; I'd humour her and dance to her merry tune.

As we were just about to reach where she had perched herself on the wall, she raised the walking stick above her head, in a very threatening manner. She hurled it onto the floor directly in front of Shane. The stick bounced up a few inches, startling Shane. Initially, he halted and took a step back, he glared at it and I could feel the lead vibrating, but I knew that he was unfazed.

"It's only a stick," I reassured him before we continued with the assessment.

"Leave it, watch me, heel."

I patted him on his head as we walked on past. Deep down my blood was boiling; no, in fact, I was bloody fuming. What was her sodding problem? Did she have a hatred of Belgium Shepherds? Or had I done something to offend her?

I could take no more of her crap.

"What's your fuc..."

Before the vile tirade of abuse could leave my mouth, Shane distracted me with a sudden tug and deep grumble that I could feel resonate through his lead; obviously, he didn't want his chance of becoming a therapy dog ruined by my foul mouth.

"Sorry dearie, did you say something?"

"Nope, you must be hearing things."

I looked down at Shane and winked. In a hushed voice I said to him, "All raving fruitcakes hear strange voices in their heads."

"Okay return to me, and could you give me Shane's grooming brush, please. The next test is not for me to groom him for you; it is actually to replicate him being heavily petted by a stranger. I assure you I will not harm him, but I will brush him aggressively, in random directions, just as if a young child may do when stroking him if Shane was to do a school or children's hospital visit. Is he okay with being brushed?"

"What chance has he got of ever doing a visit, you're going to fail him you cantankerous…"

I do believe that I may suffer from a very mild form of Tourette's. Luckily on this occasion, the words remained in my head.

"Shane's fine with being brushed."

I handed her his brush, and she beckoned him to just in front of her. Without being told, Shane sat, glaring at his brush, his tail already wagging in anticipation from side to side.

After a few minutes of brushing the assessor smiled. Surely not, my eyes were deceiving me; I think she must have wind. More notes were secretly scribbled on her form, her head shaking from side to side as she wrote.

"Right, could I have his treats please?"

I handed over Shane's bag of favourite treats; if I'd thought about it I'd have brought something that he didn't like, but at least on our behalf it would be an honest assessment. The lady took one out and held it between her thumb and index finger. She offered it to Shane; he moved his head forward, his lips barely kissing her fingers as he gently took the small biscuit from her. Again she smiled, she must have had terrible wind.

"Okay, I've read through his notes on the application form, but could you tell me some more about him please?"

Now I was baffled. I sat down next to her on the wall, and spent the next 15 minutes telling her all that I knew about Shane and about how he had come to join my family just six months earlier.

Believe it or not, I'm sure that I saw the assessor wipe away a tear.

Without a word of warning she picked up Shane's brush and took a few of his treats from the bag, and then she called his name. Sod it, he jumped up at her; his paws went straight onto her shoulders.

"Shane no! Bloody hell, get down."

I have to be honest I shouted, both out of frustration and annoyance, he'd bloody well blown his chances and failed right at the last minute. She had bloody well lured me into a false sense of security to fail him purposely.

Before I got the chance to launch into a full-blown rant at her she spoke.

"Don't be cross; it's my fault. In fact, I only did this because I wanted a cuddle. In all my years of being a voluntary assessor for Pets as Therapy, I have never met such an amazing dog. He sailed through the tests, passing each discipline with ease. For my own benefit, and I know that I shouldn't have done it, I pushed him as far as I could, to the absolute limit. Nothing phased this beautiful dog. Congratulations Shane, you passed with flying colours boy, in fact, you more than excelled. I will send off his pass form tonight, his tabard and ID tag will be sent to him in due course, he will then be able to commence therapy visits. Your area coordinator will be in touch, and she will attend your first few visits with you to explain everything and monitor you both, but believe me, you'll both do great."

Bloody hell, I had known all along that she was a lovely lady, and had guessed that that was precisely what she was doing. I thanked her for her time. She gave Shane yet another stroke, and we turned to leave.

Just as we were about to head back to the car, she called out to us and made some very kind comments that brought a lump to my throat and struck a lasting chord with me.

"Shane is an absolute credit to his breed and an ambassador for ex-rescue dogs."

She told me that I should be extremely proud of him; I already am. She also mentioned that she was not sure if there were any other Malinois on the therapy programme and that Shane could potentially become a 'pin-up' boy for the charity.

Very sadly Shane would never get to make a therapy visit, unbeknown to us within 48 hours a deplorable turn of events would tragically turn his world upside down and destroy his life.

CHAPTER SIX

My Poor Little Man's Pain

The lap, which I loved so much, the tender loving touch...

Wednesday 25th February 2015. It was just before 7 pm and we were getting ready to leave for obedience school. Shane had learnt by our set pattern of routines what tonight was, and he was already excited at the prospect of meeting up with his friends, and rising to the challenges of the evening's lesson that lay ahead of him.

He charged out into the garden to relieve himself before we set off. Toni had rummaged around for some change to pay the lessons nightly £4 fee and had found Shane's green progress card.

Hopefully, tonight he would master another discipline and be the proud recipient of yet another silver star.

The halogen security light illuminated him as he bounded down the garden steps and ran back into the lounge.

An ear-piercing horrific shriek of pain suddenly broke the excitement of the evening. Shane was whimpering loudly in agony. He had dropped to the floor and was frantically thrashing around; his eyes seemed full of fear, they appeared to have a look of hatred as the searing pain he was enduring took over his body, his mouth snapping and lashing around violently and aimlessly.

After about 30 seconds Shane was lying motionless on the floor, taking rapid, heavy breaths. What the hell had just happened? While I tried to comfort Shane, Toni was already on the phone to the emergency vet. All I could hear was her frantically explaining in full detail what had just happened to Shane to the on-duty emergency vet. The vet was also relaying instructions that Toni had to in turn pass onto me.

"He just ran in from the garden into the lounge and collapsed, it was terrifying as he rolled about on the floor yelping in agony. No sorry, I didn't see if he tripped. Are you sure that doing that won't cause him any discomfort? Paul, very gently run your hands down each of his legs, the vet suspects that he may have somehow broken a bone when he ran indoors. If so we are going to have to get a blanket to make him a stretcher, then try and manoeuvre him onto it to carry him to the car and get him to the surgery."

Warily I did precisely as I had just been instructed; Shane showed no apparent sign of discomfort as I slowly ran my hands down each of his legs in turn, carefully caressing his bones. He looked up at me, shook his body down and leapt straight up onto his paws. I looked at Toni in utter shock and disbelief; she relayed what we had just witnessed to the vet on the other end of the phone.

"Look, I am very sorry to have troubled you. I can assure you that I wouldn't have wasted your valuable time if I didn't think it was an emergency, but that is exactly how it happened. Yes, okay, thank you, we will keep a close eye on him overnight and bring him to you first thing tomorrow morning for a thorough check-up."

Toni hung up the phone.

"I'm not sure that he believed me, he said that owners do tend to exaggerate the word 'agony' and that Shane may have just placed a paw awkwardly, or he could even be playing up for a bit of affection."

This was the second time we had had cause to call Shane's vet, and the second bloody time we had been doubted as to the seriousness of the situation that had presented itself.

We knew exactly what we just witnessed, and without a doubt, Shane was in absolute agony. We kept him as calm and quiet as we could until it was his bedtime.

I was very wary as I took him out into the garden to relieve himself. In fact, I carefully put his lead around his neck to keep him as calm as possible and to be nice and close to my side. When he had finished I slowly walked him back indoors and removed his lead. Bless him, he seemed to be in a state of utter shock as to what had happened to him a few hours earlier. Slowly he climbed up the stairs to his bed. We both took it in turns to regularly check on him throughout the night.

The next morning Shane seemed absolutely fine and back to his old self, with no apparent after-effects from the excruciating painful episode he had suffered the previous evening. We had both rang our employers to tell them that we wouldn't be at work that day – we needed to get our boy thoroughly checked over by his vet.

The surgery opened for day-case consultations at 9 am; we were there anxiously waiting for the doors to be unlocked. Toni headed straight to the counter and gave a full explanation to the receptionist, who said that there were notes on the system, and for us to take a seat.

We were soon called in by one of the practice's vets, and again relayed the exact course of events in as much detail as we possibly could. I was asked to hold Shane's collar and keep him calm and still while the vet commenced to carry out a thorough muscular and joint check; his nurse was taking clinical notes as every part of Shane's body was meticulously examined.

"How again would you describe agony? I ask because to be totally honest with you I can't find a single thing wrong with him. I have checked every one of his joints, manipulated his legs, felt his bones and depressed and examined his main internal organs. To be honest with you I'm at a complete loss, and reluctant to sedate him to put him through having an X-ray if there is nothing obviously outwardly wrong with him."

We were completely bewildered. We knew that we hadn't overreacted, and both knew precisely what we had witnessed the previous evening.

However, Shane genuinely seemed fine. He was showing no apparent signs of pain, he hadn't once winced or backed away from the vet as he checked him all over. In fact, Shane, being Shane, seemed to relish the attention.

With no further way of explaining what had happened the previous evening we thanked the vet and nurse for their time and prepared to leave the examination room.

Just as we turned to leave, it happened again. As with the night before, there was no warning or apparent reason as Shane dropped to the floor, yelping loudly, lashing out with his jaws and writhing around in agony. The latest attack, just as with last night, happened so quickly without any signs or warning; the nurse screamed in shock, this, in turn, caused the vet to nearly topple off his stall.

After just a few seconds, the pain seemed to subside; I climbed down onto the floor to comfort and console him.

"Bloody hell, what just happened?" asked the vet, as he looked at us in a state of shock.

The nurse, who had now recomposed herself, was left aghast at Shane's sudden sporadic terrifying fit of agony.

"You're the bloody expert, you tell us."

My response obviously hit a nerve. The vet's demeanour changed; his body language wasn't so defensive now.

"I am going to have to be honest with you, I have no idea what the hell has just happened, but you're right, it appeared that he was in absolute blinding agony. We don't have the specialist investigative equipment here that is going to be needed to get to the bottom of this. Professionally I think that it could be a soft tissue problem, a trapped or damaged nerve, something that I have not personally encountered before. It is way above my knowledge and skills; I am going to have to refer Shane elsewhere. Wait here with him; I will get onto a specialist straight away."

"He didn't 'appear' to be in agony you fool, he was in bloody agony."

I was angry and my patience was wearing very thin. Shane needed help, and fast.

We sat in silence with the nurse in the consultation room while the vet headed off to try and make the necessary arrangements. After about ten minutes he returned. He looked down at Shane and gently shook his head.

"That really was very strange indeed. Right we're in luck; the consultant that I wanted you to take Shane to see has a cancellation. He's an old uni pal of my fathers, I've told him it's an emergency, and he's prepared to see Shane this morning. It's about an hour's drive away from here; could you take him at once?"

What a bloody stupid question, of course we could take him at once. We needed to get Shane better; there was no way on earth that he could carry on like that.

"Right this is the address, it's in Newmarket, and this is the name of the neurosurgeon. I will email him a referral letter fully outlining my observations. He is expecting him, and I'm confident he will be able to get to the bottom of this."

With a look of embarrassment, he continued.

"Look, I really am so very sorry, I can only apologise for ever doubting you."

There was no need for the apology; in fact, we didn't have time to stand and listen to it. The vet had kindly made all the arrangements for Shane to have a consultation at a specialist referral clinic as an emergency case, and that was all that mattered. We now needed to head off to get him there.

We arrived at the referral centre just after 11 am. Toni waited in the car with Shane as I went in to find out where we had to take him. I was told to bring him in, the consultant he had an appointment to see was currently with another patient, and he would summon us when he was ready.

Eventually, we were called into a consultation room by a tall Mediterranean gentleman. After our brief introduction, he carefully reread the email from Shane's vet. After a while, he looked up and asked us to elaborate upon some of the details in the referral email, and clarify a few questions that he had. The neurosurgeon was continuously watching and scrutinising Shane's movements throughout the consultation.

When he had gathered all of the information that he initially required he got down onto the floor and carried out a full body examination of Shane.

"Well, frankly I am as confused as Shane's vet was this morning. Please bring him out to our paddock and let me observe him walk and run."

The four of us headed out of the building together, and we were led around the side of the clinic to a fenced-off field. The gate was slammed and secured shut behind us; the consultant moved himself to a better vantage point and asked me to remove Shane's lead.

I was instructed to encourage Shane to run about, to jump and play with the array of toys strewn around within the paddock. I threw balls for him to retrieve; he even jumped and managed to catch some mid-air. There were some rubber 'tug' toys and I was asked to coax Shane into a gentle game of tug of war with me. This he did, his stumpy teeth and powerful jaws took a firm grip and locked onto the toy that I had selected. In fact, he managed to pull me towards him, snarling and shaking his head all the while. Shane's core strength and power were immense. I can remember thinking at the time what an intimidating and fearsome sight an attacking Malinois makes.

For the next 15 minutes or so, I followed the consultant's instructions to the letter and despite all of the rough and tumble, Shane didn't have another severe attack.

The consultant looked confused as he walked over to us, holding his chin and shaking his head.

"Mr and Mrs Viner, I totally disagree with Shane's vet's preliminary diagnosis and his recommendations. He has asked that Shane has a scan, an MRI costs about £1,200. That's on top of my consultation fee, it's a hell of a lot of money, and to be honest with you both, from what I have just observed, and after the full examination that I carried out earlier, I can't see or find anything obviously wrong with Shane. Personally and professionally I think that it will be a complete waste of your hard-earned cash, and my time to go any further with this consultation."

Bloody hell, why does everything have to have a sodding monetary value attached to it? This was Shane's well-being we're talking about, stuff the money. We knew precisely what happened last night, his vet that morning also witnessed Shane have a violent episode, I wanted the consultant to do whatever it would take to find out what was causing these vile, evil bouts of pain, and to get my Shane better, no matter what the sodding cost was.

After my almost having to plead and beg with him for nearly a quarter of an hour, he finally agreed to arrange for an MRI scan to be carried out. Begrudgingly he headed off to finalise the necessary arrangements, and we followed him back into the clinic.

The consultant appeared angered as he instructed his clinical team to prepare Shane for an MRI. He almost scowled at us as he barked his orders to the nurses. We were told to say our goodbyes to Shane and wait in the reception area.

After what seemed an eternity we were eventually summoned back into the consultant's office. Worryingly I could see that he had an anxious look on his face.

"Right, I'm sorry, but it's not good news I'm afraid. The MRI showed the pinching of his spinal cord, in particular, the C2-C3 and C3-C4 ventral slot and C2-C6 fenestrations."

He could see that we were baffled by his professional diagnosis.

"In layman's terms, this is what is causing the sporadic bouts of pain; the poor little sod must be in absolute agony. I don't want to beat about the bush, but this is very serious, and potentially it could result in his paralysis. While he is still under sedation, I think it will be best to get him straight into theatre. It is an extremely delicate and intricate procedure."

He began to explain in graphic detail the surgical procedure he was about to undertake. I couldn't listen to the gruesome words, I had to butt in.

"Please spare us the gory details. Just do what you have to do for Shane."

Bloody hell, less than an hour ago he was doubting what we were telling him and telling us it was a waste of our money, and his time. Now he was talking about paralysis, and how much sodding agony Shane must be suffering. When will these 'experts' learn to listen?

The warmth of the waiting room, combined with the very comfortable soft chairs, was causing us to momentarily nod off while waiting for any updates on Shane's surgery. Suddenly the large swing doors that led to the operating theatres burst open. Two nurses, still in their clinical green surgical scrubs, were pushing an operating room trolley. We could see the distinct colouring of Shane's fur, tucked snugly beneath a crimson red blanket. A third nurse was holding a clear plastic IV bag aloft. Eager to see him, but not wanting to disturb the nurses, we headed over and walked along beside them.

"Did everything go okay?"

"The surgeon is pleased; we are taking Shane to the recovery ward to monitor him overnight. Sorry, but it is a controlled area, not open to visitors."

The automatic doors swung open in the reception area; the nurses pushed Shane's theatre trolley across a small external walkway to the recovery unit.

We had heard the exact words that we were waiting for and needed to hear; hopefully, now he was on the road to recovery.

"Bless him, did you see his poor little head?"

Toni knew that I could have a wicked sense of humour and didn't respond.

"He looked like bleeding Friar Tuck."

We both chuckled. We were not mocking Shane, but bless him, they had had to shave the top of his head. He had a proper little bald patch. At least we could laugh now, the last 24 hours had been extremely stressful for us. Sod it, how bloody selfish of me. They had been a damn sight worse for Shane.

The doors leading to the operating theatres opened again and standing there was the surgeon, his green surgical scrubs covered in blood.

"Mr and Mrs Viner, good news. I'm more than confident that we have rectified the damaged vertebrae. His recovery period, with a controlled daily dose of pain relief, antibiotics and muscle relaxants, shouldn't be too long. You can't see him today, so I suggest that you head off home. We will contact you regularly and keep you fully updated on his progress. Can I also suggest that you buy Shane a harness to walk him with for the next six weeks? I want to avoid him pulling or putting any excessive strain on his neck for as long as possible."

With his surgery a complete success – sadly so we naively thought – we left the referral clinic. Having not eaten for almost 36 hours we needed to find somewhere to get some food. One of Shane's nurses recommended The Green Man pub to us; it was just up the road, so that's where we headed.

We both felt elated that our beautiful little man was now out of pain, so this was going to be a celebratory meal, although very sadly the celebrations were to be very short-lived.

Shane remained at referral clinic for a week; we were permitted to visit him every other day. Shane relished our visits, we always took him some fresh chicken and doggy chocolates. Bloody hell we missed him, our house felt so empty and soulless without him.

Gemma wanted to buy him a special welcome-home present.

"Dad, what can I buy him that he needs? His toy box and his treat tin are both full."

"There is one thing that he does need, a harness."

"That's not exactly what I had in mind, but if that's what he needs then that's what he will have."

The next day she very kindly went out and purchased Shane a harness – soft padding around the shoulder area, and two sturdy clasps to secure it around his forelegs and belly, just what the doctor – sorry vet – ordered.

On Thursday I received an email from Shane's neurosurgeon. He had copied me into the correspondence that he had sent to Shane's veterinary surgeon in Harlow outlining the procedure that had been carried out on him:

Shane was admitted on 26/02/2015, after diagnosis of C2-C3 intervertebral disc extrusion, for uncontrolled pain and reluctance to move.

Surgical procedure: we performed emergency C2-C3 and C3-C4 ventral slot and C2-C6 fenestrations on 26/02.

Comment/Prognosis: Shane's neurological status has progressively improved after surgery. He was receiving multiple physiotherapy sessions daily, and he was sent home in good neurological condition and with voluntary urination. Despite the persistent episodes of yelping, which are decreasing over time but which could also be influenced by his anxious and frightening behaviour, we decided to try to send him home.

Different types of pain, responding differently to treatment, have been described. Acute pain immediately follows tissue injury and is the typical type of pain observed postoperatively. Chronic pain persists after the initial pain-causing insult has resolved. Neuropathic pain is a type of pain caused by a primary lesion or dysfunction of the nervous system as opposed to nociceptive pain, which is pain resulting from the normal result of the stimulation of nociceptors. In addition, exposure to noxious stimulation may result in modifications of perceptions such as hyperalgesia (increased response to a normally painful stimulus) and allodynia (pain due to a normally non-painful stimulus), complicating pain assessment and treatment. Due to this reason, we need to evaluate his response to treatment, taking in consideration that most of his reactions could be related also to his frightening behaviour.

We suggested the following instructions provided by our physiotherapy team. Please take Shane out onto the grass four to five times daily for toileting purposes and only on a harness (please make sure he urinates independently).

Treatment:
Amitriptyline 50 mg; half a tablet twice a day
Symmetrel 100 mg; one capsule in the evening with food
Gabapentin 300 mg; one capsule three times a day

Rimadyl 50 mg; one tablet twice a day until the 27 of March, then one tablet once a day. Please give the medication with food.

Re-examination: we would like to re-examine Shane in 4 weeks, or earlier in case of any deterioration.

***

Friday 6th March. We had finally received the call we had been anxiously waiting for all week. Shane was allowed to come home, back to the people that love him and to the comfort of his own belongings. We had been told that we could collect him at 5 pm. Eagerly we set off at 3 pm. Yes, I knew that it was only an hour's drive, but we preferred to arrive well early and sit drinking coffee, rather than be late for such an important appointment.

Literally just as we are setting off there was a traffic announcement on the car's radio,

"There are severe delays on the M11 northbound due to a major accident, and the motorway will remain shut for the foreseeable future. Please find alternative routes."

Sod it, Friday afternoon rush hour and the main arterial motorway out of London through Essex was closed. The quickest and most direct route that we had to take to pick up Shane was now completely blocked. I spun the car round to start to make my cross-country detour, but the roads had already begun to clog up. In the end, the journey took four hours.

Upon arrival, we made our apologies for being so late. We handed over the new harness that Gemma had bought for him, and the night duty charge nurse headed off to go and get Shane for us.

Then there he was, Friar Tuck, sorry, our Shane, our brave, handsome boy. We couldn't contain our excitement and ran over to embrace him. The little bald patch on the top of his head had already started showing signs of slowly re-emerging sprouts of fur. The shaved section, on the scruff of his neck, where the skilful incision of the surgeon's scalpel for the intricate and complicated surgery had been initially made still had a very angry, bulbous four-inch-long scar running across it, the wound held together by a row of neat black sutures.

Shane seemed to know that he was coming home. We tried as best we could to not over-excite him, but we had missed our boy and he had very obviously missed us, and his home.

We carefully fitted and adjusted the harness that Gemma had kindly bought for him. It was perfect, with a soft padded breastplate, and two nylon straps that didn't intrude upon the surgical area on his neck.

We made him an appointment for a check-up in seven days, and then we were issued with a wad of information sheets explaining precisely how we had to care for him for the next few weeks, along with a very long list of dos and don'ts.

A bag containing a selection of pain relief, anti-inflammatory and antibiotic medication was handed over to us. The on-duty surgeon who was discharging Shane ran through and clarified the exact dosage of each and every item, although the information was printed clearly on the individual small plastic bottles.

We were also advised to monitor his food intake and to reduce his normal amount by 10% due to his inactivity during recuperation.

Shane never made his re-examination appointment. Sadly, our joy and happiness at having him home with us, where he belonged, was to be very tragically short-lived.

The very next morning after Shane had been discharged we had to urgently rush him back to Newmarket, this time to the referral centre's emergency out-of-hours clinic. He had had a severe relapse, and taken a horrific turn for the worse.

We called them en route to fully explain the awful situation. The neurosurgeon that had performed Shane's initial operation had been contacted and was waiting for us when we arrived.

I pulled up as close to the emergency access doors as I could, the surgeon walked over and carefully opened the rear door that Shane had propped himself up against. Shane cowered away from him as best he could, he was trembling with fear. For a fleeting moment, his eyes became transfixed on mine; I couldn't understand the look on his face, his glare burned into me, it bore straight into my soul. Was it fear, loathing or the hopeless look of a loved one who had just been forsaken in the vilest and most cowardly way? I'll never know, but one thing is for sure, that look will haunt me for the rest of my days.

It took the three of us almost five minutes to eventually manage to gently coax him into sitting up, enabling us to lift him from the car carefully.

I tried my upmost to reassure him.

"Don't worry my little mate; you'll be fine."

Who was I trying to kid? Was I trying to justify my actions to save myself? What a sodding liar I was.

We were not to know that when we relinquished his lead to the surgeon this would tragically be the last time that we would ever see our Shane walk again.

I knew that I had betrayed him, in the vilest, most despicable way possible.

He never even looked back as he was almost dragged away from us. Bless him, my little man was petrified, he couldn't hide his fear, with his tail firmly between his legs.

So much for the now hollow, meaningless promise that I had proclaimed to him the first day he came to live with us, the commitment that I would protect him.

By not looking back he saved me from having to endure another one of the sinister stares he had given me a few moments earlier. Did he hate me? I sincerely hope not.

I just stood there helplessly watching as he disappeared through the swing doors leading to the operating theatres, left to face his dreadful fate alone.

That sodding damn memory still haunts me to this very day; I have recurring nightmares and am continually wracked with guilt.

However, it's not about me, how the hell must Shane have felt?

He was alone and terrified and had been forsaken by the two people on earth that he trusted. He had shown us nothing but love, and now we, his so-called protectors, had let him down, like quivering cowards we had failed him.

Yet again Shane had been abandoned.

Shane was immediately sedated and given an emergency MRI scan. Not happy with the resulting images, his surgeon rushed him straight back into the operating theatre for emergency surgery.

We waited nervously for almost two hours, while the complex and intricate operation was performed on Shane.

Eventually, the surgeon appeared, his eyes were bloodshot, he wiped the sweat from his brow with the back of his hand, he looked mentally and physically drained.

"Right we won't know if it has been a success until he wakes up from the anaesthetic. He has come through surgery, and he is in our intensive care isolation unit. Please go home, I'll keep you fully updated on his progress."

Tragically, when he awoke from his second major operation, he was totally paralysed. Shane would never recover, nor be able to move his poor, once powerful body without assistance ever again. As soon as we received the phone call telling us the tragic news we jumped into our car and sped to Newmarket. We needed to be with Shane.

We were shown to where he was lying, tubes and bandages covering his body. While we were sitting stroking him, I heard a muffled cough from behind us, it was Shane's surgeon.

"Can I have a word with you please? I am so very sorry. I should never have gone in for a second time. Two of his vertebrae were still compressing his spinal cord, and there was a huge build-up of accumulated blood. As soon as I made the first incision with my scalpel it released the pressure. The built-up blood rushed straight through into his brain. I was working blind, I knew there was no room for error, just a hair's breadth out and the results could have been… I'm sorry, I shouldn't…"

I could listen to him no more, and had to interrupt his stuttering, rambling excuses.

"Save your hollow words, we trusted you with Shane's life. If you had any doubts, then why did you operate? The results are not 'could have been' are they? Listen, we've not driven here to listen to your pathetic excuses, just leave us alone and let us spend time with Shane."

For the next two weeks, every single day without fail we visited Shane and spent as much time with him as we were permitted. All we could do was caress him as he helplessly lay there. Every now and then he would muster the strength to give one of us the gentlest of licks. I can only hope that this was his way of showing us his forgiveness.

Whenever I got the chance, I would whisper my words of sincere apologies to him, for failing him in such an unforgivable and disloyal way.

Shane, I am so very, very sorry.

CHAPTER SEVEN

Anger and Revenge

The hand which stroked my fur and the sweet voice which called my name...

We had just arrived back home from our daily, emotional visit to Shane.

It was Wednesday 25th March. Physically and emotionally I was a wreck. Getting up at 4.30 am – although to be honest I had not been sleeping much – then driving to East London, carrying out a day's enforcement work, before driving back home. I had time for a quick shower before picking Toni up from work, and then we had the hour's drive to Newmarket. But I lived for that precious time, the hour or so we got to spend with Shane in the clinic's recovery ward.

His physiotherapist had been working tirelessly with him, but there were sadly no signs of improvement. In fact, that day Shane's consultant had said the very words that I dreaded ever hearing.

"I'm sorry, but there is nothing more that we can do for him. He is suffering. He cannot, and sadly will not ever be able to, stand unaided on his own. When we lift him onto his paws, he is merely weight bearing and balancing for a matter of seconds. We have to face the sad truth and reality that Shane will never be able to move again; his paralysis is irreversible. Be kind to him; he is a noble dog, do what is right. Let him pass away with a sense of pride and dignity."

For us, this was not an option. There was no way on earth that we were going to give up on him. If in our minds we thought that there was a mere glimmer of hope that he would one day walk again, then we would insist that his surgical care team continued working with him, at any expense. I felt angry how his consultant could so nonchalantly write him off. I was bloody fuming; how dare he be so sodding disrespectful to Shane.

We had failed him once in entrusting his life to the so-called 'experts', not again, now we were calling the shots.

Before we had left the clinic, I had a question that had been gnawing away at me that I needed answering.

Deep down within me, I hoped that the answer that he gave was precisely what I needed to hear. I must release my pent-up anger and had prematurely already taken the liberty of making plans for later on that day.

I took Shane's consultant to one side for a quiet word.

"Tell me the truth doc, could a trauma blow, such as a violent punch, have been the cause of Shane's suffering? The damn damaged vertebrae that has resulted in him lying there paralysed."

The consultant looked me straight in the eyes.

"I can't say for sure that a beating could have caused the initial problem, but then again, I can't rule out that it could have."

That was it; he had now lit the blue touch paper when he uttered the very words that I both wanted and needed to hear.

"It could have."

***

We were at home, and we had both made separate plans for the next few hours.

Firstly, I had to drop Toni off at Kealy's to enable them to spend some quality mother-daughter time together. Kealy has been suffering random bouts of painful contractions, and her baby was now a few days overdue.

I had to head off for a pre-arranged appointment. Perhaps not the best plan of action, I was emotionally distraught. I would generally consider myself to be a rationally well-balanced and intelligent man, but I was feeling mentally unstable. In fact, I'd go as far as to admit that I was scared of some of the thoughts that I had been having over the last few days of retribution.

I needed to release my pent-up sadness and anger; I needed to take brutal revenge on the perpetrator of the unprovoked cowardly attack on Shane. I now knew that Shane's damaged neck 'could have been' caused by the violent, inexcusable beating that he had received back in early July 2014, just a few weeks before he had joined my family.

A few days earlier I had been sitting in a pub having a quiet, reflective drink. A man came in with a beautiful German Shepherd who sat obediently by his side. I nodded and complimented him on his stunning hound. We had soon engaged in polite conversation; our topic was solely about our mutual interest in dogs, especially Shepherd breeds. I told him all about Shane, and out of the blue he mentioned that he believed that he may have met him once at a party. I clenched my fists and gritted my teeth, but needed to remain calm. I offered to buy him a pint, I needed to entice all of the information that I possibly could out of him, without turning to violence.

With some very basic detective work, I soon managed to find a social media account assigned to the name that the man in the pub had given me. Luckily the account's security was not set, and I began to trawl through the posts of his boring life, but more importantly his photos.

Suddenly without warning, I found myself recoiling in shock, horror and anger. Staring right back at me was a photo of Shane. He was at a family barbeque. I checked the image's 'properties' – the date fitted precisely, this was the very day of the cowardly attack. I had all the proof that I needed. More importantly, I now had my target.

Soon, with a bit more digging, I managed to find out his address, and even his place of work. Thank you very much social media, what an absolute godsend for anyone seeking revenge. Although in this particular case, I would be acting as judge, jury and executioner – well torturer at the very least – to a vile, despicable, cowardly bastard dog abuser. The wimpish scumbag whose potential spineless actions had resulted in my beautiful Shane lying paralysed, miles away from his home and the family who love him so very much.

Now I was waiting patiently, my heart rate and adrenaline levels were rapidly rising as I waited in anticipation for the scumbag dog abuser to return home from work.

I was plotting retribution, but my stress levels were slowly increasing. I had a tried and tested technique for dealing with stress – I call it the three, four, five method. I breathed in for three seconds, held my breath for four seconds then slowly exhaled for five seconds. After repeating several times, I felt my heart rate slowing, and a sense of serenity gradually overcame me.

The profile of the house, in particular the appearance and contents of the front garden, fitted perfectly with that of someone who had a dog, a scattering of chewed-up tennis balls lay about on the grass, two stainless steel food bowls and a pair of muddy Wellington boots sat in the covered porch way.

I had planned everything and had come equipped with the tools to inflict pain on this man. I was overwhelmed with hatred. How could he have done this to an innocent dog? I wanted him to pay the penalty for his cowardly cruelty.

Sitting there alone, my thoughts turned to Kealy, and our new grandchild that she was going to give birth too at any time. In the end common sense prevailed and I didn't carry out my revenge. But I still feel deep hatred and contempt for this man.

I have to add that after much soul-searching this chapter was heavily edited. My true intentions of revenge were removed.

CHAPTER EIGHT

Farewell My Dear Beloved Friend

I'd will, to the sad, scared shelter dog, the place I had in my loving human's heart...

It was the official start of British Summer Time, Sunday 29th March. The clocks had moved forward the night before, robbing us of yet another hour of sleep.

We were again making the 100-miles round trip to visit our special little man, a journey that we had made daily for the last few weeks, a drive that I could now do with my eyes shut. Sometimes through sheer exhaustion I probably had; I would momentarily doze and recollect the sudden sound of a fellow motorist sounding their horn, or my car hitting the rumble strips bringing me back to my senses.

But we knew that today would be the final time we would ever have to undertake the journey.

Earlier that morning we had received a phone call from the specialist taking care of Shane, and he had had to break the devastating news to us that Shane had bravely made up his mind – he had sealed his own fate. Shane had made the choice that he could no longer suffer the degradation that he was being forced to endure daily. It was as if he had accepted his fate, and enough was enough.

It was time to let him go with our love and blessing.

His once muscular body was now rapidly wasting away as he was forced to lie there motionless, tubes entering his body to give constant pain relief and administer food, his bedding having to be changed hourly where he soiled and wet himself. Intense, daily physiotherapy wasn't helping him. With the aid of straps, they could get him to bear weight on his legs for a mere matter of seconds, but there was no way that he could stand on his own. There had been a glimmer of hope a few days earlier when he had very slightly moved his head unaided, but that miracle had been a one-off, his poor frail body now couldn't make any unassisted movements.

Finally, that morning he had refused to allow them to give him water. Every half an hour they had been using a syringe to moisten his lips, to offer relief to his poor drying mouth, but that day he mustered all of his strength to prevent them, clenching his jaws shut as tight as he could. There was nothing else the nursing team could do for him. He had given up.

Shane wanted to depart this planet with a sense of dignity and pride.

The drive to Shane took us an hour. That hour was spent in total silence, neither of us wanting to invade the other's thoughts of the mentally arduous, horrific task that awaited us. Although it was now officially summer time, it was pouring with rain, the window wipers struggling to keep the screen clear as we headed up the motorway, the rain continually pelting down on us. The fact that I was being forced to drive slower than usual due to the abysmal weather conditions gave me a sense of hope – just maybe, by some miracle, he would move, so if the journey was prolonged, we may offer him that chance of recovery. I had to hope; I couldn't give up on him. Pat had come with us; she had rescued him and had been there for Shane through the good times. Now she would share with us his final moments on earth.

We pulled into the car park of the specialist referral clinic. I turned off the engine, and we sat there, the three of us immersed in total silence, none of us wanting to make the first move. Our vision of the fields where we had once walked Shane before paralysis destroyed his life slowly became blurred, then completely obscured as the rain covered the windscreen.

We knew that the inevitable final moments of Shane's life were now in our hands. The day we had met him for the first time we had vowed to him that we would love and care for him; now we were about to commit the vilest of deeds, we were going to allow his beautiful, carefree life to be snatched cruelly from him.

We looked at each other, tears rolling down our faces, and slowly got out of the car. The rain offered some strange sense of relief, we hugged each other to give some much-needed moral support, and then hand in hand we reluctantly headed into the reception area. The lady behind the desk looked up at us. We had met her many times before, and she was well aware why we were there.

"I am so sorry; I will let him know that you are here for Shane."

Before we could sit down, Shane's specialist appeared. He ushered the three of us into his office; strangely he struggled to make eye contact with me as I walked past him. Why, did he have a guilty conscience?

We were thankful that we didn't have to spend any time sitting in reception. As horrible as it sounds, we were envious, envious of the dogs that we saw being prepared to be discharged from the surgical unit. In the few moments that we were there, we had to watch a large chocolate Labrador leave excitedly with its owners to continue its recuperation in the comfort of their own home. The surgical wound on its back swathed in bandages, but the dog's tail wagged continually; even though it was wearing a large plastic 'buster collar' bountiful kisses were planted on their human family at every opportunity. I had to endure watching as it happily bounded out of the reception area.

Our beautiful Shane would not be leaving, at least not walking out proudly by our sides. Shane had a habit of strutting with an air of confident arrogance, but never again; his body would leave wrapped and zipped up in a ghastly black rubber mortuary bag.

Deep down I knew that the specialist felt a sense of guilt; he had tried so hard to save Shane; in fact, he had performed both of Shane's operations.

"You are doing the right thing for him. There is no hope of him ever moving again. We have done absolutely everything humanly possible that we could for him. I really am so sorry."

He made a full explanation of the euthanasia process, how the drug would be administered intravenously into Shane, and the involuntary convulsions Shane's body could potentially have.

To this day I have no exact recollection of the words that he said to us, I did not want even to begin to think of how my little man's life was going to end, my mind as a defence mechanism blocked the offensive words out.

As he was taking the time to explain everything in full detail to us, all I was thinking about was my Shane, lying there on his own, alone in his final moments, alone without us by his side, the two people who loved him the most in the world.

I needed to go to him, to be with him, I needed to spend the precious little time that he had left on earth lying with him, comforting him, caressing him.

Before we were shown into the adjacent nursing room where Shane was lying, the specialist handed us a consent form for Shane's euthanasia; this stinking bastard merciless form had to be read and signed. The wording was cold and heartless; obviously, whoever scribed the words had never loved a sentient being. These disgusting, vile, insensitive words were about my Shane.

The surgeon took a pen from the chest pocket of his green scrubs gown. As he attempted to pass me the pen I glared at him; an unjustified hatred towards him filled my body. I couldn't bring myself to take the pen from his hand; I started to glare at his hands, his precious skilful work tools that had saved so many beloved pets, why the hell couldn't they have saved Shane? Now they held a weapon of destruction, a pen, a damn stinking plastic pen that would end Shane's life.

"Are you sure there's nothing more you can do for him?"

"It's not down to me, Shane has made his choice. Give him his last wish, allow him to bow out with dignity and sign the consent form please, Mr Viner."

I couldn't do it; I hadn't the courage, I could not be held responsible for signing Shane's death warrant. The room began to spin; I had to sit down.

I looked up, and very bravely Toni had taken the enormous responsibility from me. She almost snatched that damn sodding pen from the surgeon's hand. I had never looked at a pen with such fear and hatred. How could that small thing Toni was holding in her hand be capable of such vile destruction? A pen, a small bloody pen, an object that is supposed to write poetry and words of love, not kill my Shane, but there again pens have signed declarations of war, resulting in the slaughter of millions. Here I was, petrified of that damn object, and there was my wife protecting me, she had stepped in to defend me from a bloody pen.

Toni eventually mustered the strength to scribble her name, and she would now have to live the rest of her life with the burden of guilt knowing that she, and she alone, had signed Shane's life away. She had signed his death warrant.

We composed ourselves as best we could before being led to where he was lying. Shane's specialist looked at us before we entered the ward where he was, and in a hushed voice he said to us:

"Before we prepared him for his final journey he was given a large dose of sedative and pain relief; we want his final moments to be as pain-free, comfortable and peaceful as possible for him. Be brave for him, tell him you love him, caress him, stroke him, and when you are ready, look at me, I will be awaiting your signal, it will be over in seconds, but please, as his life ebbs away keep telling him that you love him."

The specialist's cold, harsh words on how they had prepared Shane offered no comfort to us, and how on earth did this executioner think he could provide us with words of compassion and love to say to our little man?

How bloody dare he impose on our emotions, he knew nothing of our love, our unconditional love for Shane.

We slowly entered the small bay that had imprisoned Shane for 14 long, arduous days. Gently, not wanting to hurt him, we lay down on the soft sterile surgical bedding to be as close as we could for one final time with our brave special little man. The nurses had already removed most of the tubes that had sustained his life for the last two weeks from his body. There was just one cannula tube remaining. This was fed directly into one of his hind legs, but had nothing flowing through it at that time.

I still had doubts. How could the surgeon be so bloody sure that Shane wanted to leave this mortal coil?

Shane's beautiful eyes met mine. Was he trying to say to me:

"Please let me go; I've had more than I can take; I can't go on."

Alternatively, was he pleading with me, begging me for help? I had to be entirely sure, it was going to be hard enough living with my conscience as it was, but if he was begging me for my help and I didn't listen or recognise the signs, I would never be able to forgive myself.

The thoughts of the promise that I had made him the first day we met, that I'd love and protect him forever were still echoing around and around my mind.

What would an animal in the wild do when ill or in agony? They would crawl away from the rest of the pack; they would secrete themselves into a corner of their lair or cave. Was this precisely what Shane was trying to do? Shane was paralysed, he couldn't move, what if his natural canine survival instincts were forcing him to try and elude us?

If he'd known that we would do absolutely anything to save him would he have fought harder?

Shane knew that in the wild he would be a burden to the pack, he would slow them down, he would take much-needed food from them. Was he fearful of the pain his ancestors would have suffered had they been euthanised by the pack they lived amongst?

Questions and doubts continually reverberated around my mind. I'd failed Shane, instead of safeguarding him, I was going to allow, and had given my permission, for someone to kill him. I'm sorry it sounds so harsh and brash, but that was precisely how I felt.

I was guilty of permitting his imminent death.

The surgeon looked down at me and gently shook his head; he must have picked up on my apprehension. Who the stuff did he think he was, Dr bloody Dolittle? He was an educated man of science, one of the country's most renowned animal neurosurgeons, but what did he know about animal psychology? I respected him, but he couldn't talk to the animals. How could this man be so sure that this was what Shane wanted? Was this a guilt trip? Did his skilled hands fail Shane? Was seeing him lying there every day a constant reminder of his incompetence?

My emotional state and immense sadness was yet again mutating rapidly into anger.

Pat was in tears. She was standing next to the surgeon, they looked at each other. I'm sure that they spoke, but I couldn't hear the words they said.

Toni was staring at me. Shane's eyes were still looking lovingly, yet fearful up at me. Shane's little 'ham tongue', as Gemma called it, looked painfully dry as it protruded from the front of his mouth.

Deep down I knew that the surgeon was right. Slowly and carefully we positioned ourselves as best we could so

Shane couldn't see his executioner standing there, armed with the evil, disgusting syringe of vile yellow liquid in his hand, the repulsive solution which contained pentobarbital, the revolting drug that would end my Shane's life.

We began to caress his weakened body, gentle, soothing strokes from his neck to his tail, very slowly over and over; our words of love and comfort flowed easily and repeatedly from our mouths.

"Good boy, brave boy, our beautiful little man, we love you, Shane."

I looked at Toni, she closed her eyes, and I knew it was now time to let him go. Our soothing words of reassurance continued as I looked towards the surgeon and gave the briefest of nods. He carefully stepped over Shane, and positioned himself at Shane's rear; our brave little man couldn't see his actions. The syringe was attached to the cannula; the surgeon looked at us and closed his eyes. He very quietly muttered some words to himself and began to ease the liquid into the cannula, very slowly and gently.

Within a few moments, Shane's breathing became more and more shallow, his eyes were filling with tears, and the whites were now taking on a reddish hue, but they never left ours. Then his beautiful body became motionless; we continued with our comforting words, the surgeon remained silent, with his head bowed, allowing us to spend the final few peaceful moments with our little man while his beautiful body was still warm.

After a few minutes, I look up at the consultant, He carefully moved towards the middle of Shane's now motionless body and placed his stethoscope to Shane's chest.

"He is at peace now."

He moved out of the way to allow us to continue cuddling Shane's now lifeless body as tightly as we could, neither of us afraid or ashamed to let our emotions for our beloved Shane be heard. After what seemed an eternity we looked at each other and embraced. Toni had brought a small cuddly teddy bear with her, one of Shane's favourites. She gently placed it between his two front legs; he looked so peaceful, just as if he was at home sleeping in the comfortable bed that Leah had brought him as a Christmas present. Oh those happy days now seemed an eternity ago.

We said our final farewell to Shane – we were numb – and slowly we headed out into the car park. It had stopped raining. At last, Pat followed us out, she was carrying three plastic cups of sweet, strong coffee. I sparked up a cigarette and moved away from where Toni and Pat were standing. None of us knew what to say; we stood there, each alone in our thoughts of the disgusting, horrible event that had just transpired, we had just killed Shane.

To this day, it eludes me who first looked up towards the sky and noticed the rainbow. It had rained for the whole journey to the referral clinic – in fact, the rain could be heard hitting the window when Shane fell into his final sleep – but now the sun was shining, with a beautiful, brightly coloured rainbow adorning the sky.

"He's saying goodbye." Pat's words broke the silence.

We all looked up.

Goodbye Shane.

The three of us climbed back into my car, the engine igniting into life was the only sound that broke the eerie silence. Very slowly we drove out of the patients' car park of the specialist referral clinic.

"Please take care of him."

These were the only words that I could mumble, I did not want to leave him, I couldn't bear to leave my Shane, lying there alone. I couldn't comprehend that I was leaving him for the very last time.

We soon reached the end of the gravel drive, a few spots of rain unexpectedly landed on my window screen, the sky was rapidly darkening. In fact, even the rainbow had disappeared, it was now hiding behind a huge black cloud. As I pulled out of the referral clinic's grounds onto London Road the heavens opened. I headed back onto the A14; yet again we were soon driving in a deluge of torrential rain.

We had disclosed the events surrounding the appearance of the rainbow to very few people. Although those we spoke to never said so in as many words, the look on their faces always seemed to show an element of disbelief, as if we had imagined it to give us a sense of spiritual relief. To this end, Toni, Pat and I never spoke about it again when we were in the company of others, but the three of us know for sure what we saw, we never imagined it, and for a very brief moment, it did give us a much-needed welcome sense of comfort.

The drive home was sombre, to say the least, in total respectful, reflective silence. I can't speak for Toni or Pat, but I honestly felt that I was in a state of shock, if the truth be known I shouldn't have been driving at speed down the M11 in such treacherous weather conditions, especially in my anguished mental state.

Gemma was waiting for us when we arrived home. We had already sent each of our daughters a brief text message, for our own benefit – we knew that to ring each of them in turn, to tell them of Shane's passing, would be far too hard for either of us to be able to handle.

Luckily Gemma didn't ask us how we were; our red-eyed, tear-stained faces told her that anyway.

"You gave him the best seven months of his life."

Gemma's kind words almost reduced me to a sobbing wreck.

"Dad, if you look at it in dog years he spent almost three and a half years with you."

I could see that Gemma was now getting upset herself. She adored Shane, he could often be found during the day lying on her bed with her.

Her words did bring me a brief moment of comfort, but Shane's life had been cruelly cut so tragically short. He had only just turned three; he had his whole life ahead of him, he should have lived for at least another 12 years with us. How could life be so unjust and cruel? Two years as an abandoned rescue dog, at long last we had given him the life, love and happiness that he craved, and more than deserved. The one thing that he had yearned for had now been violently snatched from him; life was just so unfair, then again they do say only the good die young.

Most of that afternoon was a complete blank to me; maybe my internal self-defence mechanism had purposely blanked it from my memory. One thing that I can recollect though is me continually saying to Toni:

"I want my Shane back."

We spent a few hours consoling each other before showering. I needed to scrub the vile feeling of death from my body, the clinical stench that I imagined I reeked of; the disgusting aroma of Shane's final living moments on earth.

We had already made arrangements the previous day to visit Kealy, along with the rest of our family, to spend some quality time with Heath.

Our plans had been based initially around visiting Shane at lunchtime to give him his daily much-needed words of encouragement and hugs. We had also arranged to have a coffee and face-to-face catch-up with his surgeon to ascertain what his next plan of action was with regards to intensifying Shane's physiotherapy. I had told him a few days earlier that euthanasia was not an option, Shane had to be cured at any cost.

However, and more importantly, we now had a proposal to put forward. We felt that Shane would progress far better if he were to return to the love and comfort of the people that he knew, the people who genuinely loved and cared about him. Pat had already started putting contingency plans into action. The Mutts on-site hospital was going to be converted and utilised into an IC Unit, with a camp bed installed to enable someone to remain with Shane 24 hours a day, seven days a week.

Along with Toni and me, members of staff had already started rallying around and volunteering to give up their free time to help nurse Shane back to full health. I had even looked into taking long-term leave to be one of Shane's carers. A veterinary physiotherapist had also agreed to come in twice a day to continue with his treatment.

Sadly, it was not to be.

Life can be so very bloody unjust and cruel.

Thank you, Shane.

You came into and blessed our lives for a mere seven months, for one of them you were in hospital, far away from your loving family and home.

I will be eternally grateful to you, my beautiful little man, for you taught me about love.

Now you have departed, you have taught me about loss.

Until we meet again.

R.I.P my extraordinary little man.

CHAPTER NINE

Rainbow Bridge

A heart which knew no bounds.
So when I die, please do not say...

I have made my choice; I can no longer carry on living my pathetic, worthless life like this. My body will never move again, that I know for sure. My human father gave me a command, the last time he had to rush me here from the sanctuary of my new-found loving home, a mere two weeks ago. Back then the excruciating pain I was suffering in my neck was more than I could bear, I had already endured an operation, it hadn't helped me, and I remember his words as he lifted me from the car:

"You fight my little man; you fight for your life."

However, I can't. For once I have to disobey my master's' command, for I know that this is one fight I cannot win. The damage that my body suffered during surgery has sealed my fate. I am resolute that I must prepare myself to make my final journey; I must seek the bridge. I wish that I could beg for their forgiveness, I have failed them. I also wish that I could ask for their mercy, to help my soul leave my useless broken body.

Now they are back at my side, my loving family, kneeling next to me. I can see that their hands are moving over my useless body, but I feel no sensation from their gentle touch, I can just barely move my eyes to look up at them. Their eyes are looking lovingly back at me, but they appear different today. Their words of comfort fill me with joy, but I must be allowed to leave them, I must be allowed my pride and dignity. I hope that one day they can find it in their hearts to forgive me. They must give me their blessing to depart this world with a sense of honour. Their words 'Good boy, brave boy, we love you' over and over give me a sense of comfort, and now I see the man who tried to mend my pain, he looks at my family, and now he has gently stepped over me, where has he gone? What is he doing? Their faces, tears streaming as they comfort me with their words, I see him, my human father, nod, the gentle nod he would give me, our very own special sign. I knew I had done well when he gave me that nod, with a beaming smile on his face. However, there is no smile; his eyes are full of sadness. A strange sensation takes over me, my senses are slowing down, and now it is getting hazy, my vision is becoming blurred, it is getting darker and darker, my head is starting to spin gently. I am getting tired, so very tired, I can no longer stay awake.

At last, I am now pain-free and at peace.

Thank you. You have given me the ultimate gift of love.

Shane can feel a gentle refreshing waft of air blowing softly on his body. Slowly he awakes from his peaceful slumber. His eyes blink at the brightness as they very slowly open. His vision is blurred, but as his eyes slowly adjust and focus a breath-taking sight greets them – the most beautiful dog he has ever seen standing quietly in front of him. Her pure white fur is gently fanning in the breeze, and translucently glistening in the warm sunshine. Gently and unsteadily he clambers up onto his four paws, and stretches, wow, that feeling fills his body with euphoria. His mouth is dry, and as he again looks towards the beautiful dog, she averts her gaze and faces towards the direction of a small gently flowing river. Unhurriedly he begins to walk, wobbly at first, towards the water. Feeling exhilarated he speeds up his gait, his heart pounding with excitement as he reaches the gently flowing water. Steadily he leans forwards and takes a small sip, the water is cold, and tastes so pure, he begins to drink more and more, gulping down copious mouthfuls of the flawless liquid. His body feels invigorated. The water is gently flowing, but slow enough for Shane to catch a glimpse of himself in the reflection.

"Wow, I do look good if I do bark so myself."

However, something is not right; intrigued he takes another look at himself. He opens his mouth and can't believe what he's seeing. Slowly he runs his tongue around his mouth. He is not seeing things, he really does have teeth, a full set of gleaming white teeth, but how? He hasn't had teeth for as long as he can remember. Slowly he turns back to face the beautiful dog. Confused he tilts his head inquisitively; she smiles back at him. Something else strikes him; he has not been able to move for weeks, but now he can, his mind is in a total state of confusion.

"It is time," her voice is so calm and gentle.

"Time for what?"

Without barking another word, she looks towards the river that Shane had just drunk from. He turns back to face the river, and there in front of him is a beautiful, multi-coloured bridge.

"Where did that come from?"

"It is for you, Shane. In your own time, and when you feel that you are ready, cross over the bridge. My task is complete; your body is now ready for your next journey."

Is this the bridge that he had made his mind up to cross when lying unable to move? The bridge, the legend of which is past down from dog to dog, the Rainbow Bridge.

Fear and confusion are playing turmoil with his mind. Shane is scared at the uncertainty of what lies ahead of him. He knows full well of the legend, of the paradise that awaits him, but what of his family, the people he has left behind? He can only hope that the foretold legend is correct and that one day they will meet again.

He is scared; he turns back and starts to walk towards the beautiful dog for comfort. Shane stops, he knows that there is no going back to his former life. His fear slowly begins to subside, and an overwhelming urge begins to engulf his body, he is being drawn back towards the bridge, and the uncertainty of his future. For one last time, he glances towards the dog, then turns and begins to run, adrenaline pumping within his body as he runs as fast as he possibly can towards the bridge, the cool breeze blowing in his face.

It is getting closer, as his paws first touch it they bounce on its candy-floss soft surface, they gently sink a little, but it doesn't break his stride. He briefly looks behind him; she has disappeared, no longer there to protect him from whatever fate lies ahead. Onwards and upwards he runs, the multitude of colours spreading as far as he can see. All around the sides, he can make out soft fluffy clouds bouncing around in a clear blue sky, Shane keeps running, faster and faster. The vista ahead of him is changing; the rainbow is merging into a vast expanse of greenery. Soon the soft surface he has been bounding across has turned into grass, soft dew-covered grass that smells so clean and fresh, he can't help himself. Exhilarated he drops down and rolls around like a puppy, it feels so good.

"Welcome to the other side of the Rainbow Bridge Shane."

Shocked at the sudden rude interruption to his moment of self-indulgence he leaps up to his paws, his body wet from the dew that he has been frolicking about in. Shane finds himself surrounded by a pack of dogs – where had they suddenly appeared from? All he can sense is a calming peace from them. At the head of the circle is the spitting image of the dog that greeted him on the other side of the bridge. Like her, his fur is pure white, and there is a calming aura radiating from him. The rest of the pack, 12 dogs in all, avert their gaze from Shane; they all sit in a circle around him in total silence, their heads bowed.

"I am Caesar; welcome to your furever home, my friend. Your body has been through so much, and I know you have many questions. We will show you to a quiet place where you can rest a while. We have many years together to explain everything to you. Now please, come with us."

Without saying another word Caesar gets up and turns and slowly starts to walk away, followed by six of the other dogs. He turns back towards Shane, who is wholly bewildered about everything that is happening.

"Come on, Shane."

He doesn't need telling again; instincts say to him that he must follow. Shane takes his place to the rear of the six dogs that have already followed Caesar; the final six dogs take their place in the procession and follow behind Shane.

They eventually reach a small copse of cherry trees which are in full blossom; the grass beneath them is shaded and soft.

"Rest here my friend, and I will come back later."

Shane watches as Caesar turns and leads his faithful followers back in the direction they have just come from, back towards the bridge, maybe to meet another guest to the tranquillity that Shane now finds himself in. He lies down and gently falls asleep.

Freshwater can be sourced in a multitude of small crystal clear ponds, and the air is clean and pure. Food is bountiful, but consists of foraging for nutritional berries; no sentient beings are ever harmed. The sky is swathed in constant warm sunshine illuminating the lush green meadow carpet, covered in a multitude of fragrant, colourful flowers, the sweet smell of the cherry blossoms adding to the beautiful scent. There is a shallow neon blue river flowing through the centre of the meadow, full of golden fish and bright yellow ducklings; the sound of the flowing water and gentle quacking merge seamlessly with the birdsong from the turtle doves and swifts flying above. This is indeed paradise.

Startled, he opens his eyes, Caesar is alone and sitting in front of him.

"The foretold legend is true Shane. All animals that have been ill, injured or old are restored to their youthful health and vigour. Those who were hurt or maimed are made whole and healthy again, just as their families remember them in their dreams of days and happy times that have gone by. All of our guests are at peace and content, except for one small thing; they each miss someone very special to them, who had to be left behind.

"Here we all run and play together, but rest assured Shane, the day will come when you suddenly stop playing, you will look into the distance. Your bright eyes will finally catch a glimpse of your human. Your eager body will begin to quiver. It is your turn; you will run from the group, flying over the green grass, your legs will be carrying you faster and faster.

"When you and your special friend finally meet, you will cling together in joyous reunion, never to be parted from one another again. Their happy kisses will rain down upon your face; their hands again caress your beloved head, and you look once more into the trusting eyes of your special human friend. For so long they have gone from your life but never absent from your heart.

"Together you will turn and leave; you will again cross over the Rainbow Bridge for your final journey, to your eternity together."

Caesar slowly rises to his four paws and begins to walk away; he stops and turns back to Shane.

"On your seventh day here Shane, on the hour that you left your previous life, you must pick up a white feather, take it to the river's edge, close your eyes and think lovingly of the family you left behind. Gently drop the feather into the water. They will see it when it floats down to them; it is your sign, and reassurance to them that you have reached your paradise and are at peace."

Duly as commanded Shane gave us his sign, and he continues to play happily with the other dogs, living his after-life in contentment.

He has to be patient and allow me to live out my days.

However, he knows that one day we will be together again.

CHAPTER TEN

Mourning

"I will never have a pet again, for the loss and pain is more than I can stand."

I am not a person who shows my emotions freely; in fact, in the 38 years that I have been with Toni, she has only seen me cry twice. The first time was when our eldest daughter had had an horrific accident. I lay down in the road with her, trying to comfort her until the ambulance arrived. The second time my tears flowed freely was when we held Shane in our arms as his life slowly ebbed from his beautiful body. My extreme sadness seemed to manifest itself as anger, I am not proud of it, but it is what it is. I know that men do cry, but usually when no one can see them.

Over the previous 24 hours, I had found myself breaking down at the mere thought of Shane; his artefacts were still scattered and spread throughout the house. I picked up his toys and smelt them, I stroked his bed, I gazed at his collar and lead hanging next to the front door, yearning to place them around his neck and head off on one of our two-hour jaunts. As doors opened the gentle breeze disturbed small clumps of his fur that had accumulated under our settee. Gently they wafted across the floor, it was as if he was still with us. These discarded soft pieces of his tan pelage that gracefully stirred and moved through our home were all that we had of Shane.

How long would this pain last? The day before I had been told that I had joined a club, its members all had one thing in common – they had all lost a pet dear to them. Well stuff your membership, there was no way I wanted to be a member of this sodding club, it was bloody vile.

Monday was my day off. Along with my parents we had arranged to visit my father's local pub, The Bull, the pub where we had held their golden wedding celebrations in far happier times. No that's unfair, that day we were going to have a few drinks to wet our new grandson Heathy's head. Silently though I would raise my glass to Shane, my dear little absent friend.

Mentally Toni and I were not in the mood for socialising; we had only lost our Shane 24 hours earlier, the pain was still raw and intense.

Deep down, if I'm honest, I think that my main selfish worry was what if I was to break down and cry in front of everyone.

During the free-flowing drinks, I sensibly made up my mind that a day of enforcement work in East London was probably not the best thing for me to be engaging in on the following day. One wrong word from an illegal DVD, perfume or cigarette seller, well, who knows what the outcome would be. I had far too much pent-up anger to be let loose on the undesirables of the East End. I popped outside for a much-needed cigarette and decided to ring my manager.

"Sorry mate, I'm going to have to take tomorrow off. I lost Shane yesterday and to be honest I'm far too upset to come in."

"Who is, sorry, was Shane?"

His response was both abrupt and disrespectful.

"You know exactly who Shane was you sodding idiot; I spoke about him all the time."

"You're telling me that you're taking a day off because your dog has died?"

"Well done Sherlock, you've got it in one."

I could sense that the conversation was quickly going to become confrontational. To be honest, if it weren't for the several pints of strong real ale I'd already drunk I would have jumped in my car and, well thankfully on this occasion the beer spared my manager's front teeth. Anger to tears in the blink of an eye, my emotional state was bordering on irrational.

"It was only a..."

Before he could finish the uncompassionate sentence I was dreading that I'd hear, I quickly butted in.

"I suggest you think long and hard about the next words that leave your mouth."

I knew that he sensed my anger - all mouth and no action was my manager, talked a good fight, but would run a mile from any face-to-face confrontation.

My job could be perilous; to this day my overt anti-stab vest hangs in our spare bedroom. My days of working in the East End of London were tainted with violence. I had made the acquaintance of and socialised with some dangerous men, violent criminals, old-school East End villains and gangsters. These intemperate men could have you buried for looking at them the wrong way, yet I had managed to earn their respect, and to be honest I'd helped them out. Now here I was talking to a pathetic excuse of a man, a man who very nearly said the wrong thing, a man I could easily snap in half. He had come very close to crossing the line. Did he think his managerial position impressed me? Did he honestly believe it would protect him?

I'm a foot soldier. Once I was with a fellow officer, whose lousy attitude resulted in a loaded handgun being pointed at us. I've been threatened on many occasions with knives, had ferocious bull breed dogs almost set upon me, a car was once deliberately driven into me, an argument had escalated out of control, my opponent knew he couldn't physically or mentally beat me, so he used his car as a weapon. The injuries I sustained were minimal; even after he had used his two-tonnes of steel to attack me, I still tried to yank open his driver's side door. I was going to break every last bone in his head. In a state of panic he slammed his car into first gear and fled the scene, our CCTV team had monitored the whole incident and the Metropolitan police soon arrested him. It takes a lot to scare me, although blood-filled hypodermic syringes do scare me – one scratch from the needle holding the crimson coloured fluid could result in a long and mentally agonising wait to find out if you have been infected with a life-changing or threatening disease. These weapons were now becoming more widely used by thugs paid to inflict traumatic mental suffering, and potentially a death sentence on unsuspecting victims. I have had the training to know what to do if stabbed by a needle;

Do not cover the entry point of the needle, try to force as much blood out as possible and let it continually flow, hopefully forcing any contaminated fluid from out of your body.

I'm not proud of some of the things I've done in my professional role, but to make a vile comment to a person who has just suffered the bereavement of a beloved family member, even if 'it was just a dog' is not in my nature.

"Erm, I was erm, erm, I was going to say I'm sure we can manage without you."

In a moment of panic, he stuttered out his words and managed to swerve away from the vile sentence that only someone who has never loved a dog would say.

I thanked him for his 'understanding' and hung up the phone. What an utter prat he really was.

The following days were spent spending as much time as possible with our beautiful little grandson. I will be eternally grateful to Heathy for helping me through one of the darkest periods in my life.

Over the last few days sleep had become my closest ally, well not the actual sleeping, but the waking-up part. For the briefest of moments when I opened my eyes I looked for Shane; I expected to be able to hear him or to have to prepare myself for him launching himself onto my bed for a cuddle.

However, he wasn't there; the reality soon kicked in, he was gone, and would never be coming back.

It seemed that my subconscious mind, which influenced my feelings, was protecting me. While asleep I had been having recurring dreams of the loving, fun-filled times that I had the privilege of spending with Shane, while the horrors and sadness of his demise seemed to have been entirely erased from my memory.

Hence when I awoke, I still expected to see his beautiful face staring at me.

***

The following weekend was Easter. On Good Friday we had decided to book a two-week holiday on the Greek island of Rhodes in August. At least now we had something to look forward too. On Saturday, we spent the day with close relatives at Southend-On-Sea, Essex. They were also dog lovers and had experienced the heartache of recently losing both of their beloved Rottweilers in very close succession. In their company, Toni and I felt free to let our emotions show; in fact on more than one occasion the four of us were very close to being in floods of tears.

The following day was Easter Sunday. Our family was joining us for dinner, we were going to get to spend some quality time with Heath in our own home. Sadly my Shane would not be there with us; I knew that he would have utterly adored Heath, and would have looked on in bewilderment at our noisy little bundle of love and joy.

CHAPTER ELEVEN

Shane's Homecoming

Instead, go find an unloved dog…

Wednesday 8th April. Shane was finally coming home. Deep in reflection, we drove back to the referral specialist veterinary clinic, the first time we had returned since we had to say our emotional farewell to Shane. The foreboding grey sky and dank conditions matched our sombre moods.

Upon arrival, I slammed on the brakes and stopped the car violently on the opposite side of the road, nearly sending Toni through the windscreen. I felt physically unable to drive through the wooden gates; it was as if there was an invisible barrier preventing me from entering the place that held so many devastating and sad memories.

"Be brave for Shane. He's waiting for us; he wants to come home with us."

Toni's heartfelt sorrowful words broke the silence.

"I know, but I just can't bring myself…"

My words trailed off as my voice began to give way.

"It's not about you; it's about Shane. Please let him come home now, he's been away for far too long."

Toni was right; it was about Shane. I managed to muster the emotional strength to drive through the gates onto the gravel drive. The cars tyres crunched as they slowly headed across the small stones.

Sod it; the only available parking space was the exact same spot where I had to park two weeks ago, that damn horrendous day that Shane had left us.

We composed ourselves, climbed out of the car and headed into the reception area.

"Good afternoon, can I help you?"

The receptionist's demeanour was very cheery.

"Hi, we're here to collect Shane."

My response was apparently far too vague for her, as a dazed and confused expression engulfed her face. She scrutinised the computer screen in front of her, then started to shake her head.

"Sorry, can I ask his surname, and what he is in for? I can't find him on the system."

Sensing that my sadness could soon manifest itself as anger, Toni quickly stepped in.

"No sorry, Shane passed away two weeks ago; we have had a call to say his ashes have been returned and are ready for us to collect. His surname is Viner."

"I'm so sorry for your loss. Please take a seat, and I will arrange for someone to bring him to you."

We turned to take a seat. There were a few people in the reception area with their dogs, all in different stages of recovery. Déjà vu struck me, I'd been here before, the awful feeling of jealousy again engulfed me.

Some of the dogs were wearing buster collars, shaved skin exposing fresh scars where they had undergone surgical procedures, bloody successful surgical procedures – why them? Why not Shane? Their owners had obviously heard our conversation; a few smiled politely, some fidgeted uncomfortably, trying as hard as they could to avoid making any form of eye contact with us. No one spoke. Some, if not all of them, must have been through this exact same heart-wrenching and traumatic experience, and they knew just how intense and raw our pain was. But today for them was a happy day, their dogs were all on the road to recovery.

Eventually, a young nurse appeared, cradling a small wooden box. She looked over to the receptionist who pointed to where we were sitting.

"Mr and Mrs Viner, I have Shane for you."

We stood up; both of us had our eyes transfixed on the box, a small, shiny brass plaque adorning the top. Could this be all that remained of Shane? Our once large, powerful and proud dog crammed into a tiny pine box. I could feel my anger surging from deep within.

"Thank you."

Toni responded to the lady as she reached forward to take the box – sorry Shane – from her.

Angrily I scanned the room; every person within the seating area had now averted their gaze away from us as if they didn't want to impose on this very emotional moment, or to allow us to cry if we needed to without the embarrassment of an audience. The harsh reality was that probably every one of them had one of these damned boxes at home. Seeing us must have brought back awful memories for each and every one of them.

Slowly the three of us started to head out of the reception area. Before we reached the automatic doors a more senior member of the administration team came out of her office, the click-clacking of her cheap high heels speeding up as she tried to catch us before we left.

"Mr and Mrs Viner, I'm so glad that I spotted you. I am so sorry to have to ask at such a sad time, but there are Shane's final fees that will need settling. We have been in touch with your insurance company, and they have paid, but there is an outstanding balance of just over £5,000."

At a time like this and she was talking about sodding finances, had she no compassion? This sodding place was obsessed with money. There was us, standing in a waiting room of patients with Shane in a bloody wooden box, and she wanted to talk money?

"If you hadn't have stuffed up his operation then…"

"Please leave it with me. Payment will be made over the phone by the end of the week."

Yet again Toni had had to step in quickly. She knew me far too well, this could easily have turned into the moment that I totally lost it, and yes I said it out loud, 'you stuffed up his operation.'

I knew that there would be a shortfall in the final amount that would be paid by Shane's insurance. I hadn't remembered – or maybe mentally I had chosen to ignore – the additional fees for the extras such as his cremation and the sodding box that would hold his ashes. The small bloody box that Toni was clutching, the very box that would one day be placed in my own coffin, to allow Shane and I to spend our eternity together.

I was so thankful that we had insurance, to be honest, and in my own humble opinion, it should be a compulsory aspect of dog ownership. I have heard several people say that over the last 20 years or so, as pet insurance has become more prominent, that vets' fees have increased dramatically, but the charges have to be paid, one way or another. Treatment for injury or illness can soon run into thousands, if not tens of thousands of pounds, but what price can you put on your four-legged family member? It is heartbreaking to hear of pets sadly being euthanised due to their owner's inability to pay for the medical treatment that they may so desperately require.

I had already applied for and been approved for a 0% credit card to pay off Shane's bill. We were fully aware that it was going to take us several years to pay off the credit card, but we would have spent absolutely anything to save our Shane. In fact, we had spoken about re-mortgaging our house if needs be, it was only money, what price could we put on Shane's life?

With Shane now back with us, we left for home. The awful sadness of the drive home was only eased by my recollection of the meeting that we had on Monday. However, I felt unfaithful, in fact, ashamed of the thoughts that actually put a small smile on my face. Stop being a prat, it is Shane's legacy, and it's what he would have wanted.

Bless her; Sheba had already started rescuing me.

The three of us arrived at our house. Shane had sat on Toni's lap for the whole journey home. At times I could swear that she was stroking him.

"Welcome home, mate."

The exact same words that I had said to him just eight months earlier, in far, far happier times, with the promises of a long happy life with us bestowed upon him; unforgivably I had lied.

We got out of the car and headed indoors; a large white envelope was sitting on the doormat. I bent down and picked it up. There was a printed section on the front – the words read 'Pets as Therapy Visitors Pack'. This could not have arrived on a worse day, in my hands was the envelope that contained Shane's tabard and ID badge, the very tabard and ID that he had worked so hard for just two days before he was taken ill. To this day, the envelope remains unopened; it is carefully stored in 'Shane's memories box'.

We had already prepared a space – no not 'a space', pride of place – in our large wooden display cabinet for Shane's box. Even now, without fail every morning, I say good morning; every evening I bid him a good night.

I hung Shane's collar, with his shiny name tag still attached, next to our front door. Here it would remain forever more.

We were to be informed later on that evening that very sadly Shane's partner in crime, Noel the Staffy, had crossed over the Rainbow Bridge three days after Shane. You really couldn't begin to make up the unique bond that those two gorgeous boys had had.

I can only hope that wherever it is that they now are, they are running together, both pain-free and wreaking absolute havoc and mayhem.

CHAPTER TWELVE

Sheba

One whose life has held no joy or hope…

Easter Monday, April 6th 2015. Eight days ago we had been forced into making the hardest, and the most heart-wrenching decision of our lives. We had had to say our final goodbyes to our beloved little man Shane.

The previous week had been one almighty roller-coaster ride of mixed emotions. One moment extreme euphoria at spending time with my beautiful, newborn little grandson Heath, followed by the deepest depths of despair and sadness when I reminisced or spoke of Shane. Without a word of warning, the next minute I'd want to cave the face in of the next bloke I met. Bloody hell I was in a mess.

We hoped that time would eventually prove to be a healer, but we knew that there was a long emotional road ahead of us.

The stark reality was that we were going to need months, if not years, to grieve for Shane, before we could even contemplate giving a home to another rescue dog

In our minds, Shane would never leave us. He had made such a huge, positive impact on our lives. In our minds, even just considering giving a home, Shane's home, to a needy dog too soon would be disrespectful to him.

Deep down, if I'm totally honest, I knew that selfishly I couldn't put myself through the pain and trauma of ever losing another dog. My selfishness was causing another innocent dog its prolonged incarceration.

Sadly, Shane had known all too well the actual reality of what life was like living in a rescue sanctuary, and to be denied the chance of a home and loving family that he could call his own.

Shane was a caring, loving dog. He had made the grade as a therapy dog; would he begrudge us giving another poor abandoned dog the chance of happiness? Hell no, of course he wouldn't. In fact, I'm sure he would have given us his blessing.

So now, on this lovely sunny bank holiday, we were sitting in our garden, sharing a nice bottle of chardonnay with our daughter Leah. Amongst a variety of conversations, mainly about Shane, with us now trying to focus on the happy times, reminiscing with smiles rather than tears, we randomly started to talk about Maria, the disabled little German Shepherd dog that Mutts had brought over in February from Bulgaria. Sadly, Bulgaria has a significant street dog problem. The Bulgarian government claim to have the situation under control and local government officials state that approximately 6,000 strays are roaming the streets, independent charities working in the country put the figure closer to 60,000.

"I'm not too sure on Maria as her name."

Toni's statement hit me straight out of the blue, just like Christmas Eve 2013, only 16 short months ago, when she first broached the subject of us getting a dog. The consequences of that conversation had now changed our lives, for the better, beyond all recognition.

Intrigued by her comment, I pursued the question further.

"Go on then; what would you have named her?"

Toni asked for my mobile, and logged into the dedicated page that had been set up to 'Help Maria Find A Home' on the Mutts website.

"Look at her picture, her eyes, they look as if they have mascara on. The only time in paintings I have seen eyes made up like that was in history lessons at school, the Queen of Sheba. Sheba, yes she looks like a Sheba, such a beautiful name. Funnily, it sounds almost like the female equivalent of Shane."

Toni had already chosen a name for the beautiful little disabled dog on the Mutts site.

There was no need for her to say any more. I asked her to pass my mobile back to me. I dialled the founder of Mutts in Distress, Pat's phone number.

"Hello darling, is everything all right?"

Pat had been regularly checking up on us ever since Shane had passed.

"Yes mate, everything is fine and dandy. Sorry to trouble you, it's about Maria, could we pop over to meet her?"

The phone remained silent for a few seconds.

"When?"

"This afternoon if possible. In fact, we are ready to leave now."

"I'm getting goosebumps. I'll let the girls know you're on your way and to get her ready to meet you. I'm just on my way back from Enfield; we had to take a sick bird to the emergency vet. See you soon."

I could hear the emotion in Pat's voice. She had spoken to us about Maria in the past, but she had not raised the subject with us since Shane had crossed over the Rainbow Bridge, giving us the respect and space we needed to try and come to terms with his untimely passing before considering adopting another abandoned dog.

We again made the now all too familiar drive to Mutts. As we slowly pulled into the car park, we could see that one of the girls was already waiting for us in the foyer. As soon as she spotted us, she headed off towards the rear of the reception area to the kennel block where the rescue dogs were kennelled.

Excitedly we clambered out of the car and moved over towards the grassed paddock that was home to the two rescue donkeys. They had been saved from a barbaric breeder in France, and the horrific fate of being slaughtered to become salami – these two adorable donkeys were destined for nothing more than to become pizza toppings.

To add to the beauty of the sanctuary's grass areas and paddocks, the cherry blossom trees, the symbolic flower of springtime, had spread a covering of small pretty pink petals over the ground, looking like a delicate covering of wedding confetti.

The door of the reception area swung open, and there she was, Maria. Bloody hell, she really was the smallest German Shepherd we had ever seen. Straight away, even from a distance, we could see that her front right leg was distinctively straighter than her left.

Suddenly the little dog spotted us. We both shouted words of greetings and encouragement to her. She may well have been small in stature, but fired up with excitement Maria easily dragged her handler across the forecourt towards us.

The closer she got the more beautiful she looked. Blimey, she was absolutely stunning.

Just as I had done when I had first met Shane, as soon as she reached me I knelt down. Eagerly the little dog jumped up to greet me, and again as with Shane I embraced her, and yes, as with Shane, I was met with a barrage of full-face slobbery kisses. I could feel my eyes filling with tears.

"Hello, gorgeous."

I know this sounds weird, but as I was trying to talk to her, for some strange and unexplainable reason, her loving actions caused me to laugh out loud. Bloody hell, I never knew just how much I'd missed this, a beautiful, loving dog in my arms, and the ability to laugh, only now without an intense feeling of guilt for feeling happy.

Toni bent down to stroke Maria and was also greeted with a bombardment of kisses. Maria's poor little deformed leg didn't stop her from jumping about like any able-bodied dog. The scar running down her right leg from her recent corrective surgery still looked red and angry and was clearly visible due to where her fur had been shaved off.

Then it happened again. As I was kneeling embracing the beautiful little dog, my mind was suddenly hurtled back into doubt, guilt and turmoil. Shane had only left us eight days ago, and here's me, showering all my affection on another disadvantaged dog. How bloody disrespectful. I had said it would take months of grieving before I could even contemplate offering another dog a home, yet in my mind, Maria was now already our dog. Maria needed a family; she was absolutely gorgeous, she had months of surgery and recuperation ahead of her, was my 'need to be needed crisis' rearing its ugly head again? Was I acting rationally? With my head still spinning another huge sloppy kiss was suddenly planted straight on my face, bringing me back to my senses. Again, emotionally I was entirely overcome, my body filled with the warm, tingling sense of love. The question now was, was I rescuing Maria, or was Maria rescuing me?

In my desperate state at times over the previous few weeks I had often reached out for a hand, but in the end, my salvation came in the form of a paw.

Why was I drawn to the misfits? There are a multitude of able-bodied dogs waiting patiently at the rescue for homes, and some have already had formal training, why not make things easier for myself and offer one of them a home? Not a bloody chance, I had always stood up for the 'underdog', pardon the pun, and in her current state of health, Maria was definitely the underdog. Her deformed front legs, her hind legs that had dropped to compensate; we had also been made aware of her anti-social behaviour towards other canines. This aggressive defence mechanism hid her fear, probably due to the horrors she must have endured as a street dog from a faraway country. No, Maria was definitely the dog for us.

"Bless her little heart."

Toni had also fallen head over heels in love with the little doggy lapping up our affection.

"At least I may get a look in with her; us girls stick together you know. Also, to think you're going to have a houseful of women again."

Toni absolutely adored Shane – they would often head off alone together for countryside jaunts – but deep down Toni was always under the impression that Shane was a 'man's dog', if there is such a thing, with his physical stature and sometimes intimidating persona.

With us both totally engrossed and overwhelmed by the beautiful, happy little dog in front of us, not allowing her disabilities to hold her back in any way, shape or form, we failed to hear a car pull up behind us. Pat had got back quicker than expected. We were still making a huge fuss of the happy little pup as Pat got out of her Volvo and walked over. I looked up at her, the emotion of the moment had got the better of me, and I was finding it hard to speak. All I was able to do was nod my head, with a smile on my face, a genuine smile, a smile where your eyes light up your face, a smile that had eluded me ever since Shane had left us for the afterlife. Pat knew precisely what my nod meant; Maria now had a family and home to call her own.

"It's just like Shane all over again."

Pat had tears in her eyes as she struggled to get her sentence out.

"Do you mind if we rename her Sheba?" Toni asked.

"She's your dog; you can call her whatever you want. Sheba the Corgi."

Pat laughed out loud.

It has become the subject of on-going banter between the rescue team and us, due to Sheba's small stature she is often referred to, in jest, as the corgi.

"She is still recuperating from her surgery and needs plenty of cage rest to enable the bones to heal properly. She is booked in for surgery to straighten her left leg on the 23rd of April. It would probably be best for Maria, sorry Sheba, if she remains here with us until after her next operation. However, please, visit her as often as you can."

Pat's advice made perfect sense. We were allowed to return Sheba to her kennel, and say our loving goodbyes to her. Sheba, our beautiful little rescue dog.

Over the next two weeks, we visited her daily, slowly building a strong and loving bond. We took her for short gentle walks, sat in the meadow stroking her, and spent time telling her all that she had to look forward to when she eventually moved in with us. Precious time was also spent telling her about her beautiful big brother, Shane. Our emotions were still raw and continually got the better of us; but somehow the cute little dog lying on the grass with us sensed it, and she always managed to kiss us at our lowest ebb.

We were more than aware that the next few months were going to be extremely tiring and stressful for the three of us. Sadly, painful for Sheba as well, with her on-going surgery and convalescence.

However, there was light at the end of the tunnel; the pleasure of helping Sheba through the dark days would build an unbreakable bond between the three of us.

We were giving her a loving, protective home and family, and would allow her as much time as she needed to adjust to becoming a family pet, living her life with us in her new home, providing her with all of the creature comforts that she would ever require. A million miles from the existence and struggles she had endured merely trying to survive on the disgusting, violent streets of a faraway country.

The thought of what lay ahead of us sent my mind into overdrive; I needed to calm down and think rationally.

Luckily I have a simple tried and tested method that I try to apply whenever problems start to culminate. I break things down into small manageable segments and deal with them one at a time; you'll be amazed how stress-free life can suddenly become.

***

Thursday 23rd April, St George's Day. I arrived at Mutts bang on 8 am as planned. It was a beautiful sunny spring morning, although there was a bit of an early morning chill in the air. Today was a big day, we were taking Sheba for her final operation. Sheba's corrective surgery was meant to have took place the previous week, but due to her having a poorly upset tummy the operation had had to be postponed. Stool samples were sent to the laboratory, and she was put on a short course of prescribed medication to clear up any infection that may have been present in her intestine. Anyway, she was fighting fit now and ready to face the next exciting chapter in her life. As we started to prepare Sheba for the 40-mile journey, the on-duty staff and volunteers all came out to wish her well, and gave her words of encouragement. They also brought Sheba her favourite soft toy to have waiting in her recovery kennel when she awoke from the two-hour operation. Once Sheba was secured safely in the back of my car, we waved goodbye to the assembled team and headed off.

We arrived at the veterinary surgery in Cambridge at about 9.30 am, and as we got out of the car, our first port of call was to take Sheba to a small grassy area to let her do a wee. We then headed in to meet her surgeon. As soon as she saw the man who had done so much to improve her quality of life Sheba became animated with excitement, tail wagging, and almost wiggling her little bottom. The surgeon approached us and greeted Sheba, and checked on how the long scar running down the front of her right leg was healing, before Pat formally introduced me to him.

“Hi, it’s good to meet you. My name’s Chaim. How’s Maria been doing, Pat? The scar is looking nice and clean, and from here her leg appears to be pretty straight. Things are all looking very good for you, Maria. You’ll soon be standing three inches’ taller little lady.”

Chaim seemed exceptionally pleased with his very professional and neat handiwork.

“Absolutely fine. She completed her prescribed course of painkillers and antibiotics. We have been trying as hard as possible not to let her get too excitable and jump around, but Sheba, as she is now known, is one very bouncy little dog, even after her major operation,” Pat replied.

Chaim smiled and acknowledged the name change, apologising for initially calling her Maria.

“Perfect, right let’s take Sheba – you know that name actually really suits her – outside so I can see how she walks.”

The four of us headed out of the building and walked to a quiet paved area to the side of the building. Chaim positioned himself about 20 feet from us and knelt facing towards us, enabling him to get a better view of how Sheba was walking when she approached him.

“Right, walk towards me please.”

Slowly I led Sheba towards him.

He remained silent as we approached; he was carefully scrutinising her every movement. He said nothing as he got up and walked back to where we were initially standing. Again he knelt on the ground.

“Okay, walk her towards me, but very slowly please.”

As instructed, I slowly walked Sheba back towards him. I could see that as we were getting closer, Chaim’s face appeared to have taken on a look of concern. He was gently shaking his head from side to side and biting his bottom lip. Again, without saying a word to us, he got up and returned to the opposite end of the footpath. He knelt, this time he was crouching low on all fours. He asked us to repeat the slow walk back towards him. As we got a few feet from where he was kneeling, he lowered his head. Chaim almost had his left cheek pressed onto the concrete paving slab as he carefully studied Sheba's every step.

"She seems lame on her right leg, she's not placing it right, and there is almost a limp in her step. She wasn't walking like that when we discharged her. I am going to need to carry out some exploratory X-rays before I can even consider surgery on her left leg."

Feeling anxious, we followed Chaim back into the building and headed straight to the consultation area. As we entered, the three on-duty nurses walked over and began to make a massive fuss of Sheba. They had all followed and knew her rescue story; two had even been lucky enough to have been in attendance during her first corrective operation.

"Prepare her for an X-ray immediately. Her front right leg please."

There was an air of confusion at Chaim's request; one of the nurses looked over at me and whispered:

"Does he mean her left?"

To reiterate her point, she touched her left leg.

I shook my head and touched my right arm.

"You heard correct nurse, her right leg please," said Chaim.

The head nurse asked me if I could help out by lifting Sheba onto the examination trolley. A soft covering of clean 'vet bed' had already been placed on the top to make it more comfortable for her. Once she was up on the trolley, I held her collar tightly with one hand and kept her calm with soft, encouraging words and gentle strokes with the other, while the nurses gathered the necessary equipment to prepare to sedate her.

One of the nurses produced a set of electric clippers. She made an exaggerated fuss of Sheba before she switched them on. The rattling, buzzing sound initially startled her, but she soon relaxed enabling the nurse to commence shaving off a small area of fur on her leg. The exposed skin was sterilised, before a hypodermic needle was very gently inserted and the nurse administered the anaesthetic.

Slowly Sheba's eyes closed as she fell asleep. This was all far too much for me to watch, the room started to spin. Just a few weeks ago I had to lie on the floor and comfort Shane as he was injected and fell to sleep, only he was to never wake up. Shane's passing was far too raw, I had to get away.

"Are you all right, Paul? You've gone white as a ghost."

"Sorry, I need to sit down."

One of the nurses took over stroking Sheba as I sat on an adjustable stool. I could feel myself becoming clammy, the room was now starting to spin even faster and faster.

Luckily, just before I blacked out I snapped out of it. How embarrassing, I was behaving bloody ridiculously; I needed to be there for Sheba. I got up, shook my head then walked, or semi staggered, back to where Sheba was being prepped for her X-ray.

"Are you okay?" asked Chaim.

I nodded at him, although inside I did feel nauseous.

I removed her collar. Her tongue had already been secured in a retaining clamp and left hanging from the side of her mouth.

I helped Chaim wheel her trolley into the radiography area and position it under the X-ray imaging camera. I kissed her, then left the dimly lit room. Chaim closed the door behind me. Soon an electric sign burst into life and illuminated the warning:

'CAUTION X-RAYS. DO NOT ENTER WHEN LIGHT IS ON.'

After a few minutes the red warning light extinguished, the door opened, and Chaim wheeled Sheba back into the consultation area. The nurses were asked to remain with her as Pat and I were called into the radiography room to view the images on the LED screen that Chaim had taken of her leg.

"I'm afraid it's not good news, in fact it's very bad news. If you look here, you can see a small black line, sadly it's a crack. Sheba has broken her leg, just above the titanium straightening rod that I inserted. The area would have been weaker and under a lot more stress until the new bone had started to form. The problem is being exaggerated by the fact that her other leg still has the severe deformity, the load bearing on her newly repaired leg is far greater. We are going to have to repair the break before we can even begin to contemplate her having her next op. One thing is for sure, she is one tough little cookie, she's got a bloody broken leg for god's sake, yet the untrained eye wouldn't know it from the way she manages to tear about."

Forlornly we headed back into the surgery area.

I looked down at Sheba lying there so peacefully, still sedated from the anaesthetic. At least she was not in pain at that moment. I stroked the soft, velvet-like fur that covered her little ears; they twitched at the gentle touch of the back of my index finger. How much more pain and suffering would this beautiful little pup have to endure?

"Right, while she is nice and still could we please set about splints and bandages please."

Chaim's words broke the sombre mood that had engulfed the room.

One of the nurses walked over with a handful of sealed sterile packages.

"What colour bandage do you think Sheba would like?"

"Pink, it's got to be a nice bright pink one," Pat quickly butted in and answered for me.

Under the watchful eye and guidance of Chaim, the nurses set about swathing Sheba's poor little leg in soft dressing. Over this two strong plastic splints were carefully placed and secured with sticky sterile strips to brace the area of the break, and extra layers of soft padding were added to the sole of her foot area to soften and absorb the impact of her walking. Additional layers of soft gauze were added to the top of the splints; this was potentially the area that could chafe and cause her discomfort when she became mobile. Finally, several layers of the garish pink dressing were wound around her entire leg, almost up to her shoulder joint.

Once happy with the splints and bandages Chaim asked me to carry Sheba through to the recovery area. One of the nurses followed and sat with her, monitoring her as she slowly started to awake from the effects of the anaesthetic.

When I returned, Chaim was sitting with one of the nurses adding notes to Sheba's file on his computer. He stopped and looked up, his face seemed to have taken on a worried appearance.

"Right, Sheba is going to need complete cage rest, and believe me when I say rest I mean total rest, for up to six weeks, for her leg to have any chance of healing. She is going to have to be kept as calm as possible, no running, jumping or excessive walking. Also, I will advise a diet plan, due to her inactivity I don't want her piling on the pounds, the extra weight will be no good for her legs. Good nutritional food will also help aid the healing process."

I could now sense three pairs of eyes glaring at me; I didn't want to be the centre of attention. I could feel my posture changing, my head was lowering, and my shoulders were slumping. Pat was obviously worried about Sheba's on-going welfare.

"We'll have absolutely no chance at all of being able to keep her calm at the kennels. Is there any way that you can take her back with you today, and take care of her during her recuperation?"

Déjà vu punched me squarely on the jaw; this was precisely like that August day just eight months ago when we unexpectedly had to take Shane home. Now, as then, we were utterly unprepared for taking Sheba to join our family. We still had Shane's food and water bowls, collar, lead, and a couple of his favourite toys; but everything else we had donated to the dog rescue.

Now a significant concern started spinning around and around in my head; the words soon blurted out from my mouth.

"How are we going to be able to keep this little live wire calm and quiet? Shane had the full run of our house; he could freely go wherever he wanted due to the open plan design that our home has, with no downstairs doors anywhere, how on earth are we to keep Sheba restrained?"

"I have a brand-new cage I bought at Crufts this year, not even been out of the box. We could set that up for her."

Pat's offer alleviated the first major hurdle; now I had one to jump on my own, letting Toni know.

"Right, in that case I'll ring Toni and tell her what's going on. It looks like Sheba's coming home much earlier than expected."

As with Shane, an emergency action plan was sprung into operation.

I headed outside for a much-needed cigarette, and a spot of refreshing, cool fresh air before ringing Toni at work to let her know there had been an enormous change in plan. While I was telling her that Sheba was coming home with me that day, Pat was next to me on her mobile phone coordinating her staff into getting an emergency kit in place for Sheba.

When we returned to the recovery area, Sheba had fully regained consciousness from her anaesthetic. She appeared drowsy and clumsy as she tried to manoeuvre herself about in her cage. As soon as she saw me, she hobbled over to the side of her cage, poking her tongue through the bars.

"You can open the door and give her a cuddle if you want, just don't let her run around."

I took up the nurse's offer. As soon as the latch was released, Sheba was there.

"Good girl, my brave little girl."

As I was hugging Sheba and whispering words of encouragement, she planted a barrage of kisses on my face. Did she know she was coming home with me that night?

Chaim appeared holding a plastic bag of medication.

"Right, I need to see her in four days to change the bandages and check the splint. Can you bring her back on Monday?"

Luckily Mondays were my rest days, so an appointment

was arranged for 11 am.

Chaim ran through her meds, and how they needed administering, and again recapitulated his strict instructions.

"I can't reiterate how vitally important it is to keep Sheba as calm as possible, and how important it is to keep the bandages as dry as you feasibly can."

We said our goodbyes to the nurses, and headed outside with Chaim to my car. Sheba still had the remnants of the anaesthetic flowing through her body and was slightly wobbly on her paws; luckily she was also still a bit subdued.

I carefully lifted her up and onto the rear seat of my car and secured her harness. I placed a towel under her right leg to soften the blows of any bumps in the road that we might encounter on our journey home.

We thanked Chaim yet again for all that he had done for Sheba. He leant into the car, patted her on the head and gave her neck a stroke.

Now we began the 40-mile journey back to Mutts to gather together everything Sheba was going to need for the next few weeks.

As I pulled up at my house, Toni was already eagerly waiting with the front door open; I reversed onto the drive. Sheba caught a glimpse of Toni and became excitedly animated in the back of the car, her tail wagging and banging on the back of my seat. The wafts caused small strands of fur to start blowing around my car.

Pat had pulled her car up in front of mine and got out in preparation for unloading the cage, bedding and food.

I opened the rear door and unlocked the car safety harness that Sheba was wearing, connected to one of the seat belt anchor points.

"Come on little lady you're home now."

The words that I had just uttered to Sheba hit me really hard. Was it honestly just a mere eight months ago I had said almost the exact same sentence to Shane? I quickly had to compose myself, I shook my head, as if to try and expel the sadness that had engulfed me, I knelt and stretched my arms towards Sheba. She obligingly, yet awkwardly, clambered towards my unfolded arms. Once I was sure I had a secure, but gentle grip on her, I lifted her out of my car and carried her into our home, trying as best as I could to support her broken leg. Pat had followed me in, and once the front door was shut, Sheba was gently lowered to the floor.

She was off; there was no holding this little pocket rocket back. There was a strange sound on our wooden flooring – her claws clattering, mixed in amongst the thudding and clumping of her heavy bandages and splint, as she tore off to explore her new home.

Shane's unique scent must have still been everywhere. Sheba was frantically scurrying all around, sniffing every single place that Shane used to spend his time. She bounded into our lounge, her senses going into overdrive as she continued to sniff everywhere. Suddenly, Sheba appeared to be drawn to our glass-fronted wooden display cabinet, the cabinet that Shane's ashes rested in. For a brief moment, Sheba stopped and sat in front of the display unit, sniffing the area just in front of Shane's pine box. Was it her reflection in the glass she was looking at, or had she picked up on something else? Her head tilted inquisitively from side to side while staring intently at the box. After a minute or so Sheba moved on, but glanced back towards the cabinet a few more times. Eventually, she resumed exploring the rest of her new home. Toni sat with Sheba while I unloaded the cage, bedding and food from Pat's car. The enclosure was soon erected and located in a small, draft-free alcove area of our lounge. The bedding was layered to make the floor surface as soft and comfortable as possible for her.

"Right little lady, I think you've had enough excitement for one day."

I walked over to Sheba. Without any prompting, she slowly followed me, and hobbled towards the cage and carefully stepped in. Toni fetched Shane's water bowl for her.

"Here you go darling, have a drink. This was your dear late brother's bowl, but I'm sure he won't mind if you take care of it for him."

Toni's words hit me; it had been a long, emotional day. I wiped my eyes and watched as Sheba took some much-needed thirst-quenching gulps of water. She then lay down, staring up at us.

Pat got ready to leave. Reassuringly, she reminded us she was always prepared to help out, and if we needed her urgently she was only 15 minutes away.

I poured myself a can of chilled draught Guinness and headed out into the garden for a fag. I know smoking is a stinking, filthy habit, but at times like these, it did offer me a sense of comfort. Once I'd finished my pint I set about contacting my daughters to let them know our exciting, yet unexpected news.

Sheba had been lying quietly in her cage, taking in her new surroundings for about 30 minutes. I opened the door and encouraged her to join us in the lounge. She bounded over and plonked herself down. I lay down next to her and started stroking her neck, her eyes closed. Toni crept up behind us clutching one of Shane's tennis balls. She knelt and offered it to Sheba. Initially, she seemed puzzled by the small lime green sphere and appeared reluctant to take it from her, so Toni gently rolled it across the floor to her. Sheba tilted her head and looked up at me with a bemused expression upon her face.

"Bless her little heart; she doesn't know what it is and hasn't a clue what to do with it."

I lowered my head and tried to pick the ball up in my mouth, but I was unable to open my jaws wide enough. I nudged the ball with my nose to Sheba; she lowered her head and picked it up, then dropped it. The ball bounced; I moved closer and again pushed it back to her with my nose.

"She hasn't had the chance to be a pup; the poor little thing has never had toys, or the chance to play because she has had to spend her life defending herself."

What sodding horrors had our poor little feral ex-street dog endured? It broke my heart to think that she had never experienced life's simple pleasures, such as playing. I resumed stroking her with one hand while encouraging her to take the ball with the other. Eventually, she grasped the concept of play; she started to chew at the ball vigorously. Occasionally it slipped out of her mouth. She quickly grabbed it and continued gnawing at it. I lay with her playing ball for about half an hour until our daughters arrived, each laden with gifts and eager to meet Sheba.

She relished the love and attention lavished upon her; it never ceases to amaze me the way that a dog who has endured so much heartache and pain can be so forgiving, and how quickly they settle and relax into family life, their past traumas and horrors soon become distant fading memories.

The girls eventually left us at about 10 pm. Now we had to start establishing a structured routine for Sheba. I carried her out into the garden and up the steps to let her do a wee, a regime that we ended up having to follow for the next five months, every time that Sheba either needed to relieve herself or wanted to venture onto the lawn.

In June, we were kindly given money by our family as anniversary gifts. We decided to use it to employ a builder to redesign our garden steps, with shallower risers and wider treads. We were confident that these modifications would allow Sheba the freedom to be able to negotiate her way up onto the lawn by herself, when she was ready.

"I'm going to sleep on the couch tonight, don't want Sheba to feel alone on her first night in her new home. I'll keep a close eye on her; she's not going to sleep in the cage tonight."

Toni agreed with my decision. We placed Shane's bed in front of the couch, and Sheba was carried over and placed on the soft faux fur cover. Toni reappeared, clutching Shane's beloved rabbit.

"Here you go poppet; I'm sure Shane would like you to take care of his rabbit for him."

Sheba, clutching Shane's rabbit in her mouth, made herself comfortable. Obviously contented, she did not attempt to clamber off her bed. Her eyes remained fixed on my every movement. She watched me intently as I turned off the lights and climbed into my sleeping bag on the couch next to her.

Sheba's beautiful features were being illuminated by the silvery glow of the moonlight flooding in through the large patio doors. Gently I reached down and started stroking her; she started sighing, followed by a gentle, almost lip-licking sound, the same tone of contentment that Shane used to make. After a few minutes, she turned her head and responded to my loving affection by licking the back of my hand. Slowly after such an eventful day we both fell asleep.

We both awoke at about 5 am; the early morning spring sunlight flooded into the lounge, the sky was filled with a multitude of oranges and reds. Sparrows and blue tits were chirping their background melody.

"Good morning darling."

Sheba's mouth expanded into a gaping yawn. I again reached down and started to stroke her soft sable and black fur, and teasingly tickled her belly. In between caressing her, I ran my hand over the cover of her bed, the warmth of Sheba's body still radiating from it. Miraculously it was dry. What a good girl. I climbed out of my sleeping bag and opened the patio doors. I could see that the grass had a covering of damp early morning dew. Sheba would need to relieve herself, so I set about wrapping her bandaged front leg in a plastic carrier bag, which was secured carefully around the top with an elastic band.

Sheba had remained on her bed throughout, and put up no resistance. The intelligence of dogs never ceases to amaze me; it was as if she knew exactly what I was doing, and why. Carefully I lifted her; her front legs hanging over my right arm, her bottom resting in my left. I carried her out into the fresh morning air and up the small steps onto the lawn, where she was lowered carefully onto the grass. She squatted and peed, what a good girl.

Toni appeared behind us and smiled as she watched Sheba hobbling about on the grass, leaving her tracks and making a green path in the fresh, white dew. Although there was a chill in the air, the first rays of the sun were shining off the small glistening droplets of water, the rays bringing a welcome, warming brightness to the new day as it emerged in front of our eyes.

I sparked up a cigarette and turned to look at Toni. We smiled as we stood there watching Sheba roam and explore her garden, engaged in what I can only describe as 'dog intrigue', just as Shane had done eight months previously. Now and then she squatted and urinated, in the exact places that Shane used to. Was she 'cancelling out' Shane's mark on what she now perceived to be her territory? It saddened me to think that Sheba was dispelling his memory, but I would never forget my little man.

I finished my fag and called Sheba. She hobbled over to me and I gently picked her up and carried her back indoors, Toni had opened the door to the cage that had been lent to us, and Sheba showed no signs of being agitated as she was placed carefully into the cage. The door was closed and secured. The next job was giving Sheba her medication, both pain relief and antibiotics. The required tablets were removed from their foil packaging; I had been taught a simple method for administering them, just in case Sheba didn't want to take them voluntarily. The usual practice of disguising medication in a small piece of cheese would have to be avoided, Sheba was going to be immobile for weeks, and we had to avoid anything that would pile the extra unwanted pounds on her. There was no need for us to worry, Sheba swallowed the two tablets, was given a bowl of fresh water and then she lay down in the sanctuary of her temporary abode.

CHAPTER THIRTEEN

Surgery and Recuperation

And give my place to him...

Over the coming weeks, every three days we made the regular 80-mile round trip to visit Chaim and his team in Cambridge to enable them to check on how Sheba's leg was healing, and for her to have her splints and bandages changed. The nurses were amazing. They seemed to relish Sheba's visits, and took it in turns to bandage her leg – every time a more garish colour was applied, bright pink, yellow, orange, purple, camouflage. It was almost as if a paediatric doctor was caring for a young child, with the gaudy designs somehow helping Sheba overcome the mental trauma of her broken leg.

At the end of April, Sheba's dedicated care team were finally pleased with how her broken leg appeared to be healing, and arrangements were at long last made for her left leg's corrective surgery – Thursday 14th May.

The big day arrived, how exciting. Sheba for the first time in her life was now going to be the proud owner of two straight front legs. She was hungry as we had not fed her for well over 12 hours, the fasting to hopefully prevent nausea and vomiting when the anaesthetic was administered. Overnight we had only put small amounts of fresh water in her bowl, which we stopped at 7 am that morning, to ensure that her stomach was as empty as possible without causing dehydration.

As an added precautionary measure we ensured that the lids on our toilet bowls were kept down. Sheba had never, to my knowledge, drank from the toilet. However, up until her having to fast she always had a copious supply of fresh drinking water at her disposal. We were concerned that when our backs were turned her thirst may have caused her to take drastic actions in sourcing water.

The usual loving greetings were bestowed upon Sheba when we arrived at the clinic at 9 am. It was blatantly obvious that Chaim and his assembled team were all fired up with excitement; this amazing group of individuals were so pleased to be playing such a huge, significant role in Sheba's life-enhancing surgery. In fact, both of the nurses in attendance had come in on their rest days to be a part of the surgical team.

I had been very privileged to have been invited by Chaim to be present throughout Sheba's entire operation. However, I was worried – mentally and emotionally, would I be able to handle it? The sight of blood doesn't faze me at all; in fact, I've become quite accustomed to it in my job on the streets of the East End of London. However, when it came to seeing a beloved family member enduring the harshness and brutality of surgery, well that was an entirely different ball game. Oh well, time would tell, and within the following 30 minutes I would know for sure.

Chaim retreated alone into his office and sat silently, carefully scrutinising the X-rays previously taken of the bones that he would be operating on. When he was confident that he had thoroughly familiarised himself with the extent of the disfiguration of Sheba's leg skeleton, he called his team into his office for a full briefing and explanation of how he intended to conduct and carry out the procedure. The procedure was almost a mirror image of the surgery carried out on Sheba's right leg a couple of months earlier.

Once the surgical team were fully aware of the roles that they would each be playing, Chaim asked them to commence prepping Sheba for her life-changing surgery.

One of the nurses asked me to assist her while she shaved the fur from Sheba's leg. We moved to an area away from the operating theatre, I sat down and started to cuddle and make a massive fuss of Sheba as the nurse collected the clippers and selected and inserted the No. 40 blade. She plugged in and switched on the clippers, and showed it to Sheba, making a game of it as she did. The clippers had a very distinct rattling, buzzing sound, and when she was happy that Sheba was not afraid of them, she commenced shaving her left leg and shoulder, gently keeping the blade parallel to her skin, firstly following the hair growth, then finally against the direction of growth. An area of fur extending just over 10cm past the planned incision area was shaved, leaving Sheba's milky white skin exposed. She had remained motionless throughout, bless her, now and then she had planted one of her special kisses on my face. Once happy with her handiwork, the nurse retrieved a small hoover-type appliance and 'vacuumed' the shaved area to remove as much of the loose fur as possible. The shaved area was given an initial cleanse using a chlorhexidine scrub; then a sterile surgical gauze was placed over the proposed incision site before Sheba was led into the operating theatre.

I lifted Sheba onto the operating table and positioned her with her head towards the anaesthetic machine; once she eventually settled down, she was firmly, yet gently held still by one nurse as the other commenced the pre-surgery preparation. I reassuringly stroked Sheba during the administration of the calming sedatives and preventative pain relief, which was administered via an injection. By being given then, it would hopefully help her with the excruciating pain she would undoubtedly experience when she awoke.

Chaim instructed his assistant surgeon to sedate Sheba; as the propofol slowly entered her body, forcing her to take on a state of chemically-induced sleep, her eyes rolled upwards, the whites taking on a reddish hue as the drugs started to work. Within seconds she had fallen asleep. Her tongue was pulled gently from the side of her mouth and secured with a small retaining clamp, and a breathing tube slid deep down into her throat. A catheter was next slowly inserted into one of the veins in her left hind leg. Opioid analgesic pain relief, similar to morphine, would now be continually fed into her body intravenously throughout the entire operation.

The two surgeons left the theatre to scrub up thoroughly and adorn their sterile surgery kit consisting of head covers, sterile latex gloves, green surgical gowns and nose/mouth masks. As soon as Sheba was sedated, and while the surgeons were prepping for surgery, the nurses commenced a thorough, sterile cleanse of Sheba's leg. In a circular 'bull's-eye' pattern, one of the nurses sterilised the incision site from the centre working outwards, never going over an area she had cleansed with the same piece of gauze sponge. The pale blue chlorhexidine scrub was applied four times. Each time the application was thorough, yet gentle, to avoid any unnecessary skin trauma. The final application was left to remain on the skin.

Once Sheba had been fully prepped for her corrective surgery, her body was entirely covered in a green sterile surgical drape, with the leg area to be operated on exposed. With the surgical team ready and assembled, the green wrap of sterilised surgical tools was uncovered; the titanium rod that would eventually straighten her leg was still securely encased in its sterile covering. Sheba's life-changing titanium leg rod was placed alongside the rest of Chaim's surgical apparatus.

With a tense, yet exciting atmosphere, Chaim picked up his scalpel, and using his preferred 'fingertip grip' he made the first skilful, precise incision with the large curved cutting edge of the No.10 blade. Keeping the scalpel perpendicular to her skin he drew it down from her elbow to the top of her foot in one straight cut, parting the epidermis with his left hand as the razor-sharp blade sliced cleanly through skin and subcutaneous tissue. The assistant surgeon continually swabbed, with a blotting motion, away the blood as it freely began to flow, the table and green drapes soon becoming covered in the sinister-looking, macabre crimson fluid.

I stood back, well out of the team's way, mouth agape watching in awe. Luckily the room had not started spinning. I must admit beads of sweat had soon formed on my forehead, and my palms felt clammy, but so far so good, I was still upright. Hopefully, I would not embarrass myself.

The air in the operating theatre had the distinctive sterile aroma of isopropyl alcohol, infused with other more familiar disinfectants. There was also a strange, yet recognisable background scent of small animals, beloved family pets, a tang that I found somewhat comforting.

Thankfully Chaim asked for a fan to be turned on and for the overhead lighting to be adjusted to illuminate the freshly exposed bone.

I stood there motionless for the next two and a half hours, watching as initially Sheba's metacarpal bone, and the sizeable bony callus that had formed on her wrist joint, was brutally, yet skilfully shaved away to enable her leg to be arranged in a straighter formation.

As her bone was ruthlessly shaved away, the air in the operating theatre filled with a distinctive yet pungent aroma. The only way that I could describe the smell was that of burning hair.

The bespoke titanium rod was then carefully shaped to ensure it followed the exact contour of her carpal and ulna bones, before being secured in place by a series of surgical screws.

When he was pleased with the incision of the rod, Chaim asked one of the nurses to pass him the polypropylene synthetic monofilament suture and a surgical steel atraumatic needle. These needles have a channel formed in the butt end, allowing insertion of the suture. The suture would be able to follow the needle's path without causing any further or unnecessary tissue damage to Sheba's leg. Chaim commenced closing the gaping incision area, with the stitches sewn into her skin every 5 millimetres, and tied with '6 throws' to hopefully prevent wound dehiscence.

The fresh surgical site had an angry protuberant appearance; raw red skin covered the newly inserted metal rod and screws. The area had a covering of dried blood, black sutures and iodine, the inflamed wound was a gruesome, yet strangely wondrous sight. One of the nurses gently started to cleanse the wound before sterile gauze and bandages were applied to dress the incision area.

The once scrupulously clean, sterile green sheets and drapes were now totally covered in blood; discarded crimson-coloured swabs lay scattered all around. The air in the theatre area had now taken on what I could only describe as a metallic aroma, almost like that of rusting iron, a smell that I believed I could taste. In reality, I couldn't, my mind was playing tricks with me, reigniting deep down memories of how my blood tasted after a tooth extraction at the dentist, or a split lip during a punch up.

The operation went without a hitch. Chaim pulled off his face mask and head covering; he removed his bloodied latex gloves and wiped the sweat from his brow with the back of his hand.

"Well done and thank you everyone for a great job all around. Nurse, could you monitor Sheba's stats before we relocate her to the recovery area please?"

I had never witnessed anything like it in all of my life. I will be eternally grateful to Chaim and his team, they had worked their wonders. These amazing, compassionate people had just given their time and immense skills for free to help a little disabled ex-street dog from a faraway country to now live her life pain free.

The nurses kindly allowed me to become more 'hands-on' during Sheba's recovery from the anaesthetic surging through her body.

They showed me the tell-tale signs that I needed to look out for to ensure there were no complications as she awoke, such as lifting her top lip and pressing her gum. The area initially turned white as the blood was forced away from the depressed surface area, I then had to count how long it took for the colour to return to the area I had applied pressure to. I was also taught how to gently lift her eyelids and observe the colour of her eyes. All of it was such a thrill; to think in a very minuscule way I had been permitted to assist the dedicated, professional medical team.

One of the nurses returned so I took the opportunity to pop out for a cigarette, taking my much-needed strong sweet black coffee she had kindly made for me. I stood silently staring up at the clouds for several minutes before ringing Toni to let her know that as far as I knew the operation had been a complete success.

When we had finished chatting I composed myself and returned to the recovery suite.

"Good girl. No, you stop trying to climb the cage and lie down."

In the short space of time I had been gone, Sheba had awoken from her anaesthetic, and the nurse's words echoed around the small side ward full of recovery cages. Sheba's resilience towards pain never ceased to amaze me. She had just undergone and woken from major surgery, yet she wanted to get up and play. I knelt next to the door of her cage. The nurse smiled at me and got up to leave us; before she did she scribbled notes on Sheba's surgery progress chart. She logged the time Sheba awoke, the observations I had made during her sedation and any noticeable signs of blood discharge on the bandaging, also any bladder or bowel movements were noted (at present there were none).

Sheba moved towards me. I pressed my face as close to hers as I could; yet again she was trying to shower me with affection. Bless her little heart; she must have been in absolute agony.

I opened the cage door and offered her a bowl of cold water. She took some much-needed thirst quenching sips. These soon turned into gulps. Before she left the nurse had given me Sheba's first pain-relief tablet. Without hesitation, Sheba swallowed it the second I offered it to her; it was as if she knew the little white pill would help with the unbearable pain she must have undoubtedly been experiencing.

Only a few decades ago, canine surgery patients were only given a pat on the head; luckily today, veterinarians are fully aware of the post-surgical pain their patients endure and provide the medication to alleviate it as much as possible.

Any surgery will inevitably cause some damage to the local and surrounding tissues, which result in inflammation. During inflammation, chemicals are released by the body at the site of tissue damage or trauma. These chemicals act on nerve fibres to start the pain response, so a Non-Steroidal Anti Inflammatory Drug (NSAID) is being administered orally to control the resulting surgical pain. NSAIDs block the formation of some of the chemicals that promote discomfort and so by using them it should help to stop the generation of pain at the site of Sheba's corrective surgery, as well as in her central nervous system, brain and spinal cord.

I sat on the floor next to Sheba, staring at her beautiful features, promising and reassuring her over and over that today was the exciting new beginning in the next chapter of her now pain-free life. She fought as hard as she could to keep her eyes open, but every time that she would start to fall to sleep I would have to change my position as pins and needles were rendering my legs numb. My movement would pull Sheba back from the brink of slumber.

I could feel my own eyes becoming heavy; my head would involuntarily drop forwards as I lapsed into short periods of sleep. I began thinking about the research I had carried out over the previous couple of weeks with regards to the recuperation needs of dogs that had undergone surgery. I needed to learn as much as I possibly could in preparation for Sheba's eventual homecoming.

Many of the forums that I read started by telling about the inevitable pain your dog would be suffering, and the behavioural changes you should expect. Your dog may not want to be fussed or stroked too much.

It was interesting to read how a dog recovers very quickly from the anaesthetic but is unaware that it needs a long recuperation period to allow its surgical wounds to heal. The break in their routine often proves frustrating for them, so it is vital to reassure them in other ways, keeping them amused and stimulated with attention-based and gentle stimulation games, avoiding at all costs any activities that may cause them to stretch or leap about.

The 'light and white diet' was also continually mentioned, to try and help keep off the inevitable unwanted weight increase due to the dog's enforced inactivity. Sheba was now going to be put on a 'little and often' feeding regime, mainly made up of chicken and rice, that she would find easier to digest than her normal diet of off-the-shelf dog food.

A shelf in our freezer had been emptied of our food and was now full of lean chicken breast and an abundance of white fish. Tins of sardines and pilchards in oil had replaced the regular tins of meat in Sheba's food cupboard.

Chaim returned to check up on Sheba. Most of the lights in the consultation area had now been turned off or dimmed.

"Hello Sheba, how are you feeling?"

He moved closer to look at the bandaging covering her leg.

"Good, no signs of blood seepage. We'll give her extra pain relief for the next 24 hours. Dogs are so resilient to pain, but we have to remember that she won't only be feeling sore from where I made the surgical incision, but she will also have discomfort from the internal healing."

I could sense that there was something else he wanted to say. My gut instinct was right, he coughed nervously and looked at me.

"Sorry Paul, but the girls are ready to go home; we're going to help Sheba out for a night-time wee then bed her down. The two night nurses will be here soon; I'll go over everything with them; it's time for you to go home and please don't worry, Sheba is in excellent hands."

Chaim's words reassured me, I had no idea of the time, but I knew it was late. I was shattered and mentally drained, and still had an hour's drive home ahead of me.

"It would be easier if you were not here when we get her out of the cage, so could you please say your goodbyes now. We are going to try and offer her a light supper, but it can take 24 hours after surgery to regain any form of appetite. We are going to keep her here with us for two days. Anyway, it takes up to 48 hours for a wound to seal up, and if there should be any problems I want her close so I can deal with it straight away."

Knowing that Sheba had to remain calm, I said the briefest of farewells and left her. I looked back once; she was watching me from the confines of her cage, with her ears pricked up, her head slightly cocked to one side. What must have been going through her mind?

***

Saturday 16th May. Excitedly, Toni and I set off at 9 am to drive to Cambridge to pick Sheba up. At long last we could bring her home for us to continue with her post-operative aftercare.

Chaim and the two nurses who had been in attendance during her operation were waiting for us when we arrived; there was also one very excited little pup jumping around in her cage.

We had stopped en route and bought a few bunches of flowers, some boxes of chocolates, and two bottles of something special for the surgeons, gifts from Sheba to the caring people who had enhanced her life and taken loving care of her.

We had a coffee with the team before we listened carefully to the necessary instructions we were going to have to adhere to for at least the next six weeks.

Firstly, and most importantly, Sheba biting or chewing the bandages and stitches was going to have to be prevented at all costs. Over the next few days as the wound started to heal it would become extremely itchy, and naturally, she would do her utmost to relieve the sensation. One of the nurses went to give me a plastic buster collar for her; I declined, as we still had her soft Comfy Cone at home.

Chaim reiterated the importance of keeping her bandages dry, several times, before giving us instructions to apply a plastic bag or cling film before Sheba was allowed into the garden. We had already been doing this and had become quite adept at it, due to her bandaged broken right leg.

We had reduced the time that Sheba spent in her cage, but this was now going to have to revert to her being permanently imprisoned, well for the near future anyway, but at least she was going to be back in her own home with her family.

Before Sheba was discharged and allowed to come home with us, we had to go through her medication. Firstly, we were given a two-week course of synulox, an antibiotic for dogs, which contains both amoxicillin and clavulanic acid. This combination helps prevent a wide range of bacteria. We had to give her one of these twice a day. Also we were given a box of non-steroidal anti-inflammatory drugs, again one tablet twice a day to decrease both pain and inflammation.

We took Sheba back to Cambridge every four days for a check-up and bandage change. Her stitches were removed 14 days after surgery; the wound looked clean and had knitted together with just the faintest of incision scars running up the front of her leg. The skin appeared swollen along the line of neat black nylon sutures, but this would soon start to reduce. Fur had also begun to regrow, making the wound look less angry.

***

Thursday 25th June. I was feeling slightly the worse for wear, and a bit hungover as it was the day after my parents' birthday celebrations.

It was exactly six weeks since Sheba's last corrective surgery, and we were heading to Cambridge for what we were hoping would be Sheba's final check-up, and for her to at long last be signed off by Chaim. Over the previous two weeks she had been having gentle post-op physiotherapy sessions, carried out by a friend of Chaim's. The benefits these sessions had had for Sheba included a faster healing time and drug-free pain relief.

We had been encouraging Sheba to do a couple of gentle exercises that had been devised explicitly around her unique double corrective surgery twice a day, trying to make the 15-minute sessions as fun as possible.

Deep down we were also optimistic that after today's visit we would be able to, at long last, be allowed to venture out and take Sheba out for a walk. We couldn't wait to take her for a stroll across the countryside crop fields where we used to spend so much time with Shane.

Upon our arrival, and after Sheba having the usual fuss bestowed upon her, Chaim asked his standard questions with regards to her well-being and recuperation.

Just like the first time when I met him, only two months ago, he asked me to bring Sheba outside so that he could assess the way she was walking, and for him to ascertain how successful her recovery had been. He was also keen to see how she bore weight on her two straight front legs.

He knelt on the ground with his hands on his kneecaps, about 30 feet from where we were standing.

"Okay Paul, slowly walk Sheba towards me please."

"Sheba heel, there's a good girl."

We set off together, Sheba alternating her gaze between looking up at me, and then looking at Chaim.

As we were getting closer to him, I was sure that he appeared to have the same concerned look etched on his face that he had back in April. Surely not, please no, it has got to be my imagination.

"Right, turn around, walk her back, turn and walk back towards me please."

Damn it; I knew for sure that there had got to be something wrong.

"Again please."

Chaim changed position. He was now on all fours. He lowered his head, and his face was now touching the paving slabs. He closed his right eye, focusing entirely with his left. Now he could carefully watch exactly how Sheba placed her front legs as she walked. Deep down I knew that something was wrong. I knew exactly what he was looking for, and he had probably already seen it. Sheba was lame. I only hoped that it was not her right leg yet again.

We continually walked backwards and forwards for several minutes, every single movement Sheba made scrutinised. Chaim's head nurse, who was studying physiotherapy, had now joined us. She had positioned herself next to Chaim; she was also kneeling down and also carefully studying Sheba's movements. I could see that they were talking to each other, but couldn't make out what they were saying.

We had been here before, the look that now engulfed his face was the same look he had the very first time I met him back in April. Surely no, not again.

"Sorry Paul, but I'm not at all happy with her right leg. I need to get my team to prepare her for an X-ray, and if my fears are right, then we will have to take her straight in for emergency surgery."

What the hell, why? Why was Sheba being punished? She never asked to be born into this deformed little body. How much more could she take of the physical and mental trauma of her body being continually brutally butchered and hacked away at?

We all nervously headed back to the consultation room. Chaim gathered his team together and thoroughly briefed them on Sheba's potential predicament, and if the X-rays would confirm his worst fears, then the next plan of action. The nurses wasted no time in preparing her.

Sheba was sedated and brought into the radiography area on a surgical trolley for an X-ray.

Once the required radiograph images had been captured, Sheba was wheeled back into the recovery area. Unbeknown to me, Chaim had already instructed the nurses to commence preparing her for surgery – deep down he already knew what he was about to see on his screen.

We stood solemnly and anxiously waiting with bated breath to see the results.

The image of Sheba's right front leg skeleton soon downloaded and appeared on the LCD screen in his darkened office. He put on his glasses and moved in closer to the screen, his nose touching the glass covering the liquid crystals, his eyes squinting and scrutinising one specific area. Straight away his demeanour changed; I now knew for sure that there was something wrong.

"Look here; see this small black line?"

He slowly traced the nib of his pen across the screen, along the contour of a faint black line.

"It's the original fracture; the break has still not completely healed; it has slightly drifted apart yet again. Poor little thing, she must be in absolute agony. My suggestion, and to be honest the only plan of action now left open to us, is to now use an External Skeletal Fixator."

The dazed look on my face must have said it all.

"Sorry, in layman's terms, they are an external device used to securely hold the leg's skeleton in the correct position, allowing it to heal correctly. The fixator consists of an extracorporeal frame, sorry, metal rods, and fixation elements. In Sheba's case these will be large screws directly inserted into her bones. The fixation screws will be drilled into healthy intact sections of her bone, to help stabilise the leg. Sheba's fixator will then help to transfer the weight from the intact bone immediately below the elbow, bypassing as much of her weight as possible from the broken portion of the radius and ulna. In turn, the weight will be displaced down through external braces to some more pins that will be inserted into the intact bone above her wrist joint. The poor little thing's leg will be a mass of surgical steel when you take into consideration the rod I have already implanted."

He paused. I sensed that Chaim felt awkward, almost embarrassed, about the grotesque, gory surgery he was about to perform on Sheba.

With his voice now reduced to an almost inaudible grumble he continued, and managed to stumble his way through his explanation.

"I have to warn you that the device will look like a piece of medieval torture equipment, so please don't be alarmed when you see it. I was praying this wouldn't happen, not to Sheba, but with all the extra pressure being placed on this damaged, weaker section, after the correction surgery on her left leg, the bone is just not being given a chance to knit back together. Splints are just not going to hold it together firm enough to allow it to heal itself fully; this is now the only option left open to us."

Bloody hell no, not my poor little lady; life can be so unfair. Surely there was a more humane alternative, and Sheba didn't have to endure yet another sodding operation.

"As with her previous operation, I won't stop you from watching if you want to, but I have to warn you that it is really not pleasant."

He again started to repeat and reiterate in detail the complexity of the procedure.

"I have to make small incisions in her skin where I have to screw in the retaining screws, and then I have to..."

Luckily he stopped mid-sentence, aware that he didn't need to tell me the full grisly details again. If he had I'm sure that I would have passed out.

"This is going to be Sheba's third major operation in four months, and that's not taking into account and including her broken leg. I hate to say it, but when she wakes up from this procedure, she will be in a hell of a lot of pain."

In fact, this was going to be her fourth operation in five months. She had been spayed in Bulgaria, back in January, before being brought over to the UK in February.

Chaim turned away from me and looked at the image on his screen. It was as if his deliberate pause was to give me time to try and comprehend the harsh, complex severity of the awful predicament that my poor little Sheba now found herself in and to ask any questions that I may have.

"Is this because of something we have done?"

We had followed every single instruction given to us by Chaim and his team to the letter. How on earth could this have happened?

"Don't even begin to blame yourself. Her bone had become weakened and more fragile when it initially fractured after her first operation. Maybe it was inevitable that it would come to this. To be honest, I should have gone down this road initially, but I wanted to try and avoid putting her through such an operation, hoping that the leg would manage to heal itself."

It seemed as if he couldn't find the words to offer any form of comfort. However, unbeknown to him his words reassured me; I knew that it was selfish to be bringing my emotions into the terrible situation that Sheba now found herself in, but I couldn't live with myself if I thought that my lack of care could have been the cause of the problem.

In the short space of time that we had been talking, the nurses had wasted no time in getting Sheba fully prepped for surgery. The mood in the consultation area was sombre, to say the least.

The head nurse entered the still-darkened office and nodded. Chaim looked at me stony-faced.

"I need to get myself scrubbed up, Paul. It's going to take about an hour in all, so why not go and grab yourself a spot of lunch. We'll call you as soon as it's all over."

I knew that Sheba was sedated, but I gave her a reassuring hug and kiss before leaving her.

Deep down I felt that I had betrayed her, all the bullshit I'd spouted when I first met her about protecting her from harm, the same worthless vows I'd made to Shane. I felt ashamed, and like a coward, I ran away, I didn't stay to protect her from the torture she was about to endure. No not me, I ran, to seek solace in a pint of warm beer in a local pub.

I soon found myself sat alone in The Geldart drinking a pint of locally brewed Cambridgeshire ale.

Maybe it was the beer, but I had become choked up thinking about the pain Shane had endured, and how, as his life was slowly ebbing away back in February, the new exciting, pain-free chapter in Sheba's life was just beginning.

My sadness to anger issue returned; I scanned the pub, hoping for the wrong glance from another lunchtime drinker, this would have given me the excuse that I needed to release the pressure valve of anger surging through my veins.

What an absolute idiot I was; what bloody right did I have to take out my pent-up rage on an innocent man?

Luckily my thoughts became more rational, and I soon calmed down. I remembered the real reason why I was sat here drinking alone, and I began to try and comprehend the severity of the horrific surgery that my poor little lady was going through. Slowly and surely my heart rate lowered.

My mobile rang. My recently downloaded Zulu-movie theme tune ringtone shocked me back to my senses. It was the head nurse; Sheba's operation has been a complete success. One thing that I had learnt over the last couple of months was that the effects of the general anaesthetic took a fair while to wear off, and Sheba at the moment would probably be a bit sleepy. But she was lying there alone and confused in the recovery suite, I needed to be with her. I quickly swigged down the last of my beer and headed back to the surgery.

As soon as I arrived back at the surgery, one of the on-duty nurses took me straight through to the isolation unit.

"Chaim has just popped out for a coffee, he'll be back soon. Don't be alarmed, the bandaging makes it look a lot worse than it really is."

The lighting in the recovery area had been dimmed. Sheba was in her cage, lying on a soft mattress of vet bed, manufactured from a sturdy latex-lined backing and a thick imitation sheepskin top. The idea was any moisture ran straight through the fibres, keeping Sheba dry and comfortable, the dryness being a crucial aspect with the E.S.F she had had screwed into her leg. She was lying facing away from me; I could see a cannula attached by sterile strips to a shaved area on her right hind leg.

I knelt next to her cage and whispered her name. Bless her little heart, she was thrilled to see me, her bushy tail started to rise and fall onto the soft white woollen rug; the aroma of surgical disinfectant filled the air as her tail became more animated. She lifted her head and turned her neck to look up at me with her beautiful brown eyes; although they looked different, her scleras had a blood red hue about them. Frustratingly for her, she was still very woozy and unable to fully turn herself around and clamber up onto her paws. The high dose of anaesthetic that was required to sedate her was freely flowing through her body.

The bulbous bandaging on her right leg covered the torturous frame that was now screwed directly into her fragile bones. How on earth could she even bear weight on that leg? I knew that she was pumped full of pain relief, but even so, the pain she must have been suffering had got to be excruciating.

For her well-being, her care nurse had asked that I do not open the door to her cage; they needed to keep her as calm and immobile as possible. However, Sheba was determined to somehow give me one of her special kisses. She had managed to shift her body around without pulling the cannula out, and she was now facing me. She poked her little nose and tongue through the bars of her cage; I stroked them with the back of my index finger, continuously whispering her words of admiration and love.

Chaim appeared behind me. I looked up at him then back at Sheba, her little tail was now again gently wagging, maybe her way of thanking the man who had worked tirelessly to mend her deformed body.

Instinctively I could tell by the look on his face that he was pleased at how well the operation had gone. Chaim smiled and gently shook his head as he bent forward towards Sheba.

He looked at me; I could smell coffee on his breath as he gave me a stark warning.

"I don't want to scare or alarm you, but I really can't emphasise too much, the major part you will have to play in her successful recuperation. Cleanliness of the area is paramount; you will have to keep the bandaging bone dry and scrupulously clean at all times. We will need to see her back here every 48 hours after she has been discharged to change the dressing. If the bandage should become loose or fall off, any signs of blood seepage, no matter how small or an unpleasant odour then you get her straight back here, I'm on standby 24 hours a day."

After a brief pause in his instructions he continued.

"The fixing screws are screwed directly into her bones, and it will take 3–5 days for a dry scab to form where screws enter the skin, but I have to warn you that there is an extremely high risk of infection, which could rapidly spread straight into the bone marrow, and if this should happen, well the results could be…"

His voice trailed off; the worried expression on his face said it all.

Without saying another word, he got up and returned to his office to finalise Sheba's case history notes before he headed for home.

I spent an hour with Sheba before the two duty nurses came in to say that they needed to take her out to see if she needed to go to the toilet, and that my presence may cause her to become over-animated.

Sadly, I had to say my goodbyes, but I told her that I'd be back first thing in the morning to visit her.

I noticed that each of the nurses was holding a harness. The head nurse explained that she would use hers to support and take the weight of Sheba's fore end, her colleague would use hers to reduce the risk of Sheba's hind end collapsing due to the effects of the anaesthetic, which could damage her weakened, and painful, front right leg.

On the third day after her surgery, Sheba was discharged and allowed to return home with us. As instructed, she remained on constant cage rest, only allowed out to eat and drink, and to lie on her day bed in the lounge with us of an evening.

We had been advised to make room in her cage for her water and food bowls and to keep them away from her bandage and bedding. We didn't want to take any chances, so we devised a routine for her feeding, and allowed her out of her cage every hour to enable her to drink.

For two months, I carried Sheba into the garden to allow her to relieve herself. As an added precaution, we always wrapped her leg in cling film, even during the warm, dry summer months.

No matter what horrors life chucks at her, Sheba always manages to overcome them, without complaint, in her own unique, heart-melting way.

***

Sheba's recuperation had become our main priority in life; in fact, it was our only priority. Apart from the constant round-the-clock care we took it in turns to give her, we also had to take her every third day on an 80-mile round trip to Cambridge for a bandage change and check-up.

Chaim had made plans for a new exciting challenge for himself and his family and was moving abroad to set up a veterinary practice of his own; his move would hopefully coincide with Sheba finally being discharged from his professional care.

Toni and I felt that we had no option but to cancel our already-booked holiday to Rhodes in August; there was no way we could head off for two weeks leaving Sheba at such a critical stage in her recuperation.

Pat popped round for a cup of tea. During the conversation, she slipped in that after the emotionally draining ups and downs of the previous five months, it would be beneficial for us both to get away, and not to cancel our holiday. Little did we know that she had already deviously hatched a plan of action right behind our backs, and there was an ulterior motive for us being out of the country.

Pat, along with Chaim, had already spoken to the orthopaedic surgeon who was to take over Sheba's on-going aftercare. During a series of clandestine meetings, Chaim had thoroughly gone over Sheba's case notes, and a consultation appointment was arranged for mid-August, when we were away. He would finally relinquish his professional care, and pass Sheba over to the new surgeon.

After the constant bullying we endured, Toni and I did reluctantly go on our much-needed holiday.

Pat took Sheba for her arranged consultation; ironically, Sheba's new surgeon had his practice at the same referral centre where Sheba's dear late adoptive brother Shane had spent the last month of his life before he passed away.

To save us having to revisit the place that held so many sad memories for us, Pat had arranged all of this in advance in conjunction with Chaim, hence her being so adamant that we went on holiday.

Upon their arrival, and after observing her walk, Sheba's new surgeon requested an X-ray on her fractured leg.

It was fantastic news. The bone had at long last fully healed. Anticipating that this may be the case, he had already taken the liberty of preliminarily arranging for an operating theatre and surgical support team to be on standby.

At long last, and after two long traumatic months, just one more operation lay ahead of her; she was about to lose her External Skeletal Fixator frame forever.

***

Toni and I were sitting drinking gin and tonics in a small taverna in the village of Pefkos, overlooking the beautiful Askeftos Bay on the Greek island of Rhodes, nicknamed The Island of the Knights, after the Knights of Saint John of Jerusalem. Historically, Rhodes was famous worldwide for the Colossus of Rhodes, one of the Seven Wonders of the Ancient World. The taverna that we were drinking in was not far from where David Gilmour from the rock band Pink Floyd had his holiday mansion. It was also the spot where, according to local legend, he supposedly took his inspiration for the groups iconic Dark Side of the Moon album. Sorry I digress, enough of the history and rock and roll lesson and back to the story. When my mobile started to ring, the Zulu theme tune that I had as my ringtone drew attention from the bar staff. It was Pat, with her voice full of emotion and excitement she told me that Sheba's leg had repaired itself. Sheba had successfully undergone surgery number five at lunchtime; the external fixings had now been removed. She was now fully mobile for the first time on her new, now straight front legs. We both cheered and shed tears of joy for our little lady; now it was time to order celebratory cocktails. Toni had her favourite, a pina colada, I had a margarita, and we both raised our glasses and toasted our beautiful little lady, 2,300 miles away.

Sheba's good fortune back home in England turned out to be the second bit of joyous good news that I'd had that day. Earlier that morning I had had to seek medical attention after a bit of a mishap that I'd had the previous evening.

I have to admit that I'd lain awake worrying all night, my mind in turmoil and going into overdrive. I'd over-thought and overreacted, and now all I could contemplate was the potential worst-case scenario. Had I contracted rabies?

So at 9 am this morning I had skipped breakfast and was seeking the distinctive green cross neon sign that denoted the resort's pharmacy, and the surgery of Dr Stavros.

The on-duty pharmacist doubled up as Dr Stavros's receptionist. Once I had provided him with proof of my travel insurance, to which he proudly told me that he had the same name as me, Pávlos, he directed me to go around to the rear of the building, and to climb the flight of stairs. Once I was on the first-floor landing, I had to knock on the door with the orthodox crucifix hanging on it. As far as Pávlos was aware, Dr Stavros did not have a patient with him, so he should be able to see me straight away.

The white marble stairs with the bright morning sunshine reflecting off them were initially hard to negotiate; carefully I climbed them and once at the top I reached the large and very ornate wooden door with the cross. I knocked and waited.

"If you are pretty then please enter," came the strange response, in a deep, gruff Greek accent.

I don't consider myself pretty by any means, but I needed urgent medical attention, so I opened the door and walked in.

I was confronted by a middle-aged gentleman, with a bushy, dishevelled, greying beard, sitting behind a desk. He looked disappointed when he saw me, and continued stubbing out the remnants of his cigarette into a Mythos beer glass ashtray.

"Good morning my friend, come in sit down and have a cup of Greek coffee."

The doctor flipped the lid open on his packet of Karelia red cigarettes; his previous cigarette was still smouldering in the ashtray as he lit his next one.

"Do you smoke?"

Blimey, this was poles apart from the NHS. I had never received such a jovial greeting whenever I had visited my GP, and he was offering me a cigarette. But then again, this consultation was probably going to cost my insurance company an arm and a leg, hopefully not my leg.

The examination room appeared surprisingly spotless, although there was a strong smell of stagnant cigarette smoke and a dirty yellowy discolouration to the ceiling area above the doctor's chair. The air conditioning offered welcome relief from the unforgiving heat, even at this time of day it was already hitting the low 30s. The large oscillating fan behind the doctor evenly distributed the cold air – and cigarette smoke – throughout the sterile surgery; the trouble was it was also circulating an awful rancid smell that I had soon deduced was originating from the doc's armpits. I felt myself almost gagging as the smell of his offensive, pungent body odour hit me as the fan went through its motions. Bloody hell, surely he can smell it as well. Mind you, his sense of smell was probably shot by the smoke from the strong fags he continually chain-smoked.

I declined his kind offer of a coffee, although I did become tempted when he said he was going to add a large nip of Metaxa. I had convinced myself that I was going to need an urgent medical procedure and was worried that the brandy would have an adverse effect on the anaesthetic. I walked over to his desk and reluctantly sat down on the white plastic patio chair; the putrid stench of his pits was making me feel nauseous, I needed to get out of the room as soon as I possibly could. I cleared my throat, almost retching as I did, and set about trying to explain my tale of woe.

"Erm well, it's like this doc; I got bit last night."

Dr Stavros appeared to become excited at the prospect of dealing with something different from the usual holiday tummy and sunburn cases he repeatedly saw. He stared at me over the top of his glasses, which were ill-fitting and sitting wonkily on his face. I was fighting the urge to straighten them for him. He leans forward. Bloody hell, his armpits were getting even closer; I could see the underarms of his white shirt had dirty yellow stains. He was now making me feel even more anxious, with his bony elbows resting on the desk, his scrawny fingers interlocked, and the way that he was twirling and twiddling his thumbs around one another.

"Was it by one of the village's stray dogs?"

The village of Pefkos lies adjacent to a small pine tree-covered mountain, and at night the howls of the many stray dogs that inhabit the foothills can be heard echoing around the rocky landscape as packs of them prepare to head into town to scavenge for food.

"No doc, it wasn't a dog."

Dr Stavros started to stroke his unkempt beard. I suffer from mild OCD, and the thought of the bacteria and germs that I have read live in men's beards horrifies me. I hoped that he didn't want to shake my hand at the end of the consultation.

"Was it a snake?"

Blimey, this is getting seriously embarrassing.

"Nope, it wasn't a snake."

"Okay my friend, I give up. Tell me, what – or who – bit you, and where?"

"I'm warning you, you'd better not laugh."

Bloody hell, he moved even closer. We were almost rubbing noses.

"I got bit by a kitten, on my left ankle."

Dr Stavros looked down, his glasses fell off and landed on his desktop; his shoulders began to move up and down frantically. I do believe he was laughing at me. He looked up, yup, the cheeky sod was laughing.

"A kitten? You are telling me that you got bitten by a kitten, a tiny little kitten, a teeny weeny kitten, a defenceless little kitten?"

Bloody hell, how many ways are there of saying little kitten in Greek?

"Yup, the little bugger got me right on the ankle."

Throughout the resort of Pefkos, there are cat-feeding areas. These are designated, charity-run sites authorised by the local municipal units or councils, where they ask that you kindly leave fresh water and dry food in the bowls provided to help the hundreds of feral cats that live on the streets of the village. Every evening on our way out to dinner, Toni and I had taken bottles of water and fresh food to one particular site that seemed to have an abundance of kittens.

The previous evening, while we were distributing our food donation, a young family had stood watching us. One of the children walked over to ask if he could help us. It was only about 8 pm, but Greece does not suffer from the orange glow of light pollution we have become accustomed to living in our towns and cities back home in the UK. The night sky in Pefkos was a jet-black canvas, the millions of flickering bright stars and constellations formed a twinkling picture. However, although the light from the heavenly bodies that reside millions of miles away is intense, it didn't filter down to fully illuminate where we were standing. The clumsy little sod obviously didn't see the kitten waiting patiently next to my foot for its allocation of food, and must have accidentally trodden on its tail.

There was a sudden almighty high-pitched hiss, and then a loud feline scream, followed by a burning sensation in my ankle as pin-like fangs became embedded deep into my flesh.

Hence my urgent visit that morning to Dr Stavros, with the worry that I could have contracted rabies swirling around in my head.

The doctor moved around to my side of his desk. Bloody hell, his pits were revolting. He looked down, grasped my left foot and elevated it so he could take a closer look at my wound. I started frantically wafting the air in front of my nose to try and divert the disgusting, stomach-churning stench from hitting me. Dr Stavros started to prod around the area where the fangs had left their entry marks; the skin was looking red and angry, the wound resembling the neck of a fair maiden in a Hammer House of Horrors Dracula film.

"The wound has become badly infected; we will need to get you to the mainland urgently, if not, you may lose your leg."

Bloody hell, I was merely helping with the welfare of the local cat population and now this.

Dr Stavros roared with laughter.

"Do you like my Greek sense of humour? I'll give you some antibiotics as a precaution. Also, I know what you were worried about, and I will alleviate your fears; our cats here on Rhodes do not have rabies. Now go enjoy the rest of your holiday."

Sod it; the bastard had me there. To be honest, I get why he laughed. I weigh about 16 stone, stand five foot ten, I have a shaved head and am covered in tattoos, and now here I was, floored by a bleeding little kitten.

He reached out to shake my hand. The thought of the germs that resided in his beard and the fact that he had run his hands through the grey flea and lice-infested hair hanging from his face horrified me. I had to think quick, there was no way I could touch his grubby mitt.

Don't ask me why, because I honestly don't know, but a very childish plan of action sprang to mind. So I begrudgingly started to move my hand forwards to grasp the doctor's sweaty palm, but at the very last moment I quickly retracted and raised my right hand up, put the tip of my thumb on my nose and wiggled my fingers and blew a raspberry at him. Pleased with how I had gotten out of the situation I thanked him for his time and turned to leave his consultation room. The doc looked bemused, with his hand still outstretched in mid-air.

"If you could please see Pávlos on your way out, he will finalise your consultation fee."

In all, it cost my insurance company 155 euros for that sodding bite. I should have got my monies worth and drank the doctor's bloody Metaxa.

CHAPTER FOURTEEN

Sheba's Adventures

This is the only thing I can give, the love I left behind...

It would be a never-ending task for me to attempt to write a day by day, blow by blow journal of Sheba's life and on-going adventures. In this chapter, I will highlight some pivotal moments in her life with us, up to the point that this book is finalised and published.

I'll start with Sheba's regular bedtime routine. At approximately 9 pm every evening, except Wednesdays which is her school night, Sheba goes to our patio doors; she sits and looks back to where we are sitting. One of us, usually me, gets up, turns on the security light, if it is dark outside, then opens the patio door. I always step out into the garden first but will be closely followed by Sheba, who charges out like a bat out of hell. She will run about for a bit; then head to the back of the garden, where she will growl and bark at our neighbour's three-legged cat if it is sitting taunting her from the top of our vine-covered pergola – failing that she'll chase one of the many squirrels that frequent our garden.

She does her wee, then runs excitedly back towards the house, where she carefully negotiates her descent down the extra-wide steps, with the shallower riser height and wider treads that we had specially designed and constructed for her disability needs.

Once indoors she will sit and wait for her paws to be dried if the grass was wet, then she heads out into the hallway, where she sits at the bottom of the stairs, waiting for me. Due to her disability, Sheba cannot negotiate climbing the stairs herself, so for over four years now I have carefully picked her up, cradled her in my arms and carried her up to her bed which is positioned at the foot of ours.

The first thing she does is to arrange the faux fur lining to suit herself, by scuffing it up, using the same motion she does when digging a hole. Once happy, she'll walk around it a few times inspecting her handiwork, head over to the small toy box she has in our room, pick up Shane's rabbit, head back to her bed and plonk herself down, always followed by a huff and a sigh.

Usually, within five minutes she's fast asleep, one very contented little lady dreaming in the Land of Nod.

After an hour or so she wakes up and has a walk around our bedroom. That's the moment I look forward to, it gives me an excuse to lift her onto our bed. I'll give her Shane's rabbit, and once she is comfortable she'll curl up between us and again fall asleep.

Sheba has now slept with and been the guardian of Shane's rabbit for four years. To date it is the only toy she has never destroyed. She still takes it to her bed every evening and sleeps with it, gently and lovingly clasped between her front paws.

Sometimes on a dark, clear night, Sheba will head out into the garden slightly earlier. For some strange reason on these nights, there is no charging around like a manic banshee.

Instead, she sits on the top step silently looking up at the twinkling stars, nonchalantly taking in the vast vista above, her head tilting inquisitively from side to side.

I never impose upon her, nor interrupt her while she's sitting there, alone in her thoughts. I often wonder what is going through her little mind; I so wish that she could tell me.

Little sounds can be heard emanating from her, as if she is engrossed in deep conversation, I will never know what she is saying.

Often, after her little conversation, when she heads slowly back indoors, she'll glance up at me. I'm sure that I have not imagined it, but on more than one occasion, I honestly believe that I have seen a small teardrop gently trickling from each eye.

No, maybe I am just romanticising, and it is just my imagination.

***

May 25th 2015. Whitsun Bank Holiday weekend.

Just nine short months earlier Shane had had the time of his life joining in with the fun and festivities at the Mutts Family Fun Day.

These invite-only, fun-filled, fundraising days are held every May and August bank holidays at the rescue sanctuary.

I'll try to elaborate in more detail. The day is open to all ex-Mutts dogs and their families, guests pay a small nominal entrance fee, and all attendees are requested to bring a donation of a tin of dog food.

Desperately needed funds are raised throughout the course of the afternoon from the BBQ, various auctions, tombola's and a variety of homemade goods for sale, all of the aforementioned items kindly donated by members and followers of Mutts in Distress.

Then there's the dog shows in the specially constructed arena.

Throughout the afternoon there are a variety of fun classes for the guests to enter their dogs. As you enter the arena you throw a £1 donation into a bucket, every single penny raised will be allocated for the welfare and continuing health care of the poor abandoned dogs that Mutts have saved from suffering, or the threat of death.

The classes include Best Mover, Most Beautiful Eyes, Prettiest Bitch, Most Similar Brace, Best Foreign Import; in all, about 15 different categories. Members of the extended Mutts family sponsor the various classes, which includes donating the winners' cups, and runners-up rosettes.

There is also a class for the best ex-Mutts dog; it is always very emotional and poignant to see how one of the rescue's ex once-abandoned dogs have progressed in their new life.

However, there wasn't a specific class for the disabled, the not-so pretty or glamorous, those with a horror story to tell of how they had ended up, from no fault of their own, being in the care of Mutts in Distress, just like Shane and Sheba had found themselves.

With the Mutts team's blessing, Toni and I set up and continually sponsor an award, called Shane's Cup of Hope. The dedicated Mutts team select about ten dogs – these poor dogs may not have always had the chance, or been considered for entering into the arena during the fun day, this was a special award specifically for them. The guests who attend the fun day are each asked to make a vote and give a small suggested donation of just 50p to pick one of the selected dogs that they feel is the most deserving. During the course of the afternoon, Pat reads out the nominated dogs' stories; this always proves to be an incredibly moving part of the afternoon.

Near the end of the fun day, the votes are all carefully counted.

The nominees enter the arena for the prize-giving; there is a cup for the dog who receives the most votes, and runners-up rosettes for those not chosen as the overall winner – to us though they are all winners.

We purchased a large wooden trophy, adorned with 12 small metal shields for the engraving of the winners' names and the date that they won, which sits proudly in the foyer area of Mutts, as a poignant reminder of some of the beautiful ex-rescue dogs.

On the first fun day that the Shane's Cup of Hope award was introduced, we managed to raise over £300 for the rescue. Ironically, Sheba received the most nominations, bless her little heart.

Due to her surgery recuperation, Sheba was unable to attend the fun day, and accept her award in person. To this day her trophy sits proudly in the same cabinet that holds Shane's ashes.

Our little man's name would now live on forever, with his little sister Sheba's name proudly emblazoned on the first shield of the trophy that bears his name.

Shane's legacy is that he continues to raise much-needed funds for the rescue sanctuary that had saved his life. He is continually helping other abandoned dogs, innocent souls that had suffered the cruelty and injustices inflicted upon them by humans. The pain and suffering that he had very sadly once endured himself.

Sheba's story touched many people, not only those who were directly involved in her rescue and corrective surgery, but a much wider audience. The local press had been following her story and asked if it would be possible for a journalist and photographer to visit us and carry out an interview. Eventually, the local paper ran a couple of articles about her. Excerpts from one published on 11th June 2015 reads:

Disabled dog has new life after rescue and surgery.

A disabled dog which underwent surgery to straighten her wonky legs after being brought to the UK from Bulgaria is starting her new life with a family in Old Harlow.

German Shepherd dog Sheba is now on the road to recovery in the care of her new owners Paul and Toni Viner following the operations to correct her bow legs.

"We have only had her a short time but it is like we have had her forever," said Mr Viner. "She is very loving, very kind and very gentle. She is very appreciative of the life she has got and very forgiving for the life she has had. She just likes company, a stroke and a little chat."

Sheba was brought to this country from Bulgaria earlier this year after being spotted on the internet.

A Facebook campaign was launched to highlight her plight and to raise money. Once in the UK, Sheba was cared for at the Mutts in Distress animal shelter in Little Hallingbury.

Sheba underwent surgery on one of her front legs in February and on the other last month. The operations were carried out free of charge by Chaim Pilosof, a partner and surgeon at Companion Care, Cambridge.

Sheba, who was originally called Maria, is now more than halfway through a six-week rest period at Mr and Mrs Viner's home in Old Harlow.

The couple's first dog, a Belgian shepherd called Shane who they also got from Mutts in Distress after he was found in a ditch, died in March.

"Shane was a beautiful dog, a part of the family," said Mr Viner, a Street Trading Enforcement Officer in East London. "Wherever we went he went."

He added, "Sheba has helped us with the healing process of Shane. She will never replace Shane, and we will never compare her to Shane. We are helping each other in a big way."

Mr Viner was full of praise for Mr Pilosof and his team for everything they had done for Sheba.

"They were amazing, such lovely people," he said.

The lady reporter who came to our home to write the article informed me upon arrival that she was terrified of dogs. She in fact suffered from severe Cynophobia, the fear of dogs.

I was confused as to why she would have agreed to, or chosen to take on such an assignment.

To make the reporter feel safe and at ease, I ensured that Sheba did not get too close to her. Over the course of the few hours that she was with us, her fears diminished, and her confidence grew. Anyway, how could anybody be afraid of Sheba, who coincidentally behaved impeccably towards the journalist, and to the female photographer, herself a dog lover, who had come along to take the required photos for the article?

By the time they left, the journalist was happily stroking Sheba, and feeding her small kibble treats – such a huge personal achievement for the lady.

She revisited us on a couple of occasions, using Sheba as a therapy dog to alleviate her fears, which had been brought on as I was to later find out, by a frightening experience she had had with a stray dog when she was a child.

***

Early September 2015, Sheba's new legs were enabling her to walk further afield, and upon advice from her new vet, I began to increase her daily exercise regime. I had now started taking her on some of Shane's favourite trails, the same walks that just a few months ago he had lead me on. Just as Shane had done, Sheba made frequent stops to catch up on all of the local gossip and news by thoroughly checking her wee-mails.

I had already decided that on one Friday evening I was going to take her for a walk down our local High Street.

It was a warm night, with a welcome light, refreshing drizzle in the air. The sun was just setting as we headed off on our stroll.

The bright fluorescent lights from the shops, the intense, mouth-watering aromas emanating from the variety of different cuisines offered by our local restaurants, and her interaction with the early evening shoppers and rowdy revellers were going to prove to be a good life skill experience for her.

Sheba behaved impeccably and received many adoring glances. Several people commented on the beautiful little pup walking faithfully by my side, and all seemed genuinely taken aback when I told them that she was coming up to three years of age.

Sheba became intrigued by and engaged in combat with the automatic sliding doors that led into the small supermarket. The way they unexpectedly slid open as she approached offended her, leaving her to glare into the void that they had left caused her to take up a defensive stance. Sheba took a step back and raised her right foreleg, it would have been doubled up if her bones were not fused together by titanium rods. To increase her stature, her bushy tail stood erect, and her hackles were up – she was poised and ready to take on this formidable mechanical enemy.

However, a few moments later her foe surrendered and glided shut. In a moment of triumph, Sheba barked and lunged forwards to force her adversary to retreat, only for it to reopen; she backed off, took up her stance – well you get the picture, if I had let her we would have probably been there all night, much to the annoyance of the staff.

"Come on poppet, heel."

I tapped my leg and led Sheba away from the doors. As we walked away she continually turned around and scowled at them, as they slid open allowing customers to enter or leave the shop. Every time they went through their motions, Sheba would make a slight grumble, followed by a feeble, high pitched bark.

We crossed over London Road and headed down towards the pubs where Shane had had his very own little fan club in the form of the doormen. As we approached the noisy pub, I noticed one of the men, standing there with his arms behind his black Crombie coat, look in our direction. He said something to the other bouncer; they looked over at me, nodded, smiled, then looked down at Sheba; immediately I could see that their expressions changed.

"Evening gents, I'd like to introduce you to Sheba."

Sheba dutifully sat upon my command and looked up at the two thuggish brutes looming in front of her. The elder one of them was now kneeling down and had begun to stroke her.

"Good evening Sheba, lovely to make your acquaintance darling."

As the bouncer was gently stroking Sheba's neck, he looked up at me. Anticipating what he was about to ask I quickly uttered:

"We lost Shane…" I struggled to continue the sentence.

The doorman stood up and patted me on the shoulder.

"To be honest mate I'd guessed as much when you stopped visiting. I've seen you around the Old Town, alone. I'm so sorry; he was absolutely stunning."

The other doorman turned and walked back into the pub without saying a word. He soon returned holding three small glasses of dark rum and a packet of cheese nibbles. He handed his mate and me a drink each, and raised his glass.

"Shane."

Shane, the only word he said, but his kind, poignant sentiment meant so much; my little man had made such an impression on these two. He handed me the small pack of biscuits for Sheba, we said our goodbyes and continued on our walk.

After about 100 yards or so we arrived at another one of the Old Town's watering holes; the older generation of our community generally frequent this pub. They sit there whiling away their evenings, always complaining about the quality and price of the ale that they sup, in fact, they sit there moaning about every aspect of modern society.

Just as we were passing the pub, a dilapidated, dirty old builders' van pulled up beside us, the sound of heavy rock music blaring from its antiquated stereo, plumes of smoke were flooding from the slightly lowered driver's side window and the exhaust pipe.

Sheba cowered away from the rust bucket of a van and dropped to the floor in terror, right in front of a group of regulars who were standing outside smoking.

"Come on darling; there's nothing to be afraid of."

I tried to calm and reassure her, all the time stroking the back of her neck; I could feel that she was trembling.

This was not the first time that I had witnessed her have this strange, adverse reaction to the sound of a diesel engine. What was it that upset her so much? Was it something about the distinctive rattly sound made by their engines, or was it the pungent stench of the fumes that they pump out that offended her so much? What had happened in her past to cause her always to have such a repugnant, fearful response? Could it have been her being cooped up for four days in the back of a van when she endured the 1,500-mile journey from Sofia, Bulgaria to the UK in February 2015? Or had something more sinister happened to her in her past?

The driver leapt out of the jalopy and slammed the door shut; it needed a hefty kick to close completely.

"Oi, oi!" came his cheery, hollered greeting.

I look around to see that it was an old pal of mine, covered from head to toe in dried plaster and dust. He finished his roll up and threw it into the drain.

"Coming in for a beer, Paul?"

"Not tonight mate, out on a date with Sheba."

My pal looked down, gave Sheba a wink then headed into the pub for a well-earned 'dust cutter'.

Overall I was very pleased with how Sheba had so far behaved on her first social walk through Old Harlow, so I called her to 'heel', we turned and headed for home.

Two areas that I noted that I needed to work on with her were to try to help her overcome her fear of, and cowering away from diesel engines. Also, to stop her from fighting with the automatic doors at the small supermarket. Well no harm done, so I won't bother wasting my time with that one. Anyhow, to be honest with you, there was no way I'd stop her from having a bit of harmless fun, even if it does piss off the shop's staff.

***

Late September, with her two lovely straight legs becoming stronger and stronger by the day, and the traumas of surgery behind her, Sheba had been given the all-clear by her surgeon to increase and intensify her regular exercise regime even further. We now needed to start working on rebuilding the muscles that had wasted away in her front and hind legs after the months of inactivity.

Thankfully she could now start attending doggy obedience school, for her to begin learning in earnest the important social skills that are vital for any dog. Sheba would be going to the same school, run by members of the Mutts team, that Shane had attended, right up to the horrific night he had suffered his first awful attack from the spinal cord injury that was to lead to his paralysis and untimely death, just six short months earlier.

Happy memories came flooding back as we arrived for her first lesson at the Sea Cadet hall where the classes were held. Initially, I felt apprehensive about walking into the lesson. Many of the members had known Shane, and I knew that it would be difficult for them to broach the subject of his sad, premature passing with me, but tonight wasn't about me, I had to be strong for Sheba.

We stood outside for a few moments; I closed my eyes and composed myself, took a deep breath and led Sheba in through the outer set of doors. I checked, then double-checked Sheba's harness and lead in the foyer before making sure that the coast was clear of any off-lead dogs running free in the hall.

Well the little madam certainly made her arrival and presence known from the moment she dragged me excitedly through the second set of wooden doors that opened into the main hall. The other class members all spun around as we entered. Sheba became instantaneously animated with nervous energy, barking loudly, rearing up on her hind legs, and frantically waving her newly fixed front legs about aimlessly like a boxer in the first round of a fight. We knew that Sheba was very antisocial towards other dogs, but nothing on earth could have prepared us for her initial reaction upon encountering a roomful.

Sheba's barking had an immediate domino effect upon the group. The other assembled dogs, who up until that moment had been patiently and quietly sitting, waiting for their class to commence, all joined in the furore. The sound of their combined barking echoed and bounced around the walls of the hall.

On the rare occasion that she would momentarily calm down, she was constantly poised and ready to spring into action at a moment's notice. She maintained a constant deep, savage growl; her lips curled up leaving her canine teeth uncovered, her ears faced backwards, pressed tightly against her head. If one of the dogs dared even to begin to approach, she focused her eyes menacingly on them with a fixed stare. She would stand her small body as upright and stiffly as possible, with her head raised and tail held erect and rigid; the hairs along her neck and back bristled, bless her, she was trying to make herself look as big as she could. After a brief respite, her barking and growling would start all over again.

Anticipating Sheba's potential anxious reaction at being in such close proximity to so many other dogs, I had taken the precautionary measure of purchasing her an Italian basket muzzle. She was not wearing it yet; I didn't want to get her too riled up before the class.

I know that muzzles can be extremely important, and in some cases a necessary piece of equipment for our dogs in certain situations, but I absolutely despise and detest them.

I had to take the safety and welfare of the other dogs at school into careful consideration, and hopefully, with some intense work, I would soon be able to not have to bring the abhorred muzzle anymore.

Just six weeks after Sheba started school, I finally got my wish. Slowly she began to accept her classmates, and her muzzle now always remains at home.

As a footnote, the dreaded muzzle was brought out of retirement in January 2019, after a very emotional turn of events that will be explained later.

It just went to prove the necessity of close-contact training for Sheba's on-going welfare. At least by attending school, run by one of the top dog trainers in the country, this would enable her to socialise in a safe, controlled environment on a regular weekly basis.

I consider myself to be a responsible and considerate dog owner, and as an added preventative warning to other dog handlers, as a back-up form of defence, I had also purchased Sheba a bright orange lead, with the words 'No Dogs' emblazoned all the way down the sturdy nylon strap in large white letters. Hopefully, the handlers would take notice of the wording, respect Sheba's fears, nervousness and socialising problems and give her a little bit of extra personal space.

I know that many dog owners will have issues with check chains or collars, mistakenly calling them 'choke chains'. How wrong they are – used correctly, as they always are at obedience school, they are an extremely essential piece of training equipment. A few pointers are; when pulled snug, the collar should have about three inches of extra chain, any less then the collar is too tight. The correct fit is vital to the function of the collar; it is good practice to check the fit every time you use it, due to fluctuations in your dog's weight, it is also especially important when training growing puppies.

The correct way to put the collar on is to make a number '6' with the chain, while your dog is facing away from you looking at the collar; now you can slip the collar over your dog's head. Applied correctly, it will tighten and release freely.

Using a gentle tugging motion, the links of the chain 'click' as they run through each other, it's the sound that your dog picks up on, not the tightening of the chain around its throat.

At the obedience classes we attend with Sheba, as your dog successfully progresses through the required disciplines, and is entirely trustworthy around its classmates, a half-check will replace the full-check collar.

You will know that you have a fully trained and trusted dog when the class instructor tells you that you no longer need to use its lead during lessons.

As with Shane, Sheba was soon the proud owner of a membership card rapidly filling up with, and festooned with, silver stars, as she mastered and passed the required school disciplines. Due to her hard work in March 2016, Sheba advanced to the top class. Now her training was going to intensify, which proved to be both physically and mentally stimulating for her. She had grown to accept her fellow four-legged classmates; in fact deep down she had grown to like some of them, they were members of her pack, and this had allowed her to commence her 'off lead' training for many of the disciplines. I gave her the firm commands of:

"Wait, watch me and leave it."

Before I set off alone and attempted to walk down the hall. Up until now, I had always called it the walk of shame, having to continually return to Sheba who kept getting up and following me. I had to sit her down, repeat the commands, and then attempt to head off again, much to the amusement of the other handlers in the class.

But not tonight. At long last Sheba had stopped playing the class clown and duly did precisely as I told her. She sat, waiting anxiously until I had received the nod from the class instructor. I gently called her name and watched her run excitedly down the hall, ignoring all of the other doggies, culminating in her presenting herself in a nice straight sit, directly in front of me. Sheba was then commanded to heel, she circled around the back of me and sat tightly at my left-hand side, her right shoulder was no further than three inches from my left knee.

What a good girl. She received her silver star for passing the recall discipline that night.

To this very day, every Wednesday evening at 9 pm just the mere mention of the magic word 'school' gets Sheba fired up and animated with excitement. In fact, we have to avoid saying the word 'school' at any other time of the week, referring to it merely as the 'S' word. Sheba relishes the time she spends at school; yes it has been a long, hard, emotional and sometimes extremely stressful journey to get her to the standard that she is at today, and to my embarrassment, there have been times when I had thought about throwing in the towel. However, I'm not a quitter. Finally, now our consistent attendance at school and dogged perseverance are beginning to pay off.

If I could offer one piece of advice to anyone who has a dog or is contemplating taking on a dog, then it would be to please attend obedience classes. The vital handling skills taught could potentially be a lifesaver for your beloved pet. You will be surprised to learn that the majority of our dogs' problems stem from our lack of knowledge and understanding and our basic handler errors. The way that we use too many words when giving commands, the tone of our voice, foolishly using treat-oriented training, overpraising, negative body language, our own anxieties – the list goes on and on. When you eventually come to terms with and rectify your own faults, you will suddenly see your dog becoming far more responsive and obedient to the commands that you give.

A group of us at school had dogs whom all shared the same problem, their antisocial tendencies towards other dogs; miraculously though, they had settled and had become relatively accepting of the pack that they trained with every Wednesday. As a group, we could all sympathise and empathise with the associated problems of exercising our dogs in public, especially when told continuously by other dog walkers.

"Don't worry, my dog is not aggressive and is great with other dogs; it'll all be fine."

Well sorry, but no it won't be sodding 'fine'.

Moreover, it's not about our dogs being 'aggressive' they are bloody well scared. Sadly, many rescue dogs have suffered horrific traumas in their pasts, we all know that when we adopt, and welcome them into our families, we live with it and work as hard as we can to diminish their demons, so there you have it, not all dogs are 'fine' with others, Sheba being a prime example.

She suffered multiple savage attacks living as a disabled stray on the vile streets of Sofia; in fact, she suffered a damn sight worse. Her defence mechanism is to drop to the floor, taking a dismissive posture hoping that the approaching dog will avoid her; other times she will become extremely vocal. Both of these reactions always result in another stupid, brain dead handler approaching us with their dog, causing Sheba even more anxiety, stating the aforementioned bloody statement.

"My dog is great with others; it'll be fine."

People's lack of consideration to others is so bloody infuriating.

Anyway, we decided to form an Anti-Social Dog Walking Club. Every Sunday we would meet at 9 am sharp – in all about 20 of us – at a mutually agreed location. Upon arrival, there would be an inevitable massive furore as our dogs initially came face to face with one another, but they would soon calm down as we headed off on our walk. In fact, they soon became very protective of their unique little pack of misfits, bless their little hearts.

Pishiobury Park, an 'enclosed' park designed by Capability Brown in the 18th century, just to the south of Sawbridgeworth, where English Longhorn cattle graze freely in the spring and the River Stort, with its abundance and variety of wildlife that make the river and the surrounding areas their homes, soon became our two favourite walks. Come rain or shine we would meet, our only two rules were that all dogs had to remain on lead, and firm 'leave it' commands had to be given by the handler to any dog showing aggression towards others. We would walk for an hour or two, finishing up, weather permitting, sitting outside of either a pub or cafe. The walks soon proved very beneficial for all of our dogs, and it gave the two-legged members of the group a whole new social circle.

***

October 25th, my 51st birthday. Luckily for us, this day was a very unseasonably hot and sunny autumnal day. In fact, the weather was precisely the same as the beautiful day just

12 short months ago when we had taken Shane to Mersea Island, Essex, where he had spent a fun-filled afternoon playing on the soft sand and in the waters of the chilly North Sea. It was a place that he seemed to love, with its exciting new sounds and aromas and the strange textures of the beach invigorated his senses. Well now it was Sheba's turn to visit the seaside. Just like Shane, she sat contentedly in the back of the car, staring out of her window in wonderment at the passing countryside.

Mersea Island measures just five miles long and two miles wide and is a wildlife haven, with its tidal salt marshes and mudflats.

When on the island I often stop and admire the old Thames barges that have been respectfully and lovingly converted into homes, and to wander off like a child exploring the sea life in the multitude of rock pools.

Anyway back to today's visit, to enable Sheba more freedom to venture away from us and explore at leisure on our walks, I had purchased her a 30-foot horse lunge line, in a lovely shade of purple. Unlike Shane, due to her anti-social behaviour towards other dogs, Sheba is always kept close by my side and never allowed off lead.

We had brought her lunge line with us today, allowing her to swim in the sea if she wanted to – that is if she could swim – and for her to be able to run and play unrestrained on the sand.

Due to it being high tide we had to walk down the narrow wooden boardwalk to the beach, when half-way across something caught Sheba's eye. Her lead tightened as she pulled me towards the water; her head tilted inquisitively from side to side. Just below the surface, two shore crabs were engaged ferociously in combat. One of them was holding a worm; the other was frantically snapping at it trying to steal the tasty morsel. Well it certainly entertained Sheba for a few minutes.

She soon became bored with the spectacle of the fighting crabs, and we continued along the boardwalk towards the coastline. Once on the sand, we made our way towards Monkey Beach. It usually tends to be a bit quieter there. The once green flags of the leaves on the trees that make up the backdrop of the beach had now become seasonally sepia-toned.

I will never forget the look of sheer excitement that engulfed Sheba's face the second that her paws touched the warm, soft sand. At once she began bouncing up and down full of childlike exhilaration. I had never seen anything so hilarious, up and down she leapt, then around and around in circles, then up and down again, she was in her element. We just stood there laughing and watching her before heading off to find a secluded area to sit down. We filled her water bowl with some iced water, and then I took Sheba's tennis ball out of the bag. For 15 minutes we played 'piggy in the middle' with her, then suddenly she stopped, something far more impressive had caught her attention, just as Shane had done. She stood there motionless, panting heavily, her tongue hanging out of the side of her mouth, drool dripping from the end in apparent anticipation. Sheba was now staring intently at the North Sea; it seemed that the waves were beckoning her. She looked up at us, then back to the vast expanse of water.

Shane had taken a small amount of encouragement to get him to go in for a paddle; something instinctively told me that Sheba was going to take the bull by its horns and hurl herself straight in. Without any warning, she started to drag me frantically towards the water's edge. Excitedly she bounded forwards, happily snorting and barking all the way, her hind paws kicking sand up at me as she led the way. She momentarily stopped to look at the seaweed strewn all around and piled up in random tatty heaps, but the waves were beckoning. The shells had now changed, those closest to the shoreline were all fragmented and broken, they gently crunched under our paws and feet as we reached our final destination. With no fear or hesitation Sheba charged straight in, a wave broke and covered her; the immense, unforgiving power of Mother Nature spun her around and knocked her over. Unforgivingly, she was rolled over in the surf. She made a hasty withdrawal and bolted out of the massive swathe of briny water, shook herself down, turned to face her foe and began snapping angrily at the incoming waves and white hissing foam they left in their wake.

The undulating waves were continually rearing up and crashing down onto the beach, each of them violently pounding the sand; the oceanic water they were formed from arrived as a deep aquamarine, upon its retreat it had taken on a dirty golden hue from where it churned up the sand on the shoreline.

Not at all fazed by the battering that she had just received, she ran back in and started hurling and tossing the displaced seaweed that as floating on the surface of the water; she was having the time of her life. Sheba then spied a much bigger prize bobbing about ten feet out. Without any encouragement from me, off she went. Blimey, she was swimming, she was off to try and retrieve a floating lump of driftwood. I bit the bullet and ventured in deeper for a paddle with her – bloody hell the water was cold. Involuntarily my hands turned into fists, as if for some strange reason they may offer protection from the chill of the sea. As beautiful as the British coastline is, the water that surrounds our country will never match the warmth and crystal clear turquoise hues of the Aegean.

How I adore the joys of life's simple pleasures, the calming relaxing rhythm of the lapping of the blue-green waves, breaking on the shingle beach, before they gently roll back out to sea, and the sun reflecting and glistening on their small wavy peaks, way offshore. However, my real guilty pleasure is playing with Sheba in the surf.

After an hour of playing, we dried Sheba off with a soft towel and headed slowly back along the beach to our favourite seafood restaurant.

As with last October, we sat outside overlooking the anchored yachts, bobbing gently in the sea.

Our banquet of a platter containing a variety of freshly caught shellfish was served to us. Sheba joined in on our feast with a small plate of chips. Yes, I know that it's wrong, but she was at the seaside. In fact, if she carried on being a good girl she may even get an ice cream.

When we had finished, we headed to The Victory for a couple of gin and tonics, served with a freeze and a squeeze, and yes, Sheba did have an ice cream.

For some peculiar reason, Sheba didn't stare out of the window on our drive home. Oh that's right, she slept all of the way home. Dreaming about her idyllic day at the seaside, playing in the warm autumn sunshine.

***

Sheba's poor front and hind legs were showing signs of severe muscle deterioration, after the enforced inactivity during her five months of cage rest and recuperation, following her three major operations and a broken leg. Although I had increased her exercise regime, she was now walking at a faster pace, and for longer distances, for as much as her legs would allow, the muscles were not developing as fast as her vet would have liked. Sheba's surgeon, who had performed her life-changing operations, had moved to pastures new on the other side of the world, and we had registered Sheba with a new vet, local to us. For reasons that I will not divulge, we chose not to use the same local veterinary practice that Shane had been registered with.

Sheba's new vet was instantly mesmerised by her charm and resilience to all the horrors she had endured, and treats were always freely given when she visited him. Having read through her case notes, and carrying out a thorough examination, he suggested hydrotherapy, using a National Association of Registered Canine Hydrotherapists practice, as a means of rapid muscle development, with the added benefit of some quality water-based fun time.

Ironically, just the weekend before Sheba's vet had made his suggestion, we had spent a day with one of my cousins, whose own dog, an English Bullmastiff called Lolly, was herself attending regular water treadmill sessions due to a cruciate ligament injury, close to where they live in Southend-On-Sea, Essex.

Having already been told how well the practice that Lolly visited treated their patients, and the vast level of knowledge that all of the therapists had in the field of water-cure physiotherapy, we decided to use their services and book an assessment appointment for Sheba.

Saturday 14th November. We set off at 5 pm to take Sheba on the 38-mile drive to Southend-On-Sea for her first referral visit to the hydrotherapy pool. We couldn't have arranged our first trip on a more pig of a night if we'd tried. The drive was treacherous as thunder, lightning and pebble-like raindrops bombarded us all the way along the M11, M25 then the A127. Although I did find driving in the rain both comforting and therapeutic – the car felt so cosy with the sound of rain pelting down on the thin metal roof. Anyway, I couldn't get above 50 mph for the whole journey, which should have taken us an hour, but due to the dismal conditions ended up taking us an hour and a half. Luckily for Sheba, we arrived on time.

I had already spent time in the run-up to Sheba's appointment researching in depth the many recognised and documented benefits of hydrotherapy. For my happy little lady, I liked the idea that it would offer her a therapeutic, relaxed and hopefully enjoyable workout. Sheba's legs were in theory still recovering from the traumas of invasive surgery, and the controlled swimming in the warm water would enable her muscles to rebuild and be stimulated and exercised without the stress element associated with land-based exercise, that could potentially cause her pain. With a regime of strict water-based activity, and a well-balanced, veterinary-recommended nutritional diet, we would soon get her fighting fit.

As part of Sheba's diet, I had already introduced and started giving her a regular small portion of green-lipped mussels as a form of supplement. This natural product contains high concentrations of omega-3 fatty acids, amino acids, minerals and carbohydrates. I had read that omega-3 fatty acids have anti-inflammatory properties, which for Sheba will help with her joint cell structure and function. A scattering of blueberries, with all of their proven health benefits, were also added every other day to her breakfast.

Upon arrival, we introduced ourselves and Sheba to the three ladies working the late shift; we were led into the small waiting area adjacent to the pool.

Sheba became immediately animated at the new environment she found herself in. Her nose twitching as she frantically sniffed the air, her nostrils flaring, increasing the air-flow towards her three hundred million olfactory receptors which were trying to decipher the unusual aromas all around her. Poolside odours were bombarding her, such as chloramine, a combination of chlorine disinfectant, urine and other canine and human bodily oils and perspiration.

Sheba could also pick up on the sweeter scents of the shampoos that were used when showering the dogs after their swimming sessions, and the freshly brewed pot of coffee sitting on the counter.

After carefully reading through the vet's referral letter, the head hydrotherapist suggested that a gentle swim would be the best plan of action to kick-start the rebuilding of Sheba's wasted muscles.

Before Sheba's session commenced, the therapist explained to us in detail how the session would be constructed. She also told us of the full proven medical benefits, and of the stringent hygiene regime that they adhere too, including the pool's water being sanitised, preventing harmful microbes from growing in it. Cleanliness of the water was a critical factor, the quality continually tested, in busy periods; this could be several times each day. In keeping with stipulated regulations, detailed records of water quality were maintained and logged.

The part that made my ears prick up was when the hydrotherapist said that the temperature of the water would be continuously maintained at a balmy 30 degrees. After the atrocious weather we had just had to battle our way through, a relaxing swim would do me a world of good.

The warmth of the water served two primary purposes. Firstly, and for me the most critical aspect, is that it would provide Sheba with instant relief from any pain that she may be enduring. Secondly, it would keep her muscles relaxed; due to the blood vessels close to the surface of the skin expanding, allowing her an increased range of movement and a lack of stiffness.

Another plan of action the therapist mentioned that she may consider at a later date, and that may prove to be even more beneficial for Sheba's rehabilitation, would be for her to use the 'aquatic treadmill'. This piece of equipment is basically the same as an ordinary treadmill, except that it is housed in a large glass water tank. After Sheba has entered the tank and is relaxed, warm water will slowly be pumped in via a serious of water-jets along the base of the tank, up to a level just below her shoulders. The depth of water will help with weight bearing while exercising, and the therapist will be able to observe Sheba's full range of movements, under the added resistance of the water, through the glass sides of the tank. The speed of the treadmill will be continually monitored and adjusted by the therapist to match her gait.

Finally, the therapist told us that at the end of each session Sheba would be showered and thoroughly dried.

Once every aspect of the session had been covered and fully explained to us, we led Sheba up the small tiled ramp to the water's edge. We had fitted her with a dog floatation aid, which is a small harness-type piece of safety equipment.

"It can be very daunting for them on their first visit. I will get in the pool, and then my assistant will gently encourage Sheba to get in. Be prepared to get wet, in fact, very wet."

The hydrotherapist, wearing her grey wetsuit, climbed into the water.

The pool area, like any indoor public swimming baths, was completely covered in ceramic tiles. Sheba barked, the sound reverberating around the walls. She looked up at me; her demeanour didn't seem fearful, she was unsure, but not afraid. The assistant took the lead from me and began to coax Sheba closer to the water's edge. There was a raised tiled platform in the pool itself, with a gentle slope; this would enable Sheba to make her mind up whether to dive straight in, or saunter down the gradual gradient into the depths of the warm, inviting water. I had positioned myself next to the deeper end of the ramp, and started offering excitable words of encouragement to Sheba. I dipped my hand into the water; it felt so warm. I cupped my hand and splashed Sheba. She sat and tilted her head to one side, water dripping from her nose, staring at first towards me, then into the rippled water, catching a distorted glimpse of her reflection. I was asked to select a toy to try to encourage and coax her to enter the water. I chose a tennis ball. Sheba loves tennis balls, and she had already accumulated a vast collection of them at home.

Slowly she entered the water of her own accord. A couple of weeks earlier she had played and swam in the sea on our visit to Mersea Island, so I was pretty confident that she was a fully-fledged water baby. I threw the ball into the centre of the pool. Eyeing the prize bobbing in the water, she tentatively walked down the ramp, her body immersing slowly, deeper into the water. The floatation aid took over, causing her to float. Instinctively she started moving her front and hind legs. Gracefully she propelled herself through the water towards the ball.

Continued shrills of "Good girl" were excitedly yelled by the four of us. She took to swimming like a duck to water, pardon the pun, round and round the pool she swam, continually making strange, happy little grunting sounds all the time.

After five minutes, Sheba was helped out of the pool for a brief rest period. After a three-minute break, she was led back up to the ramp area. Well that proved to be a complete waste of time; she leapt straight back in, taking us all by surprise. She swam for another five minutes; then, her first swimming session was over. The research that had been commissioned estimated that the resistance produced by the water equates to one minute of swimming equals four minutes of running, approximately one kilometre per minute. Sheba needed to build up her muscles slowly, so she was led out of the pool, very begrudgingly I must add, and down to the shower and drying area.

Sheba looked so cute, with her fur all fluffed after her wash and blow dry, bless her. A follow-up appointment was booked for the following Saturday, and we headed off. One thing we had to ensure when we got home was not to allow Sheba to sleep for a couple of hours, even though she was going to be exhausted from her workout. The reason for this was to prevent her muscles from seizing up, so we had to get her up and walking every 30 minutes.

Over the course of the next six months, Sheba attended hydrotherapy every Saturday, and what a difference it soon made. Within a couple of weeks, we noticed that her energy levels when out walking had increased, and her physical strength? Well, she actually pulled me over, in fact on two separate occasions, and I'm 78 kgs heavier than Sheba!

Her vet commented during her annual health check the following February that he could feel a definite increase in her muscle tone. Her sessions were alternated weekly between swimming and workouts in the hydro-treadmill.

***

December 30th 2016. There was an adorable new little lady in my life. My eldest daughter Kealy had blessed us with a beautiful little granddaughter, Daisy. I really was the luckiest and most contented man in the world, surrounded by my extraordinary, ever-growing family.

***

Saturday 26th November 2017. We were preparing to leave for the annual Halloween party at the dog rescue. I had taken Sheba into the garden to do a wee before we headed off for an evening of drunken frivolity. Gemma had kindly offered to babysit for us. As we were standing in the garden, there was a sudden 'whoosh' followed by the sky becoming illuminated by a multitude of exploding rainbow colours, loud bangs and crackling sounds immediately; the fireworks lit up the velvet dark tranquillity of the night sky. Those sodding, bloody explosives startled Sheba; she cowered then turned to retreat to the safety of our lounge.

I was enjoying the last few pulls on my cigarette as a panic-stricken Sheba started to leave. Just as she reached the top step, she turned back to look at me, as scared as she was Sheba wouldn't desert me, leaving me there alone with the imminent threat and danger of the exploding missiles that were now being fired sporadically into the pitch-black night sky. Gently Sheba grasped the hem of my Grim Reapers gown in her teeth; she then started to try and gently pull me towards the sanctuary of her home. Bless her little heart, even though she was petrified herself, she wouldn't leave me there alone with the fearsome exploding fireworks. I had no option, I had to follow her, discarding the remnants of my cigarette into a flower pot as we made our retreat. That simple, loving little action has never left me; her natural protective instinct took over, putting her fears second, my safety had become her main priority.

***

Something had always puzzled me about Sheba; I just couldn't put my finger on it. I know it sounds crazy, but it was the way that she walked, not due to her disability, but something else, it just totally eluded me. Sheba has a lively and excitable way about her when we're out, entirely different in her mannerisms to other dogs I spend time with and see on our strolls. Shane had never been a street dog; he walked with confidence, he strutted about town almost with an air of arrogance. The answer I had been looking for hit me square in the face one day when I was sitting drinking a jug of local wine at a beachside taverna on the Greek island of Kefalonia, during our two-week summer holiday in August 2018. We had regularly fed and given fresh water to a multitude of stray cats and dogs during our break, but sitting watching two dogs one day, I realised that they walked just like Sheba. The way the two dogs continuously looked for food, a constant fox-like prowl in the way they darted towards any potential source of nourishment, their constant hunt, it is precisely how Sheba is on her walks.

It is tough to put into words, but if you have an ex-street dog yourself, you will know exactly what I mean.

They walk with a constant prowl, almost like when you watch a wildlife documentary showing big cats stalking their prey. They seem to take far less visual notice of their surroundings, but spend their time looking in every hedge, the space between and beneath parked cars, doorways, bins or any other crevice or cavity they should happen to come across as a potential source of food. Their prey drive is very high – cats, wild birds, rabbits or squirrels, they are all possible sources of nourishment. Well, they would be if our ex-stray dogs were given a chance to catch them. Ex-street dogs constantly crave and try to scavenge; their instincts have made them extremely defensive, especially if they think they have found a meal or even place of shelter or sanctuary to hold up in, in any way, shape or form.

While we were on our holiday in August 2018, Sheba had spent two weeks enjoying her own summer vacation at the boarding kennels where Mutts in Distress is based. During her break, Sheba had taken it upon herself to try and help and offer comfort to a poor little dog that had been rescued from death row. She had only recently arrived in the UK after being brought over from a hell on earth Spanish Killing Station. Mutts had given her a very fitting name – Hope.

Hope now lives her life in safety, waiting patiently for a loving home of her own, but she remains petrified. The trouble is we never know what horrors these poor little souls have been through in their lives. Sheba must have sensed the poor little dog's fears, and spent the time that she should have been enjoying herself running and frolicking in the paddock lovingly sitting outside of Hope's kennel. It was as if she was offering protection and comfort, like a little guardian angel watching over Hope. Sheba had at long last made a friend. The kennel maids told us that it was as if Sheba was trying to reassure the dear little dog that everything would be all right and that one day she too would have a home and loving family to call her own.

The one thing, no I'll start that sentence again; one of the many things that amazed me about Sheba from the very first day that she came to live with us was her cleanliness. Sheba had begun her life as a street dog living on the begrimed streets of Sofia, Bulgaria. Depending on whether you believe the Bulgarian president's press release of 6,000 strays in Sofia, or the on-the-ground charities working tirelessly to save as many of the street dogs as possible, estimates put the figure at closer to 60,000, Sheba had once been one of them. Sheba had never known the comfort of a warm house until she joined us, she had had no training, yet she has never once soiled or urinated in our house. In fact, she doesn't even like going in our, or should I say her, garden. How could this be? I wholeheartedly expected to have to 'teach an old dog new tricks' with regards to house training, but no, amazingly

Sheba is a fully house trained street dog. I listen with interest to many dog owners telling me about the problems they have encountered trying to house train their puppies; in fact, some people I know talk of their despair at their older dogs who never grasped using the garden to do their business, and still relieve themselves indoors. Yet Sheba has never once had a mishap in our home, bless her little heart.

Another thing is that Sheba has the full run of our home, absolutely nowhere is off limits to her, yet she has never once touched, played with or damaged a single item in our house that hasn't been given to her directly as a toy for her to play with.

Anyway, I had told you previously in the book how I would allow Shane to dictate the route for the first hour of his evening's walk; then I would do an hour's intense obedience training with him. Well I have had to construct Sheba's walks entirely differently. Her daily exercise routine is broken down into short and frequent strolls, the duration is entirely dependent upon the weather conditions. The summer and winter temperature extremes can be excruciatingly painful for her as the metal rods run directly under a fragile, thin layer of skin, which offers absolutely no protection or insulation for the metal whatsoever. The warmth of the summer causes the rods to expand, with the heat transferred down the screws, straight into the centre of her bones. Sheba tries as best as she can to cool her legs down by licking them, almost in the same way as a kangaroo does. Kangaroos lick their forearms until the fur is soaking wet. As the saliva evaporates, it quickly cools down their body temperature. Sadly, on the other extreme for Sheba, the icy cold winter months prove just as problematic. During this time, the cold penetrates deep into her bones through the screws. I have tried many products to try and wrap her legs in to keep her natural body heat in and the cold out, but up until now nothing has proven successful. I also have to be very mindful when trying to warm her legs up; this is something that has to be done very gradually, avoiding the potential painful shock Sheba would endure if I were to allow the rods to heat up too quickly.

Sorry, lost track, back to dictating the walk part I had initially started writing about. So one evening, while we were out for a stroll, Sheba, for no apparent reason, decided that she wanted to head home. She had initially stopped to check a wee-mail and was sniffing around a lamp post just behind me. Suddenly I felt two tugs on the nylon handle loop of her leash and looked back. Surprisingly Sheba had her end of the lead in her mouth, and she stood there looking up at me. While still firmly grasping the lead, she tugged it again, twice, turning to walk away as she did so. I was dumbfounded, and intrigued, so obligingly I followed her. Goodness knows how, but Sheba actually led me all the way back home, stopping at each corner to get her bearings, then again tugging at the lead before leading the way. She had actually learnt how I use the check collar when we were at school and had applied it in the exact same manner, two gentle tugs. The only difference was that she didn't give me a 'heel' command. Bloody hell, what a smart little girl Sheba really is.

***

I know that there's a myth that dogs don't feel pain like humans do. The reality is that they don't show their discomfort as we do. This is partly the result of a legacy from their evolutionary origins as hunting predators. Canines have inherited an instinct to hide any pain that is caused by injuries or infirmity. In the wild, an animal that is injured or infirm is vulnerable to attack, and there is a survival advantage to act like nothing is wrong even when something most definitely is. Sheba's pain threshold is something else. I can only assume that this must be down to the agony she has endured during her months of surgery, and before that, the persistent pain she suffered having to walk on her poorly deformed legs, and not down to the way she has evolved from her ancestors.

I can remember being on one of our Sunday morning countryside strolls; Sheba was on her 30-foot lunge line. She was playing in the newly growing crops and rummaging in the hedgerows; at any point, she was no more than ten feet away from me. Sheba had been sniffing around an old disused rabbit hole close to a hawthorn tree when she stopped and looked over at me. She sat down, raised her left paw, not once taking her eyes off me. I walked over to her and could see a twig stuck to the bottom of her pad. Sheba still had her eyes firmly fixed on me. I held her paw and tried to brush it off of her, but it was stuck firm. On closer inspection, I could see that it was a small sprig that had fallen from the hawthorn tree, about 12 inches long and covered in sharp dagger-like thorns. One of these had became impaled in Sheba's pad, and looking at the other spines on the twig, I guessed that it must have penetrated about half an inch. I calmly reassured Sheba, and gently pulled the small woody spike from her pad. Not once did she flinch, but if you have ever encountered and engaged in combat with one of these vicious trees, then you will be more than aware how ferocious their natural defence mechanisms can be. I always carry antibacterial gel, so I applied a small amount to the puncture wound on Sheba's paw, rolled a fag and sat with her for ten minutes to allow the pain to subside.

Absolutely nothing about Sheba surprises me anymore, but two things are for sure, she continually amazes and inspires me.

Sheba will never replace Shane, I try my damnedest not to compare her to him, but sadly inevitably I do.

CHAPTER FIFTEEN

Sky

This is my inheritance
My will and last testament ...

2019 had not started well for us. Just four weeks in and our worlds had been turned upside down by a series of unfortunate and distressing events. Again, several times I had found myself turning to Sheba for solace, and without fail she had loyally come to my rescue.

Friday 25th January 2019. I was sitting alone reminiscing about happier times; I poured myself a single malt whisky, switched on my mobile and started to peruse through the Mutts in Distress social media page. I found myself drawn to a recent post by one of the members of staff:

"Sky is just about to arrive at Mutts. He's at the gate."

It's 9.45 at night, and for reasons that I couldn't explain I was intrigued and wanted to find out more about Sky.

Sheba was lying on the floor next to me on her soft day bed with its faux fur cover, surrounded by a selection of her treasured toys. Earlier she had eaten one of her favourite meals, which consisted of two boiled eggs, a tin of sardines in vegetable oil, and a handful of fresh blueberries, two joint supplement tablets and half a teaspoon of manuka honey.

During her evening walk, we had stopped off at a pub and I had enjoyed a pint or two of real ale sitting next to the roaring open log fire.

I looked at the photos, as they were continually uploading, of Sky's arrival. What a handsome fellow he was, but it was not just his handsome features, it was his eyes, the gateway to his soul. Sky had such kind, forgiving eyes. Again, I looked down at Sheba. She had everything that her little heart could desire, and Sky, that poor little man, had lost everything.

I had an early start in the morning; I finished off my whisky, turned off the lights and headed up to bed, as per usual carrying Sheba in my arms. She got her regular goodnight kiss; I took a shower then tried to settle down.

For reasons that to this day I can't explain, all I could think about was Sky. There was something extra special about him; to me, he was a spiritual enigma, it was as if he had been sent to help Sheba get me through the emotional traumas that were tormenting me.

At about three in the morning, I could take no more and I had to give in. I got up and headed downstairs with my laptop. I made myself a cup of tea and set about reloading the Mutts social media page.

Sky's story was heart-wrenching and read:

Sky, the first Spanish rescue of 2019 and what a beauty he is! Sky was found tied to the gates of the Ourense pound in Spain, abandoned by his owner like so much rubbish. Sky is a 6-year-old beautiful, gentle GSD who will follow the volunteers for affection and cuddles. Sky is at risk from the other dogs as he is so sweet and submissive, and as he had a foster offer in the UK, he was moved from the common pound away from the other dogs. Unfortunately, this fell through, and Sky can now easily go back to where he will once again be in danger. That is until the wonderful people at Mutts stepped up and offered to take and rehome this gorgeous boy who the volunteers say is absolutely fabulous. He will be at Mutts on 24/1/19. Thank you so much, Mutts.

This blessed little soul had found himself, through no fault of his own, tied to the gates of a dog pound, which local dog rescue volunteers report operated as nothing more than an inhumane Killing Station.

I couldn't stop staring at the photographs of Sky; I just had to meet him.

Over the last few weeks, Sheba had changed; in fact, we had come to firmly believe that, beyond all belief, she may now be ready to accept a companion in her life.

Her fear of other dogs originates from the horrors she endured roaming the streets of Sofia, Bulgaria, as an abandoned, stray street dog. Her aggressive behaviour is her defence mechanism; in fact, she had been attacked while out with me, due to irresponsible dog owners, but at school, she seemed far more accepting of her classmates, her own trusted little pack.

Would she accept Sky? I was shattered and I needed to get my head down; I'd broach the subject with Toni when I got home from work that night, but beforehand I would have a quiet chat with Pat about the possibilities of us being allowed to give Sky the loving home he so rightly deserved. That was if Sheba would permit us.

***

Saturday proved to be a manic day for me at work in Greenwich, but I was now home, well not home in the sense of the word, I was sitting in the 18th century Fox Inn pub with Toni.

I took a huge gulp of my beer for Dutch courage; it was time for me to raise the subject of Sky.

"Don't know if you've seen the post on the Mutts page about Sky?"

"No, I haven't been online today, who is he/she?"

"A GSD, arrived last night from Spain, he's had an absolutely horrific time of it."

I reached into the breast pocket of my jacket and took out my mobile. The signal in the pub was terrible, so I logged onto their Wi-Fi. I handed Toni my phone, already loaded with the pictures of Sky prior to him being rescued from the pound in Ourense, Spain.

"Wow, he's beautiful. Okay, where exactly is this leading?"

"I've got to come clean, I've spoken to Pat and she fully agrees that Sheba is ready for a partner. Can we take her over tomorrow to introduce her to him, please?"

"Well, there's certainly no harm in us trying. Give Pat a ring in the morning and see if she is free tomorrow afternoon."

"I already have, we're meeting up at one o'clock. Do you want another drink?"

Toni laughed as I made a strategic, quick retreat, and headed to the safety of the bar to get her a Bacardi and Coke, with a freeze but no squeeze.

At 1 pm on Sunday, we nervously pulled into Mutts in Distress. Sheba started bouncing excitedly around on the back seat of our car, she relished her visits to the sanctuary. Today was different; I had come armed with her Italian basket muzzle, a piece of kit that she hadn't worn for over three years. I rang Pat to let her know we had arrived and were ready to introduce Sheba to Sky.

One of the kennel maids was asked to sit in our car with Sheba while Toni and I are led off for our first introduction with Sky. What a stunner he was, and so loving, the greeting we were each given by this beautiful boy was very humbling, precisely the same as those given to us by both Shane and Sheba when we first met them. We spent a few minutes making a huge, loving fuss of him before he was led outside to meet Sheba. This was the part I was dreading. If she refused to accept him, there was no way we would be able to consider adopting him.

Sheba is both very defensive and possessive when it comes to me, so it was deemed best to take me out of the equation for the first introduction. Pat took Sky's lead and headed off towards the main gate that led out onto New Barn Lane. The kennel maid who had been sitting with Sheba lifted her out of the car and led her towards the reception area; at this point, she was not wearing her muzzle, Sheba that is not the kennel maid.

Toni and I climbed into our car to observe; both of us had everything crossed. Pat raised her arm and started to walk towards us with Sky, Sheba was led towards him. As they got close, firm 'leave it and watch me' commands were given. The two dogs passed each other, just barely throwing each other inquisitive passing glances.

For the next 15 minutes, this exercise was continued, gradually the pace that they were walking at decreased, additionally with every pass, the dogs were manoeuvred closer to one another, my heart was racing. With no warning on the final pass, Pat stopped Sky directly in front of Sheba, who had already been given a 'Sit' command.

The two dogs remained in close proximity to one another for several minutes, continually staring and checking each other out, but miraculously, Sheba showed no signs of fear or aggression towards the large dog right in front of her. They both remained in silence, staring at each other, continually sniffing the air, picking up on each other's unique scents.

"Right Toni and Paul, now it's your turn." Pat beckoned us from our car.

"Paul you walk Sheba, Toni you take control of Sky."

We looked at each other, right it was now or never. I called Sheba to heel and set off towards the reception area; Toni turned and led Sky towards the hay barn.

Pat raised her right arm and slowly Toni and I walked towards each other with our respective dogs. As we got close, I started commanding Sheba to 'watch me and leave it'.

So as not to set Sheba up to fail we initially passed with a ten-foot gap between us, the dogs positioned on the outside.

It went perfectly. We turned and repeated the exercise, gradually moving ever closer to each other on each pass. For the next ten minutes we continued; on the final pass we stopped and stood next to one another.

"Right, Paul turn with Sheba and now walk next to Toni and Sky."

It all went perfectly, thank goodness.

Pat and her assistant walked over and took control of the pups.

Sky was led off towards a van, the rear doors were already open, inside were three large dog transportation cages. He was ushered to the cage at the rear of the van, the heavy-duty wire door was opened, and Sky obligingly hopped up. As soon as the enclosure was secured, Sheba was called for.

She was led around the side and lifted into another one of the cages. The only thing that now separated Sheba and Sky was the thick gauge wire that the enclosures were manufactured from. Sheba initially showed interest in the unknown dog who was now right next to her, a few random barks, but nothing excessive. This, to be honest, was not what I was expecting at all. Eventually, she settled down; completely unfazed by Sky's presence, she happily lay down; in fact, the little madam turned her back on him.

"Right, time for a cup of tea," said Pat.

I was intrigued.

"What happens now?"

"We leave them to get on with it. Let them become acquainted and happy in each other's company. We are going to ignore them for an hour or so. They can't harm one another. Believe me, this will work; we will continue using this technique every day until Sheba is ready for the next stage."

They remained in their separate cages for two hours, in silence I hasten to add, before Sky was returned to his kennel and we headed for home with Sheba. Plans were made for me to drop her off mid-day the following day to repeat the exercise.

Monday 28th January. As planned, I dropped Sheba back at the rescue, and was asked to leave; the staff now had a new plan of action to initiate. Nothing on earth could have prepared me for the series of events that were to unfold later on that afternoon.

3.30 pm, I was popping out to buy Toni a hot chocolate from a fast food drive-thru before picking her up from work, and then both of us heading back to the rescue to check on the progress of Sheba and Sky.

My mobile was on charge in my car as I was driving, and all I could hear was a series of notification alerts. Blimey, someone was eager to contact me. Then my phone started to ring. I glanced down and saw Pat's name on the screen. I accepted the call on the hands-free kit.

"Hello mate, is everything okay?"

"Have you seen the photos I've sent you?"

"No, sorry mate, I'm driving; we'll be with you in about 20 minutes."

"Well pull over and stop, you have to look at the photos."

"Is everything okay?"

"Look for yourself."

I was worried about what I was about to see. Pat's voice was full of emotion, had something terrible happened and she couldn't bring herself to tell me? Pat disconnected the call and I immediately pulled off the road, switched off the engine and warily picked up my phone.

About 20 messages from Pat were waiting for me to open on a private chat app. I started to open them. Slowly the pixelated images turned into crystal clear photos of Sheba and Sky, lying next to one another in a single cage. Admittedly she was now wearing her muzzle, but she was physically lying next to, and her body was touching, another dog's body.

My eyes filled with tears; had at long last Sheba found herself a companion?

I switched the engine on, composed myself, collected Toni's hot beverage then headed to her school; luckily for once, she had got out on time that day.

"Look at the photos on my phone."

Toni unlocked the screen and started to look through the images that had been sent to me.

"Is that Sheba?"

She was as surprised as I was, and just as I had been, she was soon also reduced to a blubbering wreck.

As we were approaching the rescue, Toni rang Pat, but she was already excitedly waiting for us at the gates. We pulled up, got out and hugged one another. There were no words to explain how we were all feeling, I could sit and try and write a whole list of emotions, but none would be strong enough to convey how I felt at that precise moment.

When we first met Sheba four years ago back in April 2015, her passport stated that she was three years old, but how did they know? She was a pitiful, fearful ex-street dog, one of the thousands who roam the streets of Sofia. She may have been older, but the consensus of the vets who helped her was that she was probably younger. I know nothing of her past, for reasons unknown the rescue team in Bulgaria refused to divulge anything to me, but one thing is for sure, Sheba endured pain and suffering inflicted by the teeth and claws of many of the feral dogs she encountered, she may have suffered even worse when she was in season. Sheba had had to learn to defend herself; she had to fight to live for pity's sake, she was severely disabled, how on earth did she ever survive that hell? She has every right to be fearful of other dogs, I have tried to teach her that dogs are kind, then we encounter an idiot dog walker who allows their dog to attack her, she can raise her middle claw at me, call me a liar and tell me to get stuffed, she'll handle things her own way.

However, now she may at long last have a companion, there is a long way to go, but Sky is unique, he radiates inner calm, beauty and kindness, and if any dog can tame Sheba, it's Sky.

Slowly we walked towards the van that Sheba and Sky were lying in. Sheba looked up at us; her tail wagged with excitement, Sky looked at Sheba, then at us, his tail started to wag too. However, there was something strange, Sheba had remained lying down, snuggled up against Sky, why hadn't she leapt up to greet us like she always did when we visited her during her months of corrective surgery? Had Sky taken over my role?

"Right, time to move on to the next stage. To be honest, we are days, if not a week ahead of schedule. We will take them into the enclosed paddock and let them play."

Pat seemed so nonchalant as she walked over and unlocked the cage. Sky leapt out, I looked at Toni, shrugged my shoulders and walked over and lifted Sheba out.

Sky and Pat entered the enclosed area, next to the rescue donkeys paddock; we walked over and joined them, closing the secure metal gate behind us.

We awaited Pat's next instructions.

The ground underfoot was sodden; a muddy quagmire as all that remained where lush green grass once grew, it was about to become even more churned up.

Sky had been released from his lead and was charging about, he continually looked over at Sheba, barking at her, enticing her to chase him and play.

Sheba was chomping at the bit and frantically trying to rip her muzzle off. Luckily for Sky it remained firmly in place.

"Let her off her lead; she can't hurt him with her 'nose bag' on, anyway, she doesn't want to hurt him. Poor little thing won't be able to catch him anyway."

I looked at Toni. I was scared to unclip Sheba's lead, what if she should…

"Go on, release her; let her be a dog."

Sod it, Pat was right, Sheba couldn't hurt Sky. I closed my eyes and released the clip. She was off, she charged down the muddy field barking as loudly as she could. Sky let her get to within a few feet, then dodged past her and ran. Sheba turned and gave chase, she'd never catch him. Bloody hell, Sky was fast, I'd never seen a dog run so fast.

In the four years Sheba had lived with us, I had never seen her run like this before. How on earth did she manage to hurtle about so fast, with her front leg joints fused in a straight formation by the titanium rods?

I looked at Toni. There was nothing we could say, we turned back and continued to watch the beautiful sight unfolding of the two, no, our two, German Shepherds tearing around the field, having the time of their lives.

Frequently Sheba would become totally out of puff, or momentarily lose interest in chasing Sky, when a football would catch her eye. When this happened, he would stand staring at her, then he'd drop to the ground and roll over onto his back; somehow he'd always manage to plonk himself down in a muddy puddle. He had soon deduced that by lying down, in the most vulnerable position there is for a dog, with his belly and private boy bits exposed, ludicrously and aimlessly scratching at the air with his paws, that Sheba would soon become interested. She couldn't resist the opportunity to attack, with him lying there doing his Pilates. Over she would charge, leap onto him, and nuzzle her face into his belly, snarling all the while. Once he had her back where he wanted her he would rollover, sending her flying; consequently, this would annoy her, she'd scramble back up onto her paws, shake herself down, bark and growl at him, then the chase was back on again, clumps of grass sent flying as their claws ripped into the turf.

We had to ensure that Sky knew his name, bless him. We will never know the name that he had answered to for the first 18 months of his life in Spain. I repeatedly called him, with an excited and over-animated voice, within 30 minutes he had got it and was responding instantly, looking at me and running to wherever I would be standing in the paddock.

It was approaching 4 pm, and the light was rapidly fading. In fact, it was almost pitch black; the late afternoon air had turned bitterly cold.

"Right, I think we'll call it a day. Tomorrow we will meet up again and do the same, before moving onto the next stage."

Curiosity got the better of me.

"So what's the next stage then?"

I was intrigued and needed to know what was in store for us, but my question remained unanswered. Time would undoubtedly tell…

I called Sheba in to heel, Sky followed, and he presented himself in a lovely straight sit directly in front of me. Sheba glared at him; I could almost imagine her calling him a 'smart arse'.

The two pups were shattered, misty clouds of condensation billowed from their panting mouths.

I could no longer feel my feet and my hands were frozen. Although I was fully aware that we needed to keep the momentum flowing, deep down I was selfishly relieved that the lesson was over.

We said our goodbyes, allowing Sheba to have a private moment with her new companion. She snuggled up against Sky, he responded by licking her right ear.

Before we left, Pat handed us a blanket from Sky's kennel.

"Let Sheba sleep with it, and leave it with her throughout the day; it's impregnated with his scent, we need to work on building a continuous bond between them. By her having something with his scent on, she will have a constant reminder of him when they are not together."

This was precisely what we had done when Shane first moved in with us, and our family had taken us to Paris. I had left a t-shirt that I had worn with our neighbour.

Hopefully, my t-shirt hadn't stank as bad as the pungent blanket we had just been given; it reeked bloody awful. To be honest, Sky stank as well. Mind you, what do you expect, what with the poor little sod being cooped up for a couple of days in the back of the vehicle that brought him over to England, and the days he had endured in the vile, hell hole Killing Station in Spain. Sheba was such a clean dog, and if Sky was going to have any chance of becoming her beau, then he was seriously going to have to work on his personal hygiene.

A thought sprung to mind on our drive home. I absolutely detested the sight of Sheba's muzzle; it looked cumbersome, in fact with it strapped to her face she looked like a hairy version of Hannibal the Cannibal. First thing in the morning I was heading to the pet store, there must be something gentler and less obtrusive available that will prevent her from inadvertently hurting Sky.

I opted for a black mesh muzzle. The accompanying gumpf sounds perfect, it was both soft and strong, and it would allow Sheba to be able to drink, breathe and pant normally, which in turn would reduce any unnecessary stress that she may be feeling during her intense socialising lessons being in such close proximity to another dog.

We had to add 'Sky' to Sheba's repertoire.

"Sky, where is he? Sky is a good boy. Sky is your pup."

Over and over we'd say his name; when we did Sheba's head would tilt from side to side and her tail would wag, other times she'd retrieve his blanket and snuggle into it. Clever girl, she knew exactly what we were saying to her.

Late Tuesday afternoon. We pulled into Mutts; Toni sat in the car with Sheba while I went and let the kennel maids know we were here. Sky had already been in the paddock for 15 minutes, charging about like a raving lunatic. I returned to our car and lifted Sheba out and fixed her new muzzle in place, and then we led her to the paddock.

Sky as the far end rolling about on the damp churned up grass; he sensed our arrival, he leapt up and stared in our direction, with his tail wagging in anticipation.

"Sky, come on mate Sheba's here."

I called to him; he excitedly bounded towards us and circled frantically on the other side of the heavy-duty wire gate, now and then he stopped and pawed at the wire.

We encouraged him to move back and slid the clasp across; I had to wedge myself in the small opening to stop him from escaping. Toni was holding Sheba's lead; she rose onto her hind legs. I grabbed Sky's collar and moved him away to enable Toni and Sheba to enter. As soon as they were in, Toni secured the gate.

"Shall I let her go?"

"Yup, unclip her lead and let them play kiss chase."

As soon as she heard the click of the spring lock on her lead, she was off. Sky turned and ran with Sheba in hot pursuit.

For 15 minutes they hurtled around the muddy paddock. Sheba had devised a cunning plan to try and catch him. She poised herself and waited halfway, and tried to head him off, but he was far too fast, he swerved past her. In fact, Sky taunted her by getting as close as he dared, every time she lunged at him he bolted off. Despite her best endeavours, Sheba never managed to catch Sky once.

Pat arrived.

"How are they getting on?"

"They're having a whale of a time mate, look at them go."

"Right, Paul call them both in."

Without questioning Pat, I called Sheba and Sky to heel, they stopped running and slowly headed back towards me; amazingly they walked side by side, taking no notice of one another. Pat handed me Sky's lead; I took Sheba's out of my jacket pocket.

I gave two firm commands.

"Sheba sit, Sky sit."

Bless their hearts, they both followed my instructions and sat in front of me, panting heavily, two misty clouds forming as the warm moisture in their breath condensed into tiny droplets of water.

Sky raised his head as I affixed his lead to his collar.

"Right I'll take Sky in my car; you take Sheba."

I looked at Toni and shrugged my shoulders.

"Where are we going?"

"To your house."

So this was obviously the 'next stage'. No wonder we hadn't been given a heads up, I probably wouldn't have turned up. There was no way on earth that Sheba was ready to let a strange dog in her home, even Sky.

"Listen, don't let her pick up on your nervousness, she'll be fine. We'll keep her nose bag on her; she can't hurt him; Sky hasn't got a bad bone in his body. I didn't think in a million years we'd reach this stage in three days, she's desperate for a companion so calm down and let her enjoy the moment."

Despite our best efforts, in our car on the ten-minute drive back to ours, the atmosphere had a definite nervous air about it to say the very least.

Our two-car convoy pulled up outside our house, we got out and carried Sheba indoors. Continually she looked back at Pat's car. I bet she knew that Sky was in there. We secured the wooden dog gate, Sheba sat staring out of the front door, her tail started to wag, wafting small clumps of fur across the tiled floor. Then he appeared. Sheba started to bark as Sky strutted into our, sorry, his home. As soon as the front door was closed, and the security chain engaged, Pat unclipped his lead from his collar. Sheba, still wearing her mesh muzzle, leapt up, her front paws on the top of the gate, and her tail wagging.

"Welcome to your home mate."

There was no sign of aggression from Sheba, so I opened the gate. She ran to Sky and nuzzled against him, then the pair of them turned and ran past us together into the lounge. Sky headed straight for the back door; he stood there looking out into the darkness and started to whine.

"What's up, mate?"

"It's all new to him, Paul; he seems overwhelmed."

No he wasn't, he needed a poop, and we had all misread his request, so he walked off, squatted, and deposited a colossal lump straight on the kitchen floor. Sheba had lived with us for four years and never once urinated or soiled herself indoors; now she stood looking both appalled and disgusted at what her pup had done. Toni cleared up the mess; Sky relieved that his bowels were now empty, started exploring his new home.

Sheba was totally unfazed and left him to it, in fact she went and lay down on her day bed in the lounge.

Pat sat down on the floor next to her while Toni put on the kettle to make us all a cup of tea and she cut some generous slices of chocolate cake. Sky had joined her in the kitchen; he sat down close to her side, watching her every move.

"This is the kitchen, this is a knife, and this is cake, but it has chocolate in it so sorry Sky you can't have any. I'm just making three cups of tea, and then we will sit and have a chat."

While Toni was giving Sky a running commentary, he sat faithfully by her side, looking lovingly up at her; although bewildered by what she was saying to him, he hung lovingly onto every word that flowed from her mouth.

Sky joined us in the lounge; he looked down at where Sheba was lying, then over at me. Okay mate, I got the hint. I went upstairs and got him a blanket, which I laid on the floor for him. He plonked himself down, with his chin resting on the floor between his two front paws; his ears were erect and scanning every strange new sound. Without moving his head, his beautiful brown eyes scoured the room; the bridge above his brow rising and twitching as he took in the strange new surroundings, his new home.

The five of us sat chatting in the lounge, drinking tea and eating cake, until about 10 pm. We all had early starts in the morning, so decided to call it a night. More to the point, it had been a hugely successful night. Both pups had remained on their respective beds, chucking the odd glance here and there at each other, Sheba occasionally tried to tear off her muzzle, but it was too early to risk exposing Sky to the ferocity of her fangs just yet.

Before Sky was taken back to Mutts, Pat asked for a soft toy or blanket of Sheba's. Toni went up to our bedroom and selected the soft pink woollen blanket that Gemma had brought Sheba for Christmas that we used as a top cover on her bed.

We were later told that Sky would cuddle and nuzzle into Sheba's blanket as he lay in his kennel; it became his 'comfort blanket'. Like a prisoner marking their cell wall with tally marks, counting down the days to their eventual release, Sheba's blanket gave him a sense of hope. Maybe he knew that his release from the rescue sanctuary was imminent and that all the visits to our home were leading up to the moment when he would finally move into his furever home with us.

***

Sunday 3rd February. Sheba and Sky have continued meeting up both at our home and in the Mutts paddock. This day Sheba was going to be put to the ultimate test. A group of friends, all blessed with 'non-reactive' dogs, had agreed to rally round and were joining us at the paddock. Sheba, wearing her muzzle and off lead, would be introduced slowly to them all. She would not be able to harm them, and today was going to show her at long last that she doesn't have to be either scared or defensive when in the company of a pack of dogs.

Sheba and Sky were already happily playing kiss chase together when one by one the other dogs started to arrive. Their handlers were asked to remain on the other side of the fence with their dogs. Sheba knew they were there, but appeared to be uninterested in any of them; she only had eyes for Sky.

Pat stood guard at the metal gate, and Toni and I were throwing balls, distracting Sheba as best we could as the first dog was let into the paddock with its handler. Sheba stopped chasing a football and stared at the beagle, who let out a loud baying bark, almost as if it was yodelling. The beagle run towards Sheba, Sky didn't want to be left out of the game and charged full speed towards the approaching dog. He cut her off in her tracks, and they stopped and stood staring at one another; they sniffed each other's nether regions, then turned and ran off together. Unfazed, and uninterested by their shenanigans, Sheba continued playing with her football. I looked over at Toni, then at Pat. She was beaming and gave me the thumbs up. An English Bull Terrier cross was the next doggy to join in. She was initially reluctant to leave her handler's side, but eventually ventured off alone to join in with the other dogs running about.

Sky led his newly formed little pack over to where we were standing. Sheba looked at us, and she slowly walked over to join us. Sky sidled up to her as if he was putting a protective, comforting arm around her shoulders. The other dogs moved in closer, Sheba didn't react; I was left gobsmacked as she moved closer and sniffed them. Bless her heart, she had now almost become a non-aggressive social dog, one week's intense work and the results had been miraculous.

The mood was euphoric as the assembled handlers stood watching and taking photos. The gate was opened, and a third German Shepherd joined in with the pack. In all, there were now five dogs happy in each other's company, and no signs of fear or aggression from Sheba. Eventually, six other dogs joined in, we remained in the paddock for two hours, and not once did Sheba rear up or attempt to attack any of them as they dispersed around the small field, either tearing about chasing one another, or retrieving balls and toys.

It was a bitterly cold winter's afternoon, despite our fruitless efforts to warm ourselves by stomping our feet, blowing into our cupped hands and drinking copious cups of tea, we were all frozen. Our cheeks and noses were reddening as our bodies tried in vain to fend off the chilly wind that was blowing. We decided to call it an afternoon; luckily the central heating was on at home because along with Sky we were heading back to ours for a couple of hours.

Sky strutted into our house, he headed straight to the water bowl, had a drink, then cocked his right hind leg. The dirty little sod peed up the wall. Toni looked at Pat, who was trying her best to stop herself from laughing.

"He's marking his territory."

"Oh, is he indeed, we'll be having none of that matey."

I rustled up a homemade vegetarian lasagne; lentils were now playing a more significant part in our diets. Sheba and Sky remained in the lounge as the three of us sat down to eat. Sky inquisitively popped his nose into our dining area, Toni looked at him.

"Go lie on your bed Sky, good boy."

He turned and plonked himself down, with a grumble. But amazingly he was already following our commands; we just needed to work on him peeing in the house now.

Over the next four weeks we continued with Sheba's extensive socialising training. Every Sunday we would meet up with the other dogs who were very kindly helping us. The evenings were spent alternating between going over to the paddock to allow Sheba and Sky to play, and him visiting our house, his new home. He only had one more little accident;

he cocked his leg up Toni's new fridge freezer, but to date he has never soiled or wet himself indoors again.

When indoors waiting for him to visit, the mere mention of his name would get Sheba excited; she'd leap up with her tail wagging, while making a deep, grumbling sound that she somehow managed to combine with a high-pitched, squeal-like bark. Her behaviour was exactly the same as when we said the 'S' word; she was cherishing every single moment that she spent with him.

***

Sunday 3rd March. After yet another very successful socialising session I looked down at Sheba. There was something different about her demeanour that day, but I couldn't put my finger on it. She was nuzzling into Sky more than ever; her little tongue poked through the front of her mesh muzzle as she tried to lick him. Then it dawned on me, deep down I knew that she was ready. I looked at Toni and Pat and took a breath before announcing:

"I think she is ready for me to take her muzzle off. She doesn't want to hurt Sky; she loves him."

I was sure that I heard two huge nervous gulps as Toni and Pat tried to comprehend my sudden crazy suggestion. Obviously, it was usually me who followed Pat's teaching, she was without doubt the expert, but on this occasion, I was taking the lead. I knew my Sheba, and I knew that she was ready; I was more than confident that she wouldn't let herself, or us down, the last five weeks had been leading up to this very moment. There was only one step left after this on the current journey that we had undertaken with her.

"If you're sure, then we'll do it. Let me get a bucket with some water in it, just in case. If she does go for him, then one of us will have to grab the bucket and chuck the water at her. I know it sounds harsh, but it won't hurt her, the shock will cause her to back away."

I was not too fond of the thought of having to do it, but just in case I had misread her and she panics, then at least using the water would give Sky a chance of running.

I knelt and grasped Sheba's collar with my left hand; with my right, I unclipped the plastic buckle that secured her muzzle. She let out a gaping yawn as if to exercise her jaw after its incarceration, she licked her lips and sat. Sky was sniffing the sodden ground a few yards away, he looked at Sheba and slowly walked over, his head lowered as if in a show of respect. Did he sense what was happening? He was not his usual boisterous little loutish self, the playful dog we had grown to know, and he seemed to know that his imminent release from the rescue sanctuary depended on what happened over the next 30 minutes or so.

"Good girl, well done Sheba, let Sky come closer, good girl, good pup."

While whispering gentle words of encouragement I was continually stroking Sheba's neck, her gaze alternating between looking at me and then adoringly at Sky. Again she licked her lips, only now followed by the familiar slurping sound that I know she makes when she is content. Sky was now sniffing her neck; she looked at him, her little tongue popped out, she moved her head slowly towards him.

"Let go of her collar Paul; she won't hurt him, she's completely at ease and happy in his company."

Slowly I slid my fingers from beneath her collar, she

shook herself. Sky initially took a step back. Sheba looked at him then rose from her sitting position, she walked the few paces towards him, he turned and off they walked, like an old married couple out on a Sunday stroll, shoulder to shoulder without a care in the world.

Pat looked over at Toni and me; she had tears in her eyes.

"My work is done."

Never did we ever think we'd see this day, this beautiful little Spanish dog, who had been saved just in the nick of time from death's door just a couple of months earlier, had brought out a side in Sheba that we had always hoped was there. Her maternal instincts were naturally inducing her to care for the, sorry her, 18-month-old pup walking by her side.

For half an hour we let them amble around, getting to know each other even better, without the hindrance of a muzzle in sight. Not once did Sheba snap at Sky. They chased the tennis balls that we threw for them, they ran together, they continually overscented each other's pee, although I did think that Sky was pushing his luck in trying to assert his dominance.

"If you're both happy then I'll bring Mr Sky over to yours tomorrow. I'll only hang around for an hour or so to make sure that they are settled; then it's all down to you."

***

6.30 pm, Monday 4th March 2019. Sheba's ears pricked up, her head excitedly tilted to one side, she got up, her tail frantically wagging with excitement, she started to circle impatiently.

Toni instinctively knew that Sheba had heard something of interest. She got up and headed to look out of the kitchen window, Sheba followed, looking up at her in excited anticipation.

"He's here."

The last few weeks of intense socialising work had been in preparation for this very momentous moment; Sky was moving in with us, his furever home.

It had been Sheba's 7th birthday the previous day, and as far as we were concerned, we were giving her the best present ever – a puppy of her very own.

Toni went to our front door, securing the new wooden picket gate I had handmade and installed behind her. I followed them out into the hallway; Sheba was up on her hind legs, her front paws resting on the wooden slats of the gate. I could feel my nerves kicking in, Sheba must not pick up on my anxiety, I closed my eyes and started on my 3, 4, 5 breathing technique.

Toni grasped the door handle and opened the front door. Sheba spied Sky in the darkness and was instantly sent into a frenzy, ecstatically jumping up and down, just as she had done the first time we took her to the seaside.

Sky leapt out of the rear of Pat's estate car, Sheba barked and Sky barked back. Pat was dragged ungracefully through our front door; the way she was grasping the lead with both hands made it look as if she was water skiing. The plastic wallet containing Sky's adoption paperwork slipped from under her arm and dropped onto the floor.

Full of excitement, they greeted each other, and were soon licking each other's tongues through the slats of the gate. As soon as the front door was shut and locked Sky's lead was removed. Toni unlocked the gate and opened it. Our two excited pups ran off together into the lounge, by the time we joined them, they were already lying together on one of the beds we had made up. Sky got up and headed to the back door. I opened it for him, out he bounded, three leaps was all it took for him to reach the top of the steps we had had specially constructed for Sheba, who had already got up from her bed and followed him out into the garden.

I know that I have said it before, but as our two dogs – you really will never know how great it is for me to write those words – came bounding in from the garden, I knelt and embraced Sky.

"Welcome to your home mate, and we hope that you will be very happy living here with us."

I moved back, Sky licked my face, he looked over at Toni and walked to where she was sitting, he jumped up at her, his front paws resting on her shoulders, and he gently planted a kiss on her forehead.

Sheba got up and wandered off, Sky followed her. We heard a loud slurping sound. I quietly crept out into the hallway; there they were, both of their faces buried in one of the new heavy ceramic water bowls we had bought for them. Yes, they were drinking from the same bowl, how beautiful.

The pups, as I now affectionately referred to them as, followed me back into the lounge. Now it was time for a celebration. I cracked open the decent bottle of Châteauneuf-du-Pape, my favourite red wine, that Gemma bought me as part of my birthday present last October. Due to her having to drive home, Pat declined a glass and opted for a cup of tea. Oh well, more for Toni and me.

"Tonight will be a real test for them, the first time they sleep together. In a pack scenario, this is when the weaker dog will attack, the only chance it will get to take out the more powerful dog. Their bond will be unbreakable when they wake in the morning."

"Do you think it would be wise for me to sleep down here with them tonight?"

"I thought Sheba slept upstairs?"

"Up until now she has, but we think that maybe it will be better for her and Sky if they sleep downstairs."

"You're probably right; let them establish themselves in their roles as protectors of the house."

10 pm, Pat wished us all the best and got ready to leave. We had completed Sky's adoption paperwork, and were given an envelope with his passport, medical card and his unique microchip number; we had to update the PETtrac database in the morning. There was also a box of antibiotics and a tube of steroid anti-inflammatory cream. Before being transported to England, Sky had been castrated, and he had a slight infection around where the stitches were removed. Twice a day for the next five days we had to apply a small amount of cream on the infected area. Well one thing is for sure, we were certainly going to get very well acquainted on a rather intimate level.

Soon it was just the four of us, the pups had snuggled down together, bless them, they were both shattered.

We finished our glasses of wine and got ready to turn in. Toni brought me down the throw from our bed, gave each of us a goodnight kiss and headed off upstairs, turning off the kitchen and hallway lights as she passed them.

"Sheba and Sky wee wees."

I opened the garden door, and out they charged, Sheba as usual ran around the garden like a raving loony, barking at anything and everything, Sky stuck to her like a shadow, following her every step, but he made no sound. While they were out running about on the damp grass, their features illuminated by the moonlight, I plumped up their beds. It was late, and Sheba was waking up the neighbourhood. Being the 'grumpy police' I called them in; they headed out into the hallway for a sip of water. Once they had each quenched their thirst they walked back into the lounge. I had already turned off the lights; the only source of illumination was the bright white-silver glow of the moonlight spilling in through the patio doors. Sheba headed straight to her bed, she circled it three times, scuffed up her blanket, which I had just neatly arranged for her, then plonked herself down, a deep grumble was soon followed by her slurping her lips, she was one very contented little pup.

Sky stood staring adoringly at her; he threw the occasional glance at me. Poor little sod, it was as if he was waiting for permission to take to his bed. I got up and walked over to the bed I had made up for him; I lay down and patted the floor.

"Come on Sky, lie down with me mate."

He walked over, I stroked his neck, he lowered his head, and then he very cautiously lay down next to me. Sky looked up and lovingly started to lick my face; I took this as him saying 'Thank you'.

"You're more than welcome my friend. Thank you for joining our family, and I will never be able to thank you enough for all that you have done for Sheba."

I awoke at 3 am, curled up on the cold tiled floor, with my arm still wrapped around Sky. I had an awful crick in my neck and terrible pain in my back, obviously caused by the awkward position I had slept in. I groaned out loud as I tried to move, the pups both raised their heads as if to say 'keep the bloody noise down'.

I clambered up onto the couch and wrapped the throw around myself to try and fend off the cold. The moonlight was flooding through the patio doors, illuminating my two beautiful dogs, contented and fast asleep on their beds. Occasionally they stirred, their dreams causing them to whimper, and their legs going through the motions of running. How different things could have been; Sheba wouldn't have survived for much longer on the mean streets of Sofia, her legs would have eventually given way, leaving her lying in the gutter, vulnerable and unable to move or defend herself. And Sky, he wouldn't have lasted a day in the Killing Station; he was literally rescued just in the nick of time. I still can't believe how very privileged I am to have these two stunners sharing my home and life with me.

I lay there staring at them in adoration; slowly I drifted off to sleep.

***

What the hell? I was suddenly rudely awoken; I could feel myself involuntarily gagging. I opened my eyes and Sky was standing in front of me, licking his lips, and I'm sure he had a smile on his face. Yup, he had kissed me, and I do believe that his tongue had ended up in my mouth. I wiped the drool off my face and laughed, Sheba raised her head and looked over at us. She slowly got up and stretched, and let out one almighty yawn. Over she walked to join us for her regular early morning cuddle and tummy tickle. I got up and opened the back door for them, out they hurtled together into the garden,

Sheba squatted and peed, Sky sniffed the grass where she had relieved herself and peed on the exact same spot. Sheba went back and squatted on the exact same spot again. Bloody hell, how much liquid had they got stored in their bladders?

Sky walked further back up the garden, to an area where they had not peed. He looked down at the damp grass, lowered his head and pushed the right side of his face down. He walked forwards a few paces, and then he turned his head so that his left side was on the ground. He then dropped down and rolled onto his back. He rolled around for a minute or so, then got up and shook himself down.

To this day, Sky repeats his freshen-up, wash routine every morning.

The upstairs floorboards began to creak. Toni was getting up. She came downstairs to join us.

"Good morning, darlings. How were they?"

"No trouble at all, they didn't stir all night. What time is it?"

"Nearly six thirty, is it too early to give them breakfast?"

"Not at all, if we feed them now we can take them out for a walk about seven thirty. It'll be quieter then, and will give us the chance to see how they walk on lead together, without any interruptions."

So at 7.30 am, after they had peacefully eaten their first meal together, we nervously attached Sheba's harness, and Sky's brand new, extra strong, collar and lead. Full of excitement they pulled me towards the door. Bloody hell, there was a combined weight of over 60 kgs of pure muscle, with a low centre of gravity, on the end of these two leads, and to be honest, I wasn't expecting the combined pulling power of these two.

Toni had gathered a handful of poo bags; she looked anxiously at me, then at the two pups eagerly chomping at the bit.

"Are you ready?"

"Not really, but it's now or never. Open the door, and let's hope that they listen to me."

Toni released the security chain, Sky leapt up at the door, his left paw caught the handle and the door opened.

"Right, from now on the front door has to remain locked, even when we are in, by the key at all times, and we mustn't rely solely on the security chain. The little sod has already managed to open it."

I firmly grasped their leads before they bounded out onto our drive; I almost took off from the sudden exertion of power.

"Sheba, Sky, heel, please!"

My command ended up more of a plea than an order.

Sheba immediately positioned herself where she had always walked, tightly against my left leg. Sky was all over the place, tangling himself and Sheba up in his lead. He was trying as hard as he could to jostle for position, he apparently also wanted to be immediately by my side. Sheba reluctantly moved over, allowing Sky to settle in between us. I again firmly repeated the 'heel' command, and off the four of us headed down Old Road.

Luckily there were no other dog walkers over the Harlowbury Chapel field, enabling us to work them hard for about an hour on practising walking Sheba and Sky side by side. It didn't take long for them to settle down and walk at ease together, Sheba now allowed Sky to permanently walk next to me, without nudging or barging him. Bless her heart, it was as if she knew he needed constant reassurance, and a hell of a lot of training.

It gently started to rain, rapidly, black storm clouds swept in, the faltering light giving the field a tinted bronze hue, the wind pushing down on us from above had turned cold. Toni took control of Sheba and quickly led us back home before the imminent downpour that was brewing. Once we were back indoors and settled, she made us both a cup of coffee, then set about reading through the wad of adoption paperwork.

To me, there was nothing cosier than being tucked up indoors, with the central heating on, when there was a storm raging outside.

"Right we need to register Sky with Sheba's vet; I'll ring and get him an appointment for a health check. While I'm doing that you can update the microchip monitoring company. Oh, can you also sort out their insurance, try and get the best deal you can squeeze out of them, see what they offer you on combined pet insurance."

"Yes dear, before I do, I'll look for a broom, I'll try and sweep the floor at the same time."

In all it took over an hour to make the phone calls; now we could sit and start looking through the photos we had taken earlier over the field. Toni picked out a few of her favourites and added them to her social media account, along with an introduction to family and friends of our newly adopted pup.

The responses she received were heart-warming, all of them were complimentary, and the recurrent theme was how handsome Sky was.

However, our family and friends were also amazed to see Sheba, playing with and lying with another dog. We had not divulged to anyone what we were trying to achieve. Anyone that knew us was well aware of Sheba's socialising issues and fear of other dogs. Our friends were truly amazed that she freely accepted Sky. What was it about him? He was undoubtedly one extraordinary little dog.

I had been advised by my GP to take some extended time off from work, although my current mental state was a bit erratic to say the least, time spent with Sheba and Sky was proving to be the best therapy that I could possibly get. The forced time off enabled us to spend much needed quality time with the pups. Taking them out for frequent short walks together, all the time working on Sky's obedience, walking to heel, sitting and laying upon command and importantly, teaching him that he could not go over to every dog that he met for a play.

After four years of having it said to me whenever I was out with Sheba, there was no way that I was going to become one of the 'Don't worry my dog is not aggressive and is great with other dogs; it'll all be fine' brigade.

Sky's presence, and gentle aura, had had an immediate calming effect on Sheba; she was not so fearful or reactive towards other dogs that she met any more, Sky did have to occasionally step in and let out a warning bark if he felt that another dog's close proximity was intimidating Sheba, she always looked up at him, her protector, and licked his ear as a way of showing her gratitude.

Within 48 hours of Sky moving in, we had developed a fully structured routine. The pups' feeding, exercise, play and sleep regimes had all slipped seamlessly into place, both dogs obediently following our every command. Although, we were sure that Sky didn't fully understand all that was said to him – he was Spanish after all – but he followed Sheba's lead. When she was excited, he became animated, wherever she went he followed, slowly picking up on the words that we said.

Within seven days he had grasped all of the main 'household' commands, along with those used explicitly on our walks. He knew where his bed was, his food bowl, lead, the toy box, and 'stop annoying her', he had so much energy and was always on the go, sometimes to Sheba's annoyance. She was getting old, and during the cold months her legs ached, so she liked to laze around, she wasn't used to having an energetic pup pestering her and wanting her to chase him all of the time.

Two weeks had soon passed since Sky joined us, and it was as if he had been here forever. In fact, we couldn't remember how life was with just one dog. Like a bickering, faithful old married couple Sheba and Sky did everything together; occasionally they snapped at each other, but they were just firing warning shots across the bow, no harm was meant or ever done. One thing was for sure though, they adored each other, we often saw them go nose to nose, then their little tongues popped out, they briefly licked each one another's tongue. Bless them, it really did look as if they were kissing.

Sheba and Sky happily drank together from the same water bowl, but when it came to feeding time, we ensured that they were kept apart. I have moderate DIY skills, but the two bespoke raised feeding stations, separated by the wooden security gate that I made, have received many complimentary comments. To use a modern cookery phrase, I 'deconstructed' a two bowl, raised feeder that Sheba has used since she joined us. I made brackets and fitted their two stainless steel bowls to the wall in our hallway. Okay, the white wall does regularly get messy when the pups slurp eagerly at their favourite meat in jelly meals, but hey ho.

On the subject of mess, I forgot about the shaking when we get home from a walk in the rain. Sky is a 'long-coat', and no matter how prepared we are with fluffy towels at the ready to rub him down, he always manages to elude us and shake his body vigorously, droplets of water sent flying up the wall. That one is still 'work in progress', but I'm sure we'll get there in the end.

It didn't take long for Sky to get his paws well and truly under the table, bless his heart. He soon found his favourite place to seek peace and solitude, on the rare occasion when he wanted to be alone – the top of the stairs, with his front legs and nose hanging over the top of them, just like Shane used to do.

It was as if Shane was back with us. When I called him, or went looking for him, down the stairs Sky bounded, as if he hadn't seen me for days, he would leap up, I would cuddle him, his face excitedly thrashing about, eager to kiss me. Inevitably in his excitement he always managed to head butt me. Bloody hell, he's got a head like a sledgehammer.

I often find myself having deep feelings of guilt. Sheba and Sky are our pups, and I am fully aware that I must stop thinking of them as, or comparing them to, my dearly departed little man Shane, but inevitably I have to admit that I do.

Shane's memory is so precious to me; he changed my life beyond all recognition, for the better, and for that, I will be eternally grateful to him. However, I can't bear to think that I am allowing the on-going needs of either of my new rescue dogs to impose upon my recollections of the wonderful times that I had the pleasure of spending with him, the memories that I have to admit are slowly fading into the mists of time. I can no longer remember his aroma or his distinctive bark. I often find myself looking through the hundreds of photos that I have of him, then, for just a brief moment, it is as if he is back with me.

In a perfect world, life would have blessed me with Shane, Sheba and Sky sharing my home with me, but the sad and truthful reality is that there is no such place as a perfect world, as any dog that has, in the past been abused or forsaken, will tell you.

EPILOGUE

Life with Sheba and Sky

Like a mischievous child on its summer holidays, about to partake in a water pistol fight, before we set off for our walks both Sheba and Sky fill their bladders with copious quantities of water. There are lots of dogs in our neighbourhood, and my two have to lay claim to every lamp post, blade of grass, shrub, tree and bush in the area. Our walks take forever, continually having to stop to let the pups overscent and spray everywhere, then they have to overscent each other's, bless them. Then there's the other toilet issue. I often have to take cover when they poop, and they often do so in unison, staring intently at one another, almost as if in a race to see who can finish first. After voiding their bowels of excrement, they often use all four paws to make a few hefty scratches backwards; poop inevitably sent hurtling skywards towards me.

***

You'll never believe the pleasure that I get from sitting and watching Sheba and Sky play together; they're like a couple of pups, well technically Sky is still a pup. They growl and bite at each other's ears and necks. Although often I do find myself having to step in with a firm shout of 'Enough' when the playing appears to be getting just a little bit too rough.

"Leave her bloody front legs alone," is a warning I frequently have to give Sky. He has to learn to stop trying to nip Sheba's front legs; I honestly believe that the little so and so knows they are her Achilles heel, and he'll always get her undivided attention if he playfully nibbles at them. Sheba has learnt to defend her legs; in retaliation she leaps back at him and lunges at his left ear, the ear that was torn when his identification tag was cruelly ripped out in the Killing Station, the inhumane, barbaric bastards just have to inflict as much pain and suffering as they possibly can on their unfortunate inmates.

Sky joined the same obedience class that both Shane attended, and Sheba still does. He is currently in the puppy class, but he is progressing rapidly through the various disciplines; in fact, he is already the proud recipient of a vast array of silver stars to prove it. One thing I have picked up on is Sky's adverse reaction to raised voices. Some of the other handlers at school feel the need to chastise their dogs very loudly; Sky will always cower behind me for protection when this happens. Maybe it is something to do with the horrors he suffered in his past, so although I give him his commands in a firm, authoritative voice, I somehow manage to do it in a calm, friendly voice. So far, as his progress card shows, my methods are working.

One thing's for sure, he's far too bloody intelligent for his own good. His antics are a constant source of amusement for us, from pulling the continental quilt off our bed to get us up, to gently taking our hand in his mouth to lead us to his treat tin under the sink, or to his lead, when he decides that he wants to go out for a walk.

One aspect of his training that thankfully he learnt extremely quickly was the 'Sit and wait' command. As I have mentioned throughout the book, every evening, I carry Sheba up to her bed, and I carry her down each morning, gently cradling her in my arms. Sky is like a bull in a china shop and has a habit of getting under our feet. Initially, we would either have to shut him in our bedroom or behind the security gate to enable me to carry Sheba safely. Sky soon learnt to remain seated until I had climbed or descended the stairs and beckoned him, he would sit, with his head tilted, watching every move that I made. Was it out of respect for the command that I had given? Or alternatively, does he know there is something extra special about Sheba?

Due to Sheba's advancing years, and her disabilities, she is gradually getting slower when we are out on our walks, and sadly she can no longer endure walking the distances that she used to. As a result, she has slowly piled on the timber over the last month or so. We have had to put her on a diet, and are mindful of the treats that we give to her. We are now giving her healthier fruit-based, between-meal nibbles. As soon as I go to the cupboard where we keep their goodies, or to the fridge, both pups excitedly race out into the kitchen. They sit bolt upright, side by side, anxiously awaiting, with their tongues drooling and tails wagging, in anticipation of the titbit that they are about to receive. In a clear and firm voice, I emphasise the name of the pup about to be awarded their morsel-sized nibble. They look at each other, and upon hearing their name, they duly open their mouth, while cheekily shuffling forwards, still in the sit position. Never once have they lunged at each other, nor tried to snatch the treat before I have said their name. Upon receipt, they quickly retreat to their individual day beds, turn their backs on one another and devour their gift, although it still amazes me the furore that can ensue if one of them encroaches on the other one's space and tries to eat the smallest crumb, or piece of fruit that has fallen from the other's mouth.

Sky is extremely needy, bless his little heart. He continually needs to be comforted, stroked and cuddled, which I'm always pleased to do. He'll nudge us, bash us with his paw or head butt us, while whining and leaning tightly into us. Once he has received his stroke, embrace and loving words of encouragement, he will contentedly lie down, with his front paws crossed, staring adoringly up at us, with his beautiful dark brown eyes. Bless him, after the horrors that he suffered and endured, is it any wonder that he needs so much reassurance? Well my little friend, let me alleviate you fears, I give you my oath that we will never harm or abandon you, so please my little man, enjoy your life with us, and rest assured.

As I have previously mentioned, we know absolutely nothing of Sheba's past. For reasons unknown her past has been kept a secret from us, but one thing's for sure, she endured and suffered both physical and mental trauma. Sky's history is also a mystery, but for totally different reasons, all we know is that he was tied to the gates of a Killing Station to await his vile demise.

Did he know? Did he sense hatred and death?

You have probably gathered by now that I enjoy a drink or two, and frequent our local public houses as often as I can with Toni and both of our pups. Sky always seems very relaxed in pub environments; in fact, he appears quite at home in a bar. This got me thinking, had he lived in a bar in Spain? I'll never know for sure, but it is not uncommon for dogs to be locked in bars and restaurants overnight in some Mediterranean countries for security purposes. Had he spent his life mingling with the punters during opening hours, then at night he earned his keep as a guard dog? Had at the end of the summer season his previous owner took him to the Killing Station? Dogs are easy to come by in Spain, so to save on the associated costs of boarding or looking after him during the winter months was it financially easier to abandon him and have him killed, only to get a new one in the spring before having that poor soul destroyed as well? I will never know for sure what Sky's background is, and can only surmise, but I do believe that something along these lines is entirely feasible. Come on, why on earth would anyone in their right mind want to get rid of Sky? He's so adorable and loving, he really is the quintessential housemate, but most importantly, he is the perfect companion for Sheba, her very own Mr Blue Sky.

A Note from the Author

Friday 29th March 2019. Miraculously, and goodness only knows how, at long last I have managed to complete my attempts at writing a book. Believe me, it was never planned this way, but today is also the fourth anniversary of my dear little man Shane crossing over the Rainbow Bridge, a day I wish I could erase and banish from my memory forever and focus on the happy times we spent together. Deep down I'd like to think that just maybe he helped me to accomplish my dream on this significant date. Throughout my life I have been told that time is a great healer when coming to terms with bereavement; well I can tell you categorically that it hasn't, the pain and grief is as raw today as it was four years ago.

My second book, a prequel, is nearing completion, and hopefully should be published within the next year; I am contemplating releasing it, hopefully, on 29th March 2020, the fifth anniversary of Shane's passing. It is a fictional story, with elements of fact that I managed to gather, and is based around Sheba's early life as a disabled, stray street dog in Bulgaria,

2019 had started abysmally for us as a family, and I have not handled the resulting stress at all well. I have to admit that I have failed and crumbled under the immense sadness and emotional strain that I have experienced. The 'silent enemy' I ironically opened this book with has crept back into my life, only this time it is not due to a midlife crisis; the culprit this time is immense sorrow, and many days filled with sadness. I admit that mentally I'm distraught, I am constantly irritable and very, very angry, and without justification or warning, I lose my temper, the violent thoughts which inevitably always ensue frighten me.

In the end, after much bullying from my nearest and dearest, I eventually caved in and somehow summoned up the strength to visit my doctor.

"Well you see it's like this doc, my family thinks I'm mad. Irrational mood swings and losing me rag."

"Not to worry, I'll give you a prescription for some magical little white pills. I'm sure they'll sort you out."

Hopefully, the magic pills that he prescribed for my condition – apparently, my current frame of mind is something to do with the levels of serotonin in my brain becoming unbalanced – oh, and the weekly sessions he kindly arranged for me with a shrink, will get me safely through the next few months, before I unintentionally do something that I may live to regret.

Like hell the pills helped, the side effects are horrendous, and as for curing the traumas that we'd suffered as a family? The drugs, to be honest, do take the edge off and enable me to think a bit more rationally, but the immense sadness remains and will do for a long time.

To make my current screwed up mental state even worse, I now feel unable to support those in my family who need me; in fact, they are supporting me, which makes me feel utterly useless in my role as husband, son, father and grandfather. Sky joining us in the middle of these traumatic trying times has brought me happiness. To watch Sheba accept him into her home, and almost become a surrogate mother to him, fills my heart with happiness and joy, not much else does at the moment. No that was a horrible thing to say, precious time with my family helps me through the darker days.

Strangely, my current mental state has helped me in my initial editing of this book. I rewrote some of the darker, violence-inspired pages; I found a new energy in the words I used, a far more graphically honest approach. Then again on reflection that's how all of these pages have been pieced together from the very start. They were not written in chronological order, but were constructed and pieced together to reflect my moods – enraged, frustrated, loving, sad, happy, angry, remorseful, you get my drift – but for a novice like me it worked, an honest memoir of my journey into the world of dogs, written in conjunction with my aggravated state of mind.

***

I began writing and putting down my innermost thoughts about Shane and Sheba during a relaxing summer holiday on the Greek island of Rhodes in August 2015. For me, it has been a very poignant and emotional four-year roller-coaster ride. I have not written continually, there have been gaps of months – in fact, one break was for over a year – where I have been unable to write any words, but it's all done and dusted now. It's out of my hands; all that is left for me to do is set it free and release the fruits of my labour.

You may think that now, more than ever, is the time to call in the men in white coats when I tell you that the original concept for this, and my future book, came to me initially in the form of a dream. I know, you think I'm totally mad. Night after night I would have a recurring fantasy nightmare, an animated, dark, scary nightmare, about Sheba living and growing up on the vile, lawless, uncompassionate streets of Sofia, Bulgaria. I initially approached an animation company with my idea; they seemed genuinely interested in the concept but told me that I needed a script. After much fruitless searching to find a writer, I decided to attempt to do it myself.

How on earth, or more to the point, why on earth have I tried to write a book of my own? Well, to be totally honest, I just wanted to share the story of my three amazing dogs with you, the simple tale of the five emotional years that I have had the privilege to spend with them, and my undying love for them. I also hope that I have managed to convey the emotions that I believe anyone who has given a home to, and suffered the traumatic loss of a beloved pet has sadly had to endure. I want to offer inspiration to potential adoptive families of rescue dogs. I know that Shane's story was emotional, but we gave him hope and a home of his own.

There's also another aspect to this book that came to me like a bolt out of the blue while driving through the Blackwall Tunnel early one cold December morning, while on my way to work. At the time of my birth in 1964, I only had one grandfather and two grandmothers. I grew up listening to stories of the grandfather I sadly never met, and of my great-grandparents. These ancestors helped shape me and my family into the people that we are today. Throughout my childhood, I heard the tales of how my forefathers moved to North London from Witney, Oxfordshire in the late 1880s, and how my great-grandfather Charles had served and fought in the First World War. I listened as my late grandfather, who was my hero and I adored, spoke of the horrific injuries his late father sustained, and of his prowess in the boxing ring. One particular fight has become a story of legend, his fight with the Hollywood actor, and heavyweight champion of the British Army 1918, Victor McLaglen. Sadly, these stories will eventually fade into the mists of time. I make no claims to have led an exciting life, one worthy of putting into print anyway, but just maybe one day my grandchildren or future great-grandchildren just may want to know more about their heritage. Hopefully, these pages may give them a snapshot or insight into a brief few years of both Toni and my lives, and provide them with a clear and honest understanding of who we were. I sincerely hope that they will be proud of us.

For the last four-plus years, a pen and small notebook have been my constant companions and have never left my side. Sudden random thoughts or observations are scribbled down at every opportunity, the backs of my hands have sometimes been covered in black ink when I had run out of paper in my trusted notebook and couldn't find anything else to scribble on. My mood, mental state or consumption of alcohol dictated the chapter or sentence that I would be working on; the prequel book is taking far more imagination to write; this book was more like constructing a journal. To make my quest in completing my immense task easier I looked into buying myself a Dictaphone, how so very 1980s. This was until one of my daughters pointed out the voice recorder app on my mobile. Bloody hell, I wish I had known about this four years earlier.

***

Again, over and over I have been saddened when reminiscing about the wonderful times that I had the honour and privilege to spend with my handsome little man Shane. Still to this day thoughts of him reduce me to tears, his paw prints will be forever embedded upon my heart. I have laid bare my thoughts and emotions; honestly, I am embarrassed to have written, and admitted that I have cried.

I have learnt a lot over the past five years about the unique welfare requirements that dogs have, as I wrote at the very beginning of this book, I had never had the pleasure of a dog sharing my life, I was a total novice when Shane joined my family. I honestly believe that Shane, Sheba and Sky have all made me a far better human being; they have taught me compassion and a form of love I'd never encountered before in my life. I have often been asked what my favourite breed of dog is. Without a shadow of a doubt, the answer is very, very simple – rescue dogs are my favourite breed. The eternal gratitude they lavish on you for giving them a loving home is very humbling. If I could be half the person that my dogs are, or were, then I'd be twice the human that I am.

Like many people every week I faithfully purchase my lottery ticket. I dream of winning the big one and often contemplate how I will spend my windfall. I will ensure my family are financially taken care of, and for myself? A modest house surrounded by the tranquillity and wildlife of the English countryside. To top it all off I'd like a few acres of securely fenced-off land, and a Land Rover Defender parked on the drive. Obviously, there will be regular financial contributions to Mutts to help with the on-going veterinary fees and upkeep of the kennels.

Shane, Sheba and Sky, along with all of the planet's ex-street or abandoned dogs who now have a loving family home have all won the doggie equivalent of the lottery. Love, comfort, security, a caring family, food, health care and toys, that's all that any dog needs, and nothing more than they rightly deserve.

I do sometimes think, no that's not true, in fact I know, because she has told me on numerous occasions that my wife does get jealous of the free-flowing words of love and affection that I shower upon Sheba and Sky. I always kiss my wife whenever I leave home, followed by "See you later", alternatively a brash "Have a good day". For Sheba and Sky, there's a stroke each, a tummy tickle each, a kiss each then another stroke, followed by:

"Daddy loves his special little girl and handsome boy, have a lovely day and see you very soon darlings."

Yup, my wife does have a fair point, sadly after 37 years together maybe I do take her for granted. The sad reality is that Sheba and Sky will each only bless my life for 12 years or so. Shane very sadly only graced my life for seven months. I want my dogs to feel as cherished as possible for every single day that they are with me. For me, love has now become a four-legged word.

While on the subject of Toni, she does have a rather annoying habit of having to give people pet names; I won't divulge mine. Sheba and Sky each have one. Toni has affectionately referred to Sheba as Sheba Doggy from the very first day that she moved in with us, and Sky? Well, he's Mr Blue Sky after a hit song by one of Toni's favourite bands, the Electric Light Orchestra (ELO). Often I hear Mr Blue Sky blaring from the stereo, with Toni singing along and serenading, badly I hasten to add, Sky, who sits there, head tilted to one side, wondering what the hell the crazy woman in front of him is going on about.

***

Apart from my sadness manifesting itself as anger, another one of my issues, and believe me there are plenty of them, is that I over scrutinise and analyse everything. This came to a head one rainy Sunday when I was struggling to try to add more words to this book. There's a saying 'Dogs do speak, but to only those who know how to listen'. I'm not ashamed to admit that I frequently have full-blown conversations with Sky and Sheba, sharing and offloading my worries and burdens with them when we are alone on our long countryside walks. In fact, Sheba and Sky have become my four-legged, wet-nosed furry psychiatrists and I almost wait in anticipation for them to give their professional diagnosis to me. The reason that I am questioning myself today was a random thought that came to me; how frustrating it must be for a dog when it is trying to communicate with us, and our not fully understanding them. True we pick up on our dogs' mannerisms, facial expressions, their unique movements and body language, but the huge concern that has hit me like a bolt out of the blue is about Shane. Did we get it right? Did the consultant mislead me? Did I fully understand Shane's final wish that he wanted me to help him, and give my blessing for him to die in peace?

I can only hope that we unreservedly understood him on the dreadful day he left us for the afterlife, the horrendous day that we authorised his death; please let us have made the right decision, and it was the decision that he himself had made.

***

I have a social media account dedicated to all three of my amazing rescue dogs. Over the four years it has now been operational Shane, Sheba and Sky have made over 5,000 friends worldwide, including several very well-known celebrities. I use the media platform as best as I can to speak up for as many of the abused and disadvantaged animals worldwide as possible. Wherever I can, I try to offer advice and encouragement on the real joys and benefits of giving a home to a rescue dog. I'm a massive advocate of the #AdoptDontShop movement. Regular pupdates are tweeted to our multitude of social media followers highlighting milestones in Sky and Sheba's lives.

We use social media to remain in contact with Chaim, the surgeon who gave Sheba a whole new lease of life through his incredible skills, kindness, generosity and dedication. He left the UK to first work in Asia, before finally settling in Australia, continuing his career helping animals in his own veterinary practice.

Social media has enabled me to become extremely vocal with issues that directly affect both Sheba and animals worldwide, and I am very proud to say that I have become one of the voices for the voiceless.

Our new circles of friends are all in one way or another emotionally attached to Mutts in Distress.

I mean this in the nicest possible way, but they're a bunch of lovely, eccentric, raving bloody lunatics. I love them all dearly, but I will never tell them that to their faces.

We laugh, volunteer at the rescue sanctuary and party together. We're there for each other through the good times, and comfort each other during the unbearably sad. Sadly, we are all fully signed up members of the 'club', the only membership criteria as I mentioned earlier in the book, is that you have to be the bereaved parent of a beloved dog.

I have been privileged to have been allowed to become a member of the Mutts in Distress volunteer team. From fundraising, home-checking potential new families to adopt one of the sanctuary's poor abandoned dogs, to helping with the necessary on-going, never-ending repair or building work at the shelter. The sense of self-satisfaction from a day's work in the Hertfordshire countryside is humbling, rewarding, therapeutic and soul cleansing.

***

2018 for us as a family proved to be a year of love and celebration, a million miles away from how 2019 has begun.

On 14th July, my youngest daughter Leah got married; yet again I had the privilege and honour of walking the beautiful bride down the carpeted aisle, on a glorious summer's day. Leah and her husband had chosen a stunning lakeside venue in Churchgate Street, Essex, aptly named That Amazing Place.

In June, my middle daughter Gemma held her 30th birthday celebration in our garden, and in August she finally flew the family nest and moved into her own countryside abode.

On a personal note, I managed to quit smoking, completed an emergency first aid course for dogs, something I would highly recommend to everyone. In August, we had a beautiful holiday, staying at a quaint, beachside hotel, on the Greek island of Kefalonia. In June I was invited to, and spent an awe-inspiring day with, the prison dog unit at HMP Belmarsh, London.

***

On the now more frequent occasions when I have had a dismal day, one thing is for sure; I have the best therapists on the planet. Minutes before I reach home I genuinely feel my heart rate increasing, in anticipation of the loving welcome I am soon to receive from Sheba and Sky, the same greeting that I used to receive from Shane. Nothing on the planet is more humbling than the reception you get from your adoring and faithful dog. Sheba and Sky's excitable 'welcome home dad' reception melts my heart. Toni tells me how their ears will suddenly prick up with excitement when they hear the sound of my car's engine in the distance; their heads both tilt to one side, their tails wag, and off they both trot to sit patiently side by side behind the small security gate. I hear them both become excited as my key turns in the lock, gently barking their greetings in unison and spinning in manic circles waiting for me to close the front door, open the gate and embrace them. Sheba will always then run to their toy box at the end of the hallway and select a toy that she'll drop at my feet. That's all I need, the day's problems melt and fade away into oblivion.

When I am feeling sad, thinking about the unbearable loss I suffered when I had to say my final farewell to Shane, I look down at Sheba and Sky, they look up at me, and yet again they will both come to my rescue, kissing away my tears.

I asked myself the question the very first time I met Sheba, and it still stands to this very day, who really rescued who?

I will be eternally grateful to Shane, Sheba and Sky

My beautiful, loving, inspirational and amazing rescue dogs.

Final Thoughts

I know that this is a long shot, but if the scumbag who previously owned Sky should, by a slim chance, happen ever to read this book, all I can say to you is thank you. Sky has made my family complete; our gain is your loss.

Also, you failed dismally; you didn't break his soul, free spirit or caring nature. You'll be pleased to know that you have managed to scar him mentally, but your vile actions have turned him into probably the most loving dog I have ever had the pleasure to meet. So sorry my old china, as I said, you failed, and you didn't manage to destroy his beautiful inner beauty or loving nature.

Just a question, did you by any chance clout him with his water bowl? The reason I ask is because he's petrified whenever we approach him with a bowl of water, no matter how thirsty he is. He backs off, occasionally he will even cower, what the bloody hell did you do to him? I first noticed it the night he moved in with us, just after I climbed up onto the couch in the early hours. I could hear Sky panting, so I went out to the hall and got one of the pups' stainless steel water bowls, and filled it with fresh cool water. I knelt in front of him and offered him a drink. He was showing signs of anxiety, and retreated away from me, I put the bowl down, and wiggled my fingers in it trying to make a game of it, all the while I was gently trying to coax him to come to me. Tentatively he eventually moved closer, but would not take a drink until I had backed off. Bloody hell, poor little sod, what other traumas has he suffered? I guess time will tell, but no matter what, we will slowly work through, and conquer any fears he may have.

To my beloved Sky's previous owner, please could you pass on a message from me to your acquaintances at the Killing Station that you dumped and tied Sky to the gates of. I know that they'll be sorry to hear that Sky's left ear has fully healed now. The cruel bastards tore out an identification tag. They know that they are very simple to remove humanely, but they ripped it out of him anyway, just for their pure sadistic pleasure. Anyway, yes, they did maim him for life, his ear has a huge chunk missing, and the tip has been left permanently turned down, but it doesn't bother him now. The throbbing pain he would have endured stopped long before I had the pleasure of meeting him. Every single day I caress him and stroke the deformity they left him with, every day I promise him no one will ever hurt him again. He snuggles closely into me, he doesn't understand the kind, soothing words I say to him, but I'm more than sure that he picks up on my emotions. I look at his ear and wonder how on earth they could have done it to him, I wonder how loudly he would have yelped in pain. How many days would it have taken for the blood to stop flowing from the huge gaping tear that was left? Every time he shook his head he would have reopened the wound and showered his beautiful face with blood. I bet they relished in seeing his discomfort, didn't they?

I know what I am talking about because Sheba endured a similar wound when she had her ear bitten by a dog. We took her to the vets, who cleaned the wound with a diluted solution of Hibiscrub. Luckily she didn't need stitches. Daily we bathed her ear with warm salt water and applied soothing antiseptic cream. But it still took a month to completely heal, our walls had a constant splattering of blood. She walked with her head held tilted to one side, and frequently reopened the wound when she scratched herself with one of her hind paws when grooming in the morning. She'd again yelp in pain, and again the wound would reopen, but she got there in the end with constant care. Sky? I bet he suffered, and I am sure your friends loved seeing that, didn't they?

Bloody heartless inhumane bastards.

Although we have never met, and for your sake I hope that we never do, I hate you for what you had planned for Sky – to be slaughtered, mercilessly in one of the many vile Killing Stations that operate within Spain. I despise you, along with all of your fellow, despicable, cowardly animal abuser scum. None of you will ever be shown forgiveness, and don't deserve any mercy or compassion.

I have had the sad, unfortunate misfortune of encountering many of your types in my life – cowards, bullies who take their pleasure from inflicting mental and physical abuse on those who they believe are weaker than them, those poor souls who are unable to defend or protect themselves. You, and your fellow abusers, are nothing more than sewer-dwelling manipulative abusive control freaks, spineless excuses of men who prey on women, children and animals, you don't care who your next victim is, as long they can't fight back or speak up for themselves.

PHOTOS

Shane and Paul, Day 2 August 11th 2014

(From left to right) Gemma, Leah and Kealy (Shane relaxing)

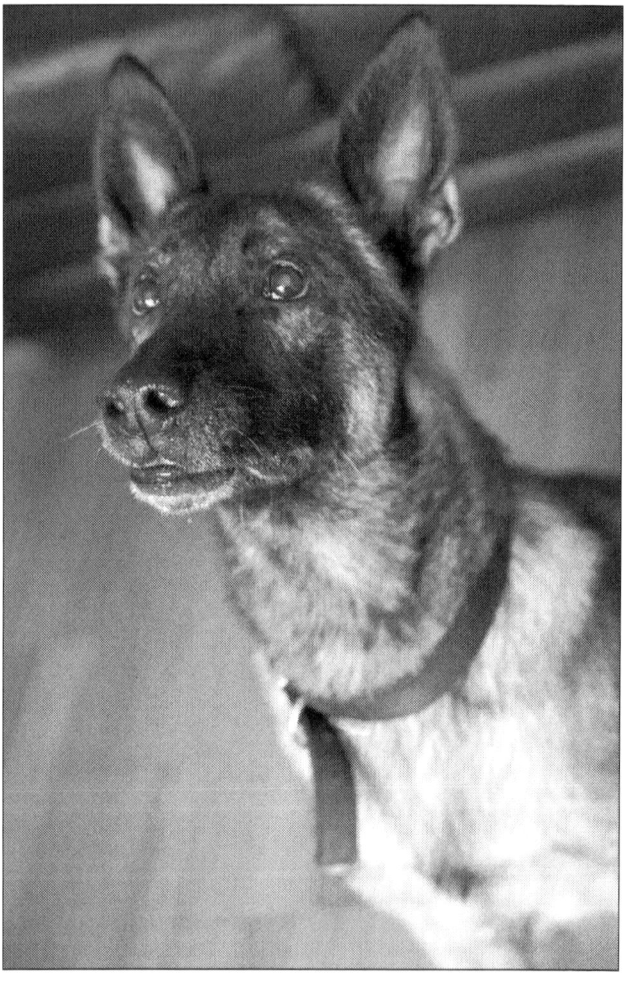

Shane February 2015

Shane having a treat February 2015

Artist's portrait of Shane and Sheba (Niki Firmin)

Sheba on the streets of Bulgaria

Sheba at Muts in Distress February 2015

Sheba in so-called Rescue Compound, Bulgaria

Paul and Sheba, day 1, Easter Monday 2015

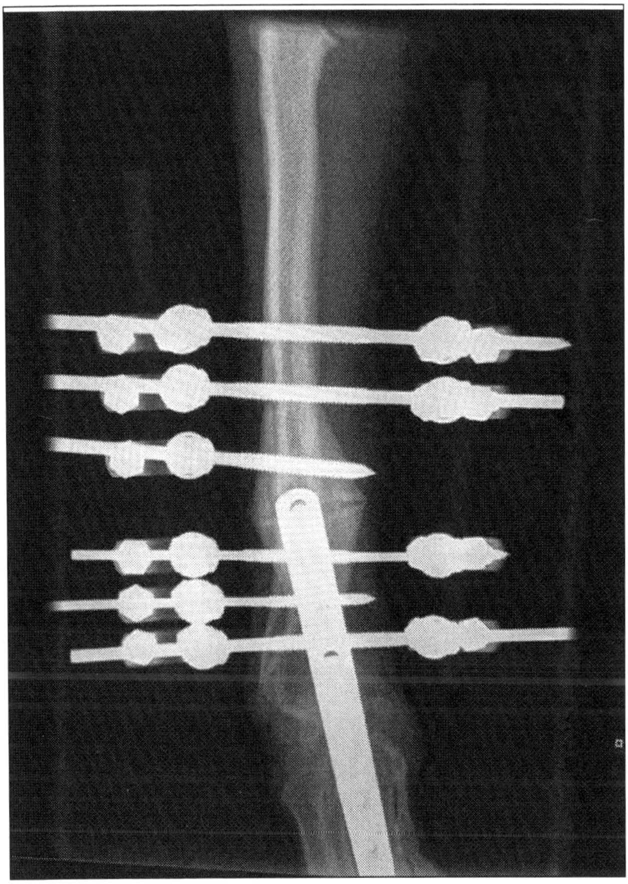

Sheba's external fixator and corrective rod and break

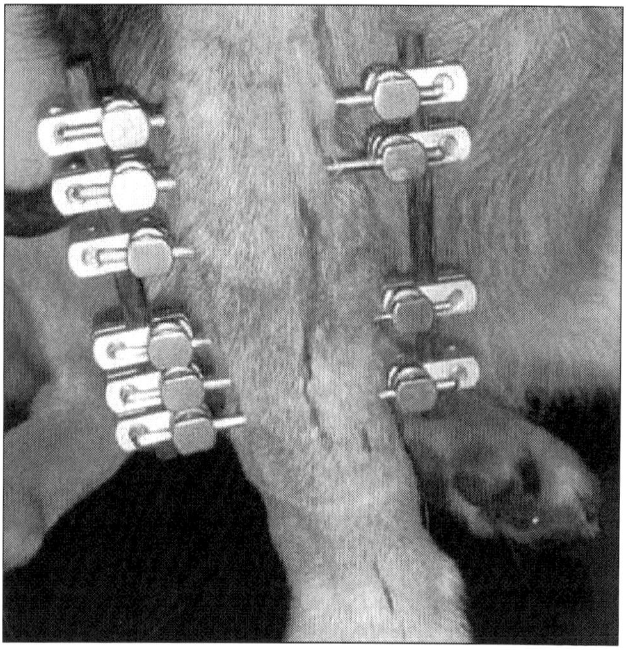

Sheba's external fixator

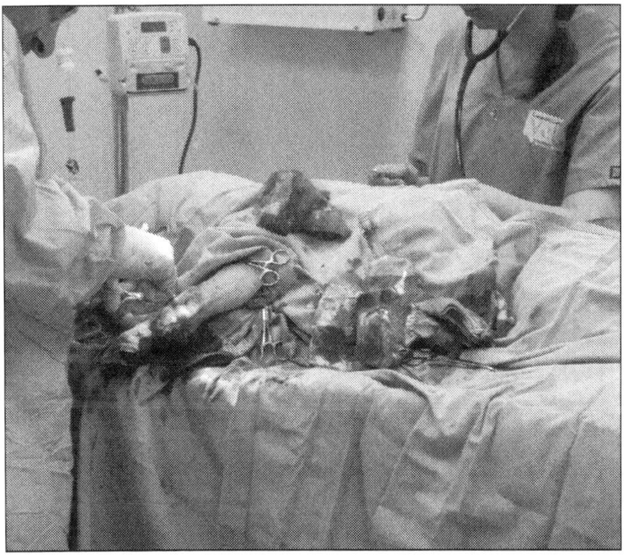

Sheba's final corrective surgery

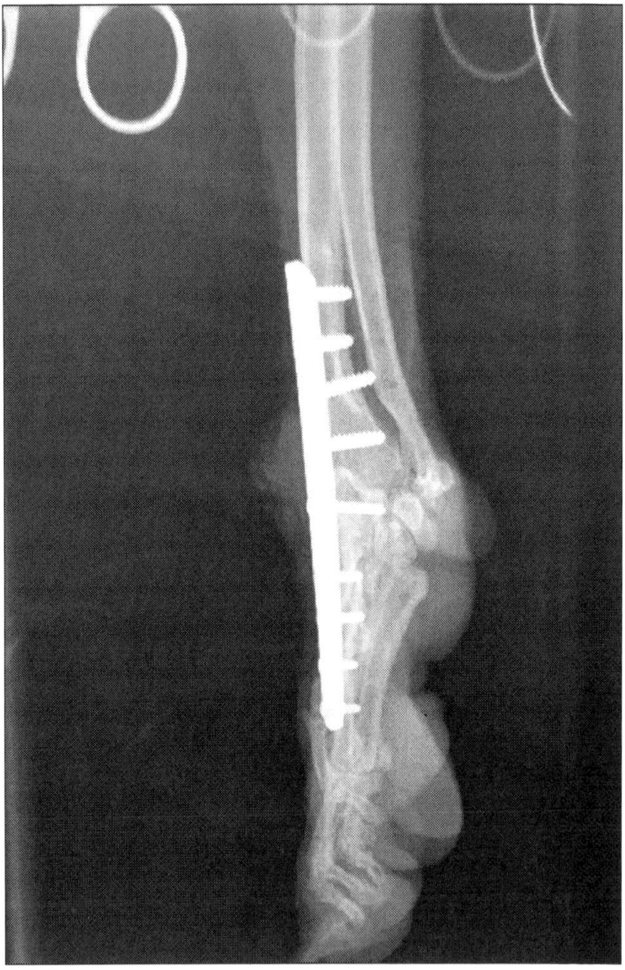

Sheba's left leg X-ray June 2015

Sheba's newspaper portrait May 2015

Toni and Sheba

Toni and Sheba on Mersea Island Autumn 2015

Sheba seeing the sea for the first time

First meeting, January 2019

When Sheba first met Sky, January 2019

Sheba and Sky playing Kiss Chase

Sheba chasing Sky March 2019

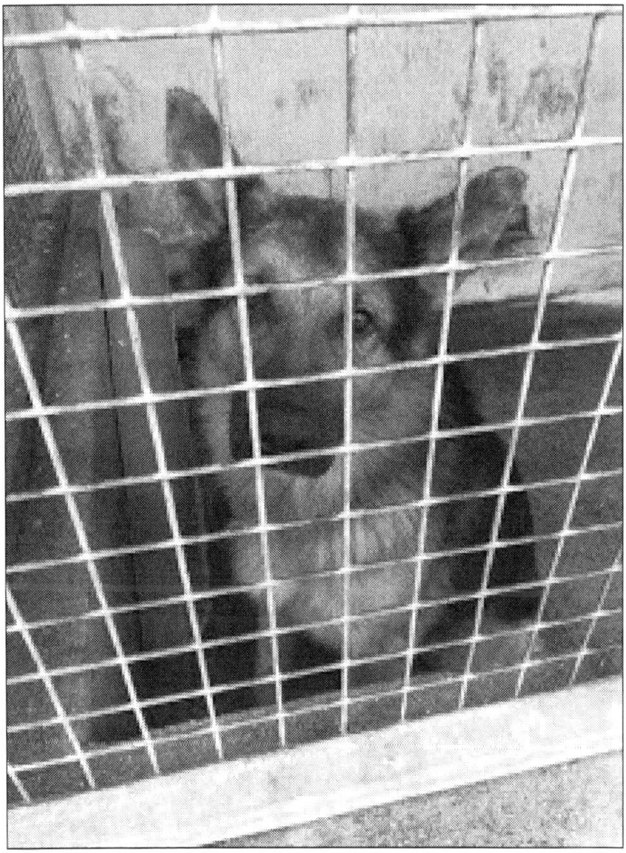

Sky in the Spanish Killing Station January 2019

Sky March 2019

Printed in Great Britain
by Amazon

33519327R00194